The Longest Cocktail Party

The Longest Cocktail Party

An Insider's Diary of
The Beatles,
Their Million-Dollar
Apple Empire and
Its Wild Rise and Fall

RICHARD DiLELLO

Published in the UK in 2000 by
MOJO Books, an imprint of
Canongate Books Ltd,
14 High Street,
Edinburgh EH1 1TE

First published in the US in 1972 by Playboy Press
Copyright © 1972, Richard DiLello

10 9 8 7 6 5 4 3 2 1

British Library Cataloguing-in-Publication Data
A catalogue record for this book is available
upon request from the British Library.

ISBN 1 84195 089 0

Typeset by Hewer Text Composition Services, Edinburgh
Printed and bound by CPD, Ebbw Vale, Wales

For Candace and Francesca

FOREWORD

It was the best of times and it was the best of times.

It was London, it was 1968 and I was 22 years old; an American by birth and working for The Beatles by the grace of God. Could there have been anything cooler? Yes. I could have been a Beatle. But then, we are all accidents of birth, and we must all accept our lot in life.

It's over thirty years later. The memory of the Apple years still retains its potent, amber glow. It's still seared into my brain bank, and though certain specifics have dimmed, the vibe is still what it was back then. Great. What made it great for me was that The Beatles, as people, were wonderful to work for. Yes, they were demanding. Yes, they were utterly spoiled and pampered. Yes, sometimes they were out of touch with the universe outside of their own universe. Yes, they could occasionally be thoughtless and frequently self-absorbed. But who cared? They were The Beatles. They Were The Greatest Band In The History Of The World Who Changed Our World Forever And The Way We See Our World. They had earned the right to be anything they wanted to be. But they were never assholes.

Someone once asked George Harrison, "What's it like being a Beatle?" His answer – "What's it like not being a Beatle?" They had lost all reference to the world of mere mortals because they had been Beatles for almost as long as they could remember. They moved from one brilliant, creative success to the next brilliant, creative success, seemingly without effort, dazzling us all with the fecundity of their extraordinary talent. But still they were cool, still they stayed cool. And, while the rest of us spend most of our lives being told "No", no one ever told a Beatle "No." It's hard to imagine what that must be like.

I always wanted to be a writer. But from the very first day

that I started working in the Apple Press Office I wasn't a writer and I wasn't an observer. I wasn't taking notes and I never kept a diary. Never. I was without reservation a focused and dedicated participant, an ecstatic and willing slave to the machinery that surrounded, coddled and supported The Beatles. I only became a writer afterwards, when it was all over.

And it was quite a shock when Apple collapsed after The Beatles had dissolved their globe-shattering union. Because while it was all going on it was so intense, so vital and vibrant, that I never stopped for a moment to think what it would be like if this grand and privileged adventure I was involved in should someday end. Because it was impossible to conceive of it ever ending.

But of course it did end. For a brief period I was adrift after Apple self-destructed and the Press Office was officially closed in August of 1970, lost in my own spaced-out space. But then someone suggested that I write a book about my "experience." What a good idea. Because now I actually had something to write about. And that's very helpful for an aspiring writer. And I knew if I didn't do it then I would never do it. If I let too long a period of time go by the edges of the picture would become blurred and the reality of what happened would be lost forever.

Sometime in the late autumn-winter of 1970 I rented a dun-colored IBM electric typewriter. I bought a Mont Blanc pen, a half-dozen ledgers and a couple of reams of foolscap paper. I closed the door of my bedroom at Number 9 Bina Gardens in the flat that I shared with three other raving hippie lunatics in South Kensington and I stopped smoking hashish.

I had my Apple Files – a mountain of press cuttings, memos and Press Office releases that I had obsessively and diligently catalogued and preserved. The Apple Files gave me the foundation for an accurate time line. I also had an extraordinary memory despite all the hashish and magic mushrooms I had consumed non-stop since 1963 with such ardent devotion. The experience of working at Apple was so intense, so part of every micro-fiber in my body, that I had little difficulty in pulling up events and conversations I had taken part in and/or overheard going back to Day One. It was just there. All I had to do was sit in a room and talk to myself. It was something I had been doing all my life.

The actual process of writing is a pain in the ass. It's hard work. At least for me it is. But writing this book was not that, it was something else, and it pretty much wrote itself. *The Longest Cocktail Party* became a joyous journey, a personal souvenir of those incredible years. It was a creative feast that I gorged on and couldn't get enough of. It was like being back at Apple – I couldn't wait to get up in the morning and go to work.

I wrote in a white heat, flat out, from early in the morning until late at night. And then, when exhaustion would set in, I'd pop a couple of Ritalin, dose myself with a pot of tea and keep on going. Nothing distracted me. All of the temptations of swinging London ceased to exist. The only sirens I heard were the ones singing in my head, telling me to write on. At the end of three months I had a book.

My master plan was to go to New York, sell the manuscript for a fortune and return to London, which I loved more than life itself, and live happily ever after, rich and famous. It didn't work out that way. *The Longest Cocktail Party* was rejected by twenty-two publishers. They all had the same line – "The Beatles have broken up and no one is interested anymore." I couldn't believe it. So much for the wisdom of adults.

But there I was, back in New York, the city of my birth, with a book no one wanted to publish, broke and depressed. But an even worse fate had befallen me – I was once again living with my parents. To their credit they had grown up considerably in the seven years since I had last seen them. They were supportive and caring and shared my pain. They knew how much getting this manuscript published meant to me. But what could they do? And what could I do but slog up and down Madison Avenue in search of publisher Number Twenty-three.

Twenty-three was the magic number. Playboy Press bought the manuscript. My original title was *The Longest Cocktail Party Ever Held*. My publisher didn't appreciate the overblown hyperbole and suggested that I shorten the title. Actually, they insisted that I shorten the title. I figured it was only two words, so big deal. Other than that the manuscript was published word-for-word, just as I had written it, as it is here.

The Longest Cocktail Party was published in the fall of 1972. The reviews were extensive and mixed. I had a feeling that the book was selling well, but then, it was only a feeling. A British and Japanese edition followed. I still had a feeling it was selling well. But, in the years that *The Longest Cocktail Party* was in print, I don't recall ever receiving a royalty statement or a single check after my initial advance. Then the book went out of print. After John Lennon's death Playboy Press bought the book back from me and republished a paperback edition. After a few more years the book was once again out of print.

What did The Beatles think of *The Longest Cocktail Party*?

John Lennon told a very close friend of mine – "That was the only good book ever written about us." My feeling was that John should know. After all, it was his band.

I'm sure Paul McCartney hated the book. If he didn't actually hate it then he must have at least hated the idea of it. But, I have absolutely nothing to substantiate that theory, because it's just a theory.

Whoever called George Harrison "The Quiet Beatle" didn't know George. George Harrison is an extremely high-verbal human being, he rarely stops talking and he has an opinion about everything. Like all of The Beatles he has an exceedingly strong personality. And, like all of The Beatles, when you are in a room with a Beatle, you know you are in a room with a Beatle. I spent a day with George a couple of years after *The Longest Cocktail Party* was published. We talked of many things that day but George never mentioned the book, for better or for worse, and of course I was too intimidated to ask.

Ringo? I don't know. I hoped he liked it. It liked him.

The publication of *The Longest Cocktail Party* didn't alter the course of my life by a single jot. However, I did what I had set out to do, which was to write a book about an important part of my life that would never come again. By 1975 I was still broke and floundering. So, with nothing to lose and no particular place to go, I packed up my camera bag, my portable Remington typewriter and with my faithful Wire Hair Fox Terrier, Asta, I headed to Los Angeles to be a screenwriter.

Once again things didn't work out the way I thought they would. For five years I scratched out a minimal existence as a rock & roll photographer in the music business, living in a cramped, converted garage in an alley next to the railroad tracks in West L. A., writing screenplays and trying to get a foot in the door of the movie business. It wasn't happening.

Then one day in the City of Eternal Summer the sun was at last turned on. I wrote and sold a feature screenplay called *Bad Boys*. It wasn't exactly a box office sensation but it got made and suddenly I was no longer a starving writer. Life got better, more work kept on coming. Before I knew it I was living in a movie star's house in Bel Air and I had a car that started when I turned the key in the ignition. Asta dined on sirloin steak and slept on an embroidered velvet pillow. And, as the years racked up, I was given the greatest gift of all, really the only true gift – a beautiful family. I was a lucky man.

But, the movie business wasn't like Apple, it wasn't rock & roll. It lacked the spontaneity and the feeling that anything great could happen at any moment; in comparison it was uptight and codified, rigid and unforgiving, where something bad was almost guaranteed to happen at any moment and usually did. And actors weren't musicians, not by any stretch of the imagination. I missed the insanity of the rock & roll minstrel's free-for-all, non-stop life. No doubt about that.

Writing for a living forced me to grow up – after a fashion – and to deal with the reality of my craft and everything that went with it. Another feature film followed and then came a long stint in the trenches of American television. I put several TV series on the air with varying degrees of success and failure. Along the way, like every other writer I know, I bitched a lot, but I wasn't really complaining.

The supreme rush that came with the writing of *The Longest Cocktail Party* never quite happened again for me. I was never able to recapture that first pure moment of creative joy where everything fell into place just the way I wanted it to.

That moment never resonated again in the same way. Maybe it was because I wasn't 25 anymore. Maybe it was because the world had changed and I didn't want it to change. I think that's it. I liked it better the way it was.

The Beatles helped us stay forever young though they themselves could not stay forever young. Life dealt out its hand of horrors to The Beatles like it deals out its horrors to the rest of us. When we first discovered the magic of their youthful genius it was inconceivable that someday they would be visited by murderous insanity, divorces, the death of a beloved spouse, near-murderous insanity and a darkening of the days. But it happened.

Apple was a noble experiment that failed. When The Beatles announced their vision of helping creative people in all walks of life they were honoring the tradition of the philanthropic giants of industry of bygone eras. The Beatles were four individuals who had exceeded their own wildest dreams and who believed it was their obligation to give something back to the world, never losing sight of their own hard-scrabble origins. It was clear that their sense of social responsibility remained intact and untainted by success and cynicism.

Yes, we are all accidents of birth and we must all accept our lot in life. And indeed, who amongst us, at one time or another, hasn't dreamed of being a Beatle? But, if you weren't you, and you were a Beatle, then think what you would have missed. You would have missed The Beatles.

Richard DiLello
Los Angeles, California
July 2000

CONTENTS

PART TWO – 1969
''HEY, MAN HOW DO I GET IN TOUCH WITH RINGO STARR?''

PART THREE – 1970
"WE DO NOT WISH TO ADD ANY MORE TO THE DIALOGUE ALREADY IN THE MEDIA"

PART FOUR –1971
SILENCE IN THE COURT TIL THE JUDGE
BLOWS HIS NOSE

PART ONE

1968

THE ENGLISH AT WORK AND PLAY

Ringo Starr

SO HOW DID you come to get this job? What were you doing before and where are you from?"

"I don't really like talking about myself –"

"Well look, this book is your idea not mine. I mean you've got to say *something*."

"I was born on September 28, 1945, at 8 A.M. at Flower Fifth Avenue Hospital, New York, New York.

"And then what? You can't just say, 'I was born on September 28, 1945, at 8 A.M. at Flower Fifth Avenue Hospital, New York, New York.' You've got to go on from there. Then what happened?"

"At twenty-two I found myself in San Francisco in the summer of 1967 trying to figure a way *out* of California where I'd been for five years because I really wanted to come to England."

"So you came to England."

"Yes, in November of '67 and London was miserable so I went to North Africa for four months and when spring rolled around I made it back to England."

"How did you land this job?"

"I was at someone's house one night and I picked up one of the musical papers and there was this picture of Derek Taylor, the Beatles' Press Officer; he looked like he was walking right out of the paper and he was talking about this thing called Apple."

"Where did you know Derek from?"

"My Hollywood days. *Everybody* knew Derek."

"And?"

"So I went in to see him and say hello and asked him for a job."

"Just like that?"

"Yup."

"What did he say?"

"He told me he'd think about it for a while and told me to call him back in a few days."

"And what happened when you called him back?"

"He said, 'Come in next Monday and start work.' But there was the problem of a work permit. He wrote to the Home Office requesting an application for working papers for a foreigner already in Great Britain. In reply to the standard Home Office query that was sent him he wrote a charming but rambling abstract letter which must have raised a few question marks because a few days later a man from the Home Office called Derek. He said, 'Mr. Taylor, we have your application for working papers for a Mr. DiLello but your letter has me a bit confused as to what it is that Mr. DiLello does that an Englishman can't do.' Well, Derek was in there like *that!* "He's a young man of great importance to a company such as ours which has to deal with artists who happen to be much closer to his age than to mine and, I might add, to our employers, The Beatles, who themselves are rapidly approaching thirty. He's able to relate to them in such a manner that I find at times impossible. I've got a wife and five children that I go home to every night and at times jumping this generation gap is a very strenuous ordeal. He's in touch with the current record scene in America where the largest percentage of our record sales come from. *He has his fingers on the pulse beat of the times!* He's literate, informed and in fact totally indispensable to this company. Because of his previous background as what we call a gofer in the record business, he has a practical working knowledge of this very important overseas market. This is an industry that is as elusive and erratic as quicksilver. We cannot afford to be out out of touch with its needs, direction and fluctuating whims.'"

"And what did the guy from the Home Office say to that!?!"

"He said, 'Yes, well I understand a bit better but, uhh, *exactly* what is it that he *does?*'"

"He's The House Hippie!!!"

"Ahh! Now I understand *perfectly*, Mr. Taylor. I'll be putting in my recommendation this afternoon for the young man's working papers. We'll say he's the Client Liaison Officer rather than The House Hippie. It sounds better. Well, sorry to have taken up so much of your time. Best of luck to you and the company. Good-bye."

And that's how I became The House Hippie of Apple Corps, Ltd.

Derek Taylor, The Beatles' Press Officer and Apple Publicist.

Gene Mahon, the man who designed the Apple label

2

**MORE MONEY
THAN GOD**

APPLE. A FINE NAME. Easy to remember and not very difficult to spell. Apple. Sounds fresh and pleasant. Apples. Good for the teeth and great for the digestion. Paul McCartney *probably* thought of the name.

In June 1963, The Beatles set up Beatles, Ltd., a company which received the major percentage of The Beatles' income as performers and recording artists. It was their piggy bank for profits earned from records, television, live appearances and merchandising royalties.

Apple Corps, Ltd., was the new name given to the old Beatles, Ltd. It was founded in February 1968. It was the mother company of the following divisions: Apple Electronics, Ltd., Apple Films, Ltd, and Apple Music Publishing. Further divisions included Apple Wholesale, Apple Retail, Apple Television and Apple Records.

Apple Records was incorporated so that Capitol Records, The Beatles' former American record label, became their distributor for retailing Apple Records in the United States of America, Canada and Mexico. EMI (Electrical and Musical Industries), their former British and European record label, was to distribute for the rest of the world.

WHEN GENE MAHON returned to the advertising agency from lunch that afternoon there was a note asking him to call Neil Aspinall at Hunter 1931. That number spelled The Beatles in not very abstract pop hieroglyphics, and the message inspired sufficient excitement to make dialing the number pleasantly difficult. When he got through, Neil asked him to come over to 95 Wigmore Street as soon as possible. It was February 1968.

Gene Mahon is an Irishman from Dublin whom everyone assumes is American because of his singular way of talking. Except, of course, another Irishman. It's an accent unconsciously cultivated from a score of Lenny Bruce records and too many American movies to remember.

Gene worked on the design of the "Sgt. Pepper" album cover. He art-directed the back sleeve which contains the lyrics to the songs along with the photograph of The Beatles in which Paul McCartney has his back turned to his audience. It was during those "Sgt. Pepper" days that Gene Mahon met Neil Aspinall, the Managing Director of Apple Corps, Ltd.

When Gene Mahon arrived at 95 Wigmore Street, Neil was there with Mal Evans, another top Apple executive. Neil and Mal share a common cultural heritage: they road-managed the Most Famous Group in the World. They're also both Liverpudlians and both were branded for life with that one unforgettable memory.

Neil told Gene that he wanted a photograph of an apple for a record label. Well, that seemed simple enough. Suddenly on the pickup – in that one instant – his flash came to him! It was one of those illuminating rushes in which the entire design universe

3

"WHO?"
"THE MAN WHO
DESIGNED THE
APPLE LABEL."
"WHO?"
"YOU KNOW,
MICHELANGELO,
THE GUY WHO
PAINTED THE
MONA LISA."

opened up. "Listen," he said, "why don't we have the A side of the record as a completely whole apple with no writing on it whatsoever. On the B side we can have an apple sliced in half with all the label copy. To avoid any confusion as to what is on which side we'll write on the left-hand side of the sliced apple *This Side*, and then give the song title, artist's name, running time, publishing, etc. Now on the other side of the sliced apple put *Other Side* with the title and the copy for the A side."

It was the ultimate Acid-Purist design concept for a record label. Neil and Mal looked at him and nodded silently. The next day Gene went to a photographer named Paul Castell and asked him to take photographs of apples: a red apple and a green apple, a whole apple and a sliced apple against a variety of colored backgrounds. Two days later Paul Castell returned with an assortment of apples on black, red, blue, green and yellow backgrounds shot on 2¼-inch transparencies.

The days melted into weeks. March became April. One Monday Mal would be drawn and pale. The next Friday he would lope into the office berry brown and glowing from long hours in the sunshine of India with The Beatles. The love affair with the Maharishi was running parallel with the birth of the Apple label and the founding of Apple Corps, Ltd.

Neil was juggling his days in much the same way. One morning London, next afternoon New York. Conferences, brain picking, dialoguing, more meetings, strings of intercontinental phone calls, a car to the airport, eight hours plastered to an airline seat, another airport, another drive into London, up to Wigmore Street, into the office and a desk full of While-You-Were-Out memos, contracts, an unending rush of paper work and responsibilities bouncing off his head. The Beatles had gone into corporate business.

Paul McCartney was the Beatle who was lavishing his days and energies on the newborn baby Apple, trying to work out the definitive Apple with Gene. When Gene had delivered the transparencies to Neil he told him, "These two are the ones I recommend and here are some others for you to consider."

The transparencies were masked in an oval so that when projected on a viewing screen they would resemble a record.

Then masses of color prints were made. Six every time. There were four Beatles, one managing director and the divisional head of Apple Records, Ron Kass. All six had to know at all times what the other five were seeing. Gene Mahon still gently insisted that the best-looking label would be the one he had initially suggested with the virgin apple face. Further weeks of deliberation followed. More high-speed trafficking back and forth between London, India and New York for Neil Aspinall and Mal Evans.

The Beatles in India. The last weeks of the Maharishi. The English press was going beserk in an orgy of abuse hurled at The Beatles and their guru from Rishikesh. The press knew no restraint and made no attempt to exercise any. Their ridicule had turned The Beatles into front-page pop fodder.

A decisive prediction was being made every other day that *this* was really the end of that celebrated four-cornered friendship. Their sublime careers would not withstand this latest flirtation with Eastern mysticism so soon after their last announcement that drugs were good for you, that they made you big and strong and creative and very, very wealthy. All of this on the heels of their *Magical Mystery Tour* film. Eyes were bright in all the dark corners of Fleet Street.

Gene Mahon's concept of a clean, unadorned apple was on a collision course with the legal requirements which bind a record company to state the contents clearly on *both* sides of a disk. The A side of the whole apple would have to have the appropriate dialogue on it. Ditto for the B side.

It was a shiny green Granny Smith apple on a black back-ground that was finally chosen as the definitive Apple apple. A great moment in the history of the fruit and record industries.

From London the artwork was sent to New York where the dye transfers were made up from which the label would be master-printed. When it was returned to London for the final touches it was handed over to another young and talented designer, Alan Aldridge, for the completion of the copyright lettering that skirts the perimeter of the record.

The entire project had taken six months from conception to completion. The Apple record label had been born.

4

THE DECLARATION OF INNOCENCE

THE PRESS INFORMED us that only two to three hundred fans were waiting at Kennedy Airport to greet their idols when they arrived on that afternoon in May of 1968. The logical explanation for this noticeably large reduction in mass adoration was best explained by the fact that there were only two of them instead of four as in previous years. Nonetheless, even halved, their reception at Kennedy Airport was warm and enthusiastic.

John Lennon and Paul McCartney were in New York to dialogue with the national media. With them was a brainy business entourage that included Derek Taylor, Neil Aspinall, Mal Evans, Ron Kass and many more. Hiring a Chinese junk to sail around Manhattan, Lennon, McCartney and staff held their first major heart-to-head business conference concerning Apple Corps, Ltd.

The first confrontation was the St. Regis Hotel press conference with Derek Taylor refereeing. It was a slightly scaled-down version of the Beatlemania of past days. From there it was onto the *Johnny Carson Show*. With Johnny Carson on holiday, Joe Garagiola subbed. The Beatles had a very unsympathetic reception. Before Lennon or McCartney had a chance to open their mouths they found themselves in the middle of a verbal blizzard of antagonism generated by a sad, gravel-voiced, burned-out movie star who for decency's sake shall remained unnamed. She tried very hard to throw a wet blanket of ridicule on their about-to-be-announced project.

In spite of her, John and Paul told an audience of 11 million viewers that The Beatles were now prepared to use their considerable influence and personal wealth to help the young people of the world. Apple was going to make it possible for an infinite number of artistic ventures to reach fruition. No longer would it be a world in which the young and the creative had to put up with unspeakable humiliations to achieve artistic freedom. The Beatles had formed an organization which would seek to finance and encourage projects of a cinematic, literary, scientific and musical nature. Apple was the company where you didn't have to come in on your hands and knees to get what you wanted. It was going to attempt to end forever the philistine conspiracy of artistic suppression and tyranny that had run rampant through the world for too long.

That night on the *Johnny Carson Show* the foundation was laid for one of the greatest experiments in show-business history. It was the start of one of the biggest snowballs of the decade. The Longest Cocktail Party had just begun.

5
WHO'S WHO IN THE ZOO; SOME OF THE PLAYERS

PETER ASHER, 23, Artists and Repertoire (A & R) man for Apple Records. A longtime acquaintance of The Beatles. Peter had run the pop gauntlet himself as one-half of a singing duo named Peter and Gordon.

NEIL ASPINALL, 26, from Liverpool. The ex-Beatle road manager, now managing director of Apple Corps, Ltd.

MAL EVANS, 32, from Liverpool. Top Beatle attaché and road manager, just a shade to the right of Neil Aspinall in the psychological Apple hierarchy.

DEREK TAYLOR, 36, from Liverpool. The Beatles' Press Officer and Apple publicist. He had to bear the weight of the top-heavy title of Ace Publicist of the Western World.

ALEXIS MARDAS, 27-year-old hush-voiced Greek electronics wizard. Mr. Apple Electronics.

RON KASS, 33, American. Division head of Apple Records and the former head of Liberty Records International Divisions. Immaculately tanned, groomed and tailored, he moved between continents, setting up record deals with the mobility of the United State Army.

DENNIS O'DELL, 45, Irish, head of Apple Films. A ruggedly handsome movie producer with a mile-long string of credits and a smile that went on forever, even when saying "No."

BRAIN LEWIS, 44, from Wallasey. Thin, gray-haired and cosmopolitan. Apple's specialized business consultant and expert in all matters of the law.

PETER BROWN, 32, from Liverpool. The late Brian Epstein's

personal assistant. The impeccable Signor Suave of the Apple diplomatic corps and personal assistant and social coordinator to The Beatles.

ALISTAIR TAYLOR, 33, from Liverpool. Ex-NEMS (North Eastern Musical Stores) general manager and currently Apple's office manager and chief fixer.

TONY BRAMWELL, 23, from Liverpool. Ex-Brain Epstein office boy. Specialized Apple Films troubleshooter and Apple's single-handed record plugger.

JEREMY BANKS, 33. The silver-haired photographic coordinator for Apple and The Beatles.

RICHARD DILELLO, 23. The House Hippie.

"Is that everybody? I mean you haven't told us what they're *really* like."

"Well, that's just a thumbnail rundown and of course it's by no means *everybody*. There's a lot more to come. Be patient. *Notre petite histoire curieuse* is only just getting off the ground."

6
PRE-APPLE APPLE

THE FIRST BEATLE venture bearing the legend Apple was their *Magical Mystery Tour* film, which was scripted, directed, cast, filmed and edited for BBC television between September and November of 1967.

The second was the Apple Boutique at 94 Baker Street, The Beatles had acquired a small building on Baker Street and commissioned a young team of designers, known collectively as The Fool, to outfit the place and inspire the line of clothes that the boutique was to sell.

The mural they art-directed on the building's facade somehow made a greater impression on the world than the clothes being sold inside. While the majority of the designs were copied after the originals of The Fool's own creations, they lacked the punch of the handmade originals. In only seven months the Apple Boutique completely degenerated into a

Terry Doran, George Harrison's personal assistant; the man who knew how many holes it took to fill the Albert Hall.

13

bog of bad taste. The only sensible solution was to give what was left away free. That was done at John Lennon's instigation in July of 1968 in what turned out to be an unprecedented and extremely undignified scramble for £20,000 worth of colorful rags.

The Baker Street location above the boutique was the first to house Apple Music Publishing. In its infancy it was looked after by Mike Berry, onetime Sparta Music gofer, and yet another old Beatle friend from Liverpool, Terry Doran, and his personal assistant, a young Londoner, Jack Oliver. There were two secretaries, Dee Meehan and Carol Paddon. The bulk of Terry Doran's time was spent managing Apple's first signed publishing quartet, Grapefruit.

Paul McCartney spearheaded Apple's initial, far-reaching, repercussive publicity campaign. He art-directed a poster that was responsible for the soon-to-follow avalanche of musical offerings of a young and extremely overstimulated public. He had his man Alistair Taylor photographed Terry Doran, George Harrison's personal assistant; the man who knew how many holes it took to fill the Albert Hall. in full busker's paraphernalia, playing a guitar, blowing a harmonica, keeping time with a drum strapped to his back and his foot glued to a washboard tub, all the while mouthing some unheard tune. The blurb above the photograph read, *This Man Has Talent*!!!

Below the photograph the copy went on to explain: ''One day he sang his songs to a tape recorder (borrowed from the man next door). In his neatest handwriting he wrote an explanatory note (giving his name and address) and remembering to enclose a picture of himself, sent the tape, letter and photograph to APPLE MUSIC: 94 BAKER STREET LONDON W1. If you were thinking of doing the same thing yourself DO IT NOW! This man now owns a Bentley!''

Coinciding with this poster campaign that blanketed London and the provinces were identical half-page ads placed in the English musical trade papers. Two weeks after the first poster hit the streets over 400 tapes had accumulated in the small office at 94 Baker Street. All with notes saying, *Listen to me first.*

The Baker Street premises were able to function as a mailing address for the incoming musical tapes, but for the remainder of the sprouting tentacles of the empire an entire floor in an office building behind Oxford Street was rented in early February of 1968.

7

SO LISTEN, this is what we do. Tomorrow we call up Apple and fix an appointment to see that guy who's the head of their film department, uhh, what's his name now –"
 "O'Dell –"
"Yeah, that's it. So then we go in, very calm like, and lay it on him! Say, 'Look, we want to make this movie see, and uhh all we need is twenty thousand pounds on the *outside*, dig? It's a film about this guy, a real genius, astrophysicist type of brilliant cat. Anyway, he's come up with this pill, you dig?, that's the pill of the century. See, whenever you take this pill you immediately become whoever you want to become. Like if I wanted to be Alexander the Great and I took this pill then I'd suddenly be Alexander the Great –"
"Sort of a man of a thousand souls, huh?"
"Yeah, you got it. Now we tell him that a deal like this, with the script we've got, can't lose. It's not like we need big lavish sets or anything, just a few special effects."
"What about Ringo?"
"I'm getting to that. *Then* we tell him that we've written this really wild part for Ringo to play. And with Ringo in it how can you lose?"
"Right!"
"And this is a very important movie –"
"It's *got* to be made –"
"It's about the malaise of our age –"
"The *what* of our age? –"
"You know, the *hang-ups* of our times –"
"Oh yeah, right –"

15

"It's about someone who doesn't want to be himself. It's about all of us really."

"It's got to be a winner."

"They can't say no –"

"Besides, what's twenty thousand pounds?"

"Right!"

Meanwhile, halfway across town:

"It's not like I'm on any kind of a *personal* ego trip, I mean I'm not asking for anything for myself, this is something for all our brothers and sisters. So I'm just going to tell it to him straight. I'm going to say, 'Hey man, I'm not out to hustle you for bread or anything like that!' I'll tell him. I'll say, 'Hey, look, John, I myself, *personally*, can raise a million bucks like that! (Snap!) This is the deal. We buy six square miles of land in southern Arizona from the United States government, but we don't tell them what it's for because it's none of their business and anyway they'll probably just hassle you. So then we start building the place up, toilets, parking lots, campsites, the whole number. So that by next summer it's ready. Do you realize that this is going to be the greatest rock 'n' roll festival of all time!!! Every band in the world is going to be there, with acreage like that we'll be able to get a million people together at once, maybe two million, even three million if we do it right. We fix it so that it goes on for two weeks, running day and night. On the last day of the festival we fly The Beatles in to close it. Can you see that! The Beatles doing an hour-and-a-half spot!' So I'll tell Lennon, I'll say 'You guarantee me that The Beatles will show up for the gig, you know announce it to the papers, and I'll get the rest of it together.' I'm really going to get into his head. You wait, this is really going to be fucking far out!"

While not even halfway across town but just downstairs in the very same building:

"I'm not into being a star or anything like that, man, I just wanna play the blues. I'm sick of these record companies with their lame bullshit riffs, a lot of jiveass cats! You get really hassled with that business scene, fucks your head up right-eously. I figure that McCartney cat really knows where it's at. I get that buzz from his music, you dig? So I'll tell him I just need

16

some studio time, that's all. He can produce me for the first album. I mean I don't wanna get into any big scenes or anything. All he has to do is just *be* there. Anyway it's not gonna take that long. I've got enough material for *two* albums. Shit! you should hear what I hear inside my head –''

''Well, I'd like to –''

''This record's gonna fuckin' blow your mind! Like I said, man, I just wanna play the blues.''

And even more than halfway across the world:

''I have the very strong conviction that our problem is solved. I'll write a letter to Mr. Harrison and explain the unfortunate circumstances that we find ourselves in at the moment, my dear brother. It is well known that Mr. Harrison is very fond of Mother India and its inhabitants. I will tell him how you arrived from India this month to study television production at the university for the next two years and how you intend to then return to your country where you will be a pioneer in this new medium and how great things can be expected to come from all this. I will of course look after your accommodations while you pursue your studies but as I am unable to afford your tuition, and seeing how the immigration laws prohibit you from gaining employment while you are in this country, perhaps Mr. Harrison would be so gracious as to give us assistance towards this matter of your education and tuition costs. I know that he is a very kind person and it will be a pleasurable experience communicating with him''

T HE FIRST NEWSPAPER Derek Taylor ever worked for was the *Hoylake and West Kirby Advertiser*, joining at 17 as an indentured apprentice at the standard salary of 30 shillings a week. A score of newspapers were to employ his considerable cerebral talents in the years that followed.

He was working as the northern theater critic for the *Daily Express* when the news desk instructed him to cover the Roy

8

DEREK TAYLOR OF THE HOYLAKE AND WEST KIRBY ADVERTISER

Orbison/Beatles Show at the Manchester Odeon, London Road, on May 30, 1963. His orders were to bring back a negative story. The word was that The Beatles had deserted their fans and their newly acquired popularity was on the brink of extinction.

After seeing them up close during the first half of that show, he knew he was going to have to refuse that request. He did so, bringing back an ecstatic review. That night Derek Taylor was transformed into an unregenerate Beatlemaniac.

On The Beatles' first American visit in February 1964, their Press Officer was Brian Sommerville. When they landed at Kennedy Airport and found themselves in the midst of that unprecedented crush of hysteria, Sommerville's comment was "This entire affair has gotten completely out of hand."

Soon after that Derek Taylor graduated from the post of northern theater critic of the *Daily Express* to Brain Epstein's personal assistant. He ghosted the Epstein autobiography, *A Cellar Full of Noise*, knocking it together in a few weeks under immense pressures and on the run. Shortly after publication of that book he became the new Beatles Press Officer. From there it was Take-Off-Around-The-World-With-The-Beatles. Barnstorming had been rejuvenated.

On the last night of the Beatles' 1964 American tour at their New York charity concert, Derek and Brian Epstein got into a raging, blood-boiling row over some minor point of protocol and Derek resigned, but there were no hard feelings between him and The Beatles.

He returned to England and his wife, Joan, and their four children, Timothy, Gerard, Victoria and Vanessa. Then the offer from Hollywood came. A Los Angeles disk jockey named Bob Eubanks asked him to go to work for radio station KRLA as publicist and ex-Beatles Press Officer. They offered him a Hollywood salary and all expenses paid.

By the time Derek Taylor hit Hollywood he was bigger than Coney Island and pizza pie. KRLA had used the full force of its airwaves in a prearrival Derek Taylor publicity campaign, shamelessly turning him into a major Los Angeles freak-show attraction.

The KRLA gig didn't last long. In a few short weeks the lurking truth became the obvious reality. There was nothing that even vaguely resembled an excuse for a continued relationship with Eubanks and KRLA. Head contact was non-existent.

The break was painless. Derek acquired a secretary, two desks, three chairs, a telephone, two typewriters and moved further down Sunset Boulevard to the 9000 building. He was in business.

It was the summer of 1965 and the Byrds. They became his first clients. In those days he could announce with supreme conviction and without fear of contradiction that the Byrds were the Best Group in America. After that he took on Captain Beefheart, the Beach Boys, Paul Revere and the Raiders, and his stable of clients continued to grow.

In 1967 along with Lou Adler, John Phillips and Alan Pariser he pulled off the Monterey Pop Festival. After the success of the world's first pop festival he retired to the Hollywood Hills. His fifth child, Dominic, was born and it was time to sit by the pool and think it all over. The children had begun to lose their accents and Joan began remembering the past beauty of English springs and The Beatles wanted him back. Apple was one month old and in need of someone to stand between *them* and *it*.

Then came the task of moving five children, one wife and a houseful of worldly possessions back to England. He decided the best way to do it was to throw a party. He sent a letter to all his friends.

1416 N. La Brea Avenue/Hollywood, California/461–9931
Date . . . now or never.

My dear American friend,
It's been wonderful to be here, certainly a thrill; you've been a lovely audience, I'd like to take you home with me, I'd love to take you home but I can't afford the fare for all of you. Alas.
On Friday, March 29, I have to leave for England after three magic years and because Hollywood deserves some repay-

ment in freakery for the freakish leaps, loops and twists and tantalizing trickery which have enabled me to turn three years into an enchanted garden of fun and fantasy, I thought I would manipulate Thursday, March 28, into a final phantasmagoria of a warm, nostalgic dance.

You are invited to attend with a partner because you have been so much a part of the fun and frenzy with which the family and I have been so generously surrounded since 1965.

The dance will be held at Ciro's. Do you remember Ciro's? When the Byrds first flew? It became, "It's Boss." It became, "Spectrum 2000." Oh dear.

It's closed now but on Thursday, March 28, at 8:30 P.M. it will reopen as *Ciro's* – Ciro's for one night for *us*, and the Byrds will return; older Byrds now, but still the Byrds. Dear deadpan Captain Beefheart will be there too, to play and belong. Everyone will be there. It will be a lovely night and it will be what we all deserve.

Admission will be by invitation only – a pretty invitation card which will smooth you with ease past benign un-uniformed friend/doorman to an evening of music, color, wine and love. It is regretted that having given all my money to the Black Panthers, the E1 Monte Geranium Fund, and the Friends of Elks, I have to charge $5.50 per ticket to float the flight fare home, to pacify Pacific Telephone and set Seaboard straight. Time is short – the invitations are ready and will be forwarded on receipt of your kindly check. The impertinence of it all astounds me but won't it be great, folks. Love as ever, Derek. Good-bye, Hollywood, California!

He made it back to England and a rambling house in the Berkshire countryside and The Beatless all over again. The Longest Cocktail Party had just acquired its most eloquent number-one Toastmaster.

Once installed at 95 Wigmore Street, The Press Officer didn't waste time. He surveyed his new employee. "Now that you're a sanctioned, bonafide member of the recording industry of Great Britain it's time to get to work," he said to The

Jackie Lomax

House Hippie. "Come with me." Inside his office he pointed to an enormous cardboard box filled with press cuttings.

"You see those cuttings –"

"Yes –"

"Well, I want you to go through them and break them into the following categories: Beatles Maharishi, Beatles Favorable, Beatles Hostile, Beatles Apple and Beatles Brief – that's anything having the single word Beatle in it, like Beatle haircut – then Beatles USA and Beatles Duplicate. When you're done that, let me know."

"Ok, chief."

"And don't take all day to do them either because there's another five boxes just like that in the next room."

9

THE EARLY DAYS OF A RECORD COMPANY'S STRUGGLE TO REACH THE TOP; THE ACQUISITION OF APPLE TALENT

*T*HE FORMULA FOR success is a combination of the right talent and the proper handling and packaging of that talent. You can have a genius going for you and still screw it up if you don't channel that genius properly."

"Right –"

"First off we've got this American singer and songwriter named James Taylor, who from all indications is going places. He's penned quite a few songs for Tom Rush and now he's coming into his own.

He's got himself a piano player and bass player and they're hard at work rehearsing a dozen of his own compositions. He knows just what he wants and is going to get there. His choice of musicians has been well thought out and they've proved they can do the work and complement his style of playing. So far so good. By the last week in June he'll be ready to start recording his first album. His publishing position with Apple is still open to discussion as he's unsigned. If we're smart we'll scoop him up right now. It looks like Peter Asher will be handling his personal management and producing his records.

"There's a lovely seventeen-year-old Welsh singer named Mary Hopkin who has been on *Opportunity Knocks* three times and won each time. She's cast in the mold of the Joan Baez school of folk singing but is very much her own singer. Her father has handed over a letter of agreement to Apple. Also we've had someone from the record company with her each time she's made a television appearance. If we don't sign her soon someone else will. And a few have already made tentative approaches. In the event that Paul's time is not soaked up with his own music, it's likely he'll produce her records. He's already said that he's got a single in mind for her debut. She hasn't started writing her own material yet, so consequently her publishing is open for negotiation.

"Mal Evans has discovered a group called the Iveys. They've never recorded before outside their demo tapes, which sound very interesting. John and George are very impressed with them. We've also played their tapes to Denny Cordell, who's an excellent group producer, and at the moment it looks as though he's willing to produce a single for them when they're ready. They write all of their own songs and are really quite prolific and hardworking and happily they're signed to us.

"There's a solo singer from Liverpool named Jackie Lomax who used to be with a group called the Undertakers and then moved on to form another group in America called the Lomax Alliance. Brian Epstein brought them back to England. Jackie wants to be on Apple and George recognizes his potential and is probably going to produce him.

"That Swedish group, Bamboo, sent Peter Asher a record they made for Swedish EMI and Peter played it to Paul who thought the lead singer all right but that the song didn't make it. Peter wrote them and said we were interested in the group and they called him up to make it quite clear to us that they were only signed to Swedish EMI and therefore they were free and clear for the rest of the world. Peter sent another letter to them just to find out if they had anything else they'd recorded and they got so excited that they sent us a telegram saying they'd be here by the end of the week. Anyway, if they show up we'll give them an audition and take it from there.

"This very strange group called Contact has approached us with some very far-out ideas. Musically they don't make it but their lyrics are good. Peter's not too hot about them but he played their tapes to John and he said give them a few days in the studio to see what they can come up with. They've got this song called *Lovers from the Sky*, which is a song welcoming the flying saucers which the group leader, Trevor, says are going to be here *very* soon. It may sound like a load of crap but it would be embarrassing if the prophecy came true and Apple was the company that rejected their representatives on earth. Stuff like that makes for very bad press. We've got to take all that into consideration.

"The Black Dyke Mills Brass Band is going to record one of Paul's songs that he's written as a theme for a television show. They've been consistent first-place winners in brass-band competitions in England for several years running now. They record for Pye on a record-to-record deal and get paid by session money and the band's conductor, Geoffrey Brand,

23

gets a small royalty. We've got the session arranged for June 30, which is a Sunday, at 9 A.M. at the Victoria Hall in Bradford. The B side of their single will probably be a Lennon/McCartney number; someone suggested *Yellow Submarine.*

"There's a French group signed to Barclay Records in Paris called the Pebbles. Their manager, Rikki Stein, says their records have been released all over the world except for England. He's been onto Peter about a deal between Barclay and Apple which would give them a better distribution deal with a possible mutual swap on their masters. Peter likes their stuff but at the same time he's undecided and Paul feels the same way.

"Keith Moon would like to produce some records for us as well as Denny Cordell. Manfred Mann, who's doing pretty well as a freelance producer, also wants to do something with us and says he'll come to us before he goes anywhere else. He figures he'll get the best up-front deal from us.

"It also looks like the Modern Jazz Quartet is going to be signed very soon and it's pretty certain that Nilsson also is going to be one of our next scores. Publishing and Records have been swamped in the past couple of weeks with tapes. Publishing says they've pulled quite a few promising songs out of the mailbags. The way it looks now is we can't help but come up winners but there's always the chance that we could trip over our own egos and blow the whole thing but that doesn't seem very likely, does it?"

"Nahh."

10

**THE FUN
CONTINUES**

I F YOU DID A quick walk-through and caught it all from the corner of your eye, the reception lounge at 95 Wigmore Street in that summer of 1968 looked like the waiting room at a VD clinic in Haight-Ashbury at the height of the Acid Madness of '67. Ground traffic control had a hard time scheduling the flow.

It seemed that every singer, songwriter, fast-buck artist,

apache and second-story man in town was hitting the fan and winding up at Apple. Well over half the Apple staff had been recruited from NEMS and the Liverpool days when Brian Epstein had actively discouraged his employees from talking to The Beatles beyond a brisk "Hello." Thank God the world had changed a little since then. Everyone from that old scene had to make rapid, major readjustments in their psyches to survive.

It was a matter of self-preservation. A fairly effective system of filtration had been worked out by July to protect The Beatles and their senior staff from abrasive situations that could prove embarrassing and potentially volatile. The underground had come up blinking into fluorescent lights and proved surprisingly aggressive.

And Poetry and Prose just kept rolling through the doors, wave upon wave. If it didn't come in tucked under a clutching arm, dogeared and coffee-stained, then it found its way through the mail. The pile of manuscripts was inflating itself to grosser proportions day by day.

The majority of the letters that accompanied these offerings shared the same mood, no matter what corner of the globe they came from. The running order was very much the same.

The first paragraph was always an apology for having written in the first place. It was intimated by the writer of the letter and the creator of the verse that obviously the reader (especially if it were a Beatle) had better things to do than read stuff like this, having by now forgotten that it was Apple that had invited the submission in the first place.

The second paragraph apologized for the actual contents of the package, making it quite plain from the start that what was inside was not as gifted an offering as any of the Beatles might have produced had he made the same effort.

The third paragraph apologized for the presentation and was usually crammed with footnotes. The more desperate ones then sank to demand that the unclean be cleansed. It was that old hangover from the barnstorming days of Beatlemania; only this time the supplications took on the guise of artistic faith healing.

But Poetry and Prose was only a fraction of the hustle.

For the most part it was the young who were attracted. The hopelessly straight and middle-aged shied away. But the gutter publicity had spread lavalike over London. Apple was a soft touch if you could crack the security cordon. It was actually a soft touch only because everyone was determined that the experiment should succeed.

One afternoon, as The House Hippie moved through the reception lounge heading for The Press Officer's room, he felt a sharp tap-tapping on his shoulder. Turning in that direction he heard a voice asking for a few minutes of his time. "Sure man, a few minutes is my middle name."

And then The House Hippie took a good look at the man who had asked the question. It was the Deranged Filthy Faun Raincoat. The only color the poor fellow seemed to radiate was the green, carpetlike moss on his teeth. Flecks of salvia were gathered at the corners of his mouth. His eyes were dissolute pools of the most intense grayish madness and the accumulation of old sleep seeds made him look like the victim of terminal conjunctivitis. His neatly water-combed, slicked-back hair was as greasy as the ventilation shaft of a third-string hamburger emporium. The dandruff on top looked like a heavy snowfall in January. The House Hippie took one step back.

"You see the reason I'm here, young man, is because I've evolved a system and I must speak to John Lennon about it."

"What kind of a system?"

"Ahh! It's an amazing system really. I've cracked the barrier that separates humans from the creatures of the animal kingdom and the only person who will be able to understand me is John Lennon."

"Uhh –"

The Faun Raincoat pulled from his pocket a sheet of crumpled paper covered in some private, incomprehensible shorthand.

"And this poem here," he pointed to some inky gibberish, "I wrote this afternoon at the zoo while I was having my lunch. The first verse is by *me* and the next verse is by *them*. It goes on like that to the end of the poem."

26

And then he pulled out the uneaten half of his lunch, a rancid-looking, dried-out tomato and cheese affair and offered it to The House Hippie.

"No thanks, I've just eaten."

"Well, in that case I'll finish it myself."

He did it in three chews with a huge grin, never taking his eyes from The House Hippie.

"Delicious! Well, you know all the animals in the Regent's Park Zoo are my friends, all of them, and I'm going to write a book about them but, uhh, I'm a little short on funds. However with a little financial support; well, perhaps it would be more appropriate if I discussed this matter with John Lennon."

"Uhh –"

At that moment The Press Officer's secretary's lovely face came into focus.

"Richard, Derek wants to see you right now."

"Excuse me, sir –" and The House Hippie was gone, leaving the Faun Raincoat breathless with darting eyes sweeping the reception lounge for someone else who might get him to John Lennon.

"Derek doesn't want to see you but I just had to rescue you from that fucking maniac out there. He latched on to me a few weeks back and wouldn't stop."

The House Hippie shook his head up and down in silent appreciation, wilting from relief. He had just been "Beatled" for the very first time.

All systems were go. Mid-July 1968 was a very crucial month for Apple. In addition to the projects on the board in films, electronics and merchandising there was the one that assumed precedence above all others: the launching of Apple Records. The music was, after all, the rock that the dream was built on.

The response to the ads placed in the trade papers and the poster campaign had in fact proved too successful. The number of tapes coming in was out of all proportion to the Publishing and Records Departments' ability to give each one a fair share of a listen. Most of the musical discoveries were coming by word of mouth.

Frankie Hart

Ron Kass was winging his way back and forth between America, London, Europe and South America with a singular, determined regularity, tying up all the last-minute strings with Capitol and EMI for the August world debut of Apple Records.

By now two songs had been recorded and regarded as Apple's royal flush: *Hey Jude* by The Beatles and *Those Were the Days* by Mary Hopkin. Everyone said they couldn't help but become number-one worldwide smash hits.

11
YOU LEARN SOMETHING NEW EVERY DAY

I N HIS CAPACITY as Apple librarian, The House Hippie was eventually forced to read what he had to catalogue. It was the beginning of his introduction to the English press. And he was in for a surprise.

For some uneducated reason he had always been under the impression that the American and French press were the world's most hostile journalists. But it didn't look that way anymore. Somehow it seemed only fair to yield that unsavory distinction to the English press, hands down.

Dipping into his backlog of cuttings from the critics' reviews of the *Magical Mystery Tour* film, he was shocked to witness the English press's sudden about face on their own homespun heroes. To err on the side of generosity, it was a bit harsh. More truthfully, it was downright cynical and aggressively hostile. The character assassination of The Beatles had begun. The full moon was up and the press wanted to see its effects on this latest escapade called Apple.

The Press Officer had been through it all. He had been a journalist and a very successful one. It helps to be a good journalist if you can contain great quantities of beer, gin and whiskey. It's most important to have a zinc-coated stomach that can survive wretched, infrequent meals in whatever place you can grab them. It's not an easy life. You've always got to be perched on someone else's doorstep poking a cold nose into business that you've got to make your own when it isn't.

Alternatively you have to be rude, charming, unfeeling, sympathetic, dogmatic, ruthless and perceptive. You have to know your adjectives from your dangling participles. You have to take shorthand and rapid-type with two fingers with smoke in your eyes and hard lights burning overhead, with the roar of a thousand telephones in your ears – and never once have the satisfaction of running screaming down the corridor of some musty, ink-sodden building shouting out your most cherished fantasy summed up in the three words, "*Stop the Press!*"

The Press Officer hated the press for what they could do to a person's life when they'd set their minds to it. He was particularly unsympathetic with them for what they were doing to The Beatles now. It was a very schizophrenic position to maintain, as he had to dialogue with them every day of his life.

12

A HOT BREEZE IN JULY

CHRIS O'DELL, 22, slim and blonde, left her home in Tucson, Arizona, for a life as a gofer in the jungle of the Hollywood record business before she got the English bug, found herself working in London for a company called Apple and became a line in a popular song of the day.

Someone had told her if she were ever going to London, "I'll give you a letter of introduction to Peter Asher at Apple Records." That's all she had to hear. Two shakes later she had sold everything she owned, brushed her hair, put on her lipstick and, clutching her single suitcase and letter of introduction, took off. Within two weeks she had graduated from Apple receptionist to secretary to A & R man Peter Asher.

Francie Schwartz was a slim, short-haired brunette from Pennsylvania who had spent time in New York City getting herself educated. She came to London in the late spring of '68 with a film script that needed backing. She arrived at Apple.

One afternoon she saw Paul McCartney in the Wigmore

Street reception lounge and told him her reason for coming to London. He expressed a courteous interest in her project but did not commit himself to a yes or no. He could see straight off that she was bright and New York hip. He told her she could hang around the office and help out where she could. "All heads on deck" was the order of the day.

There was an astrologer named Caleb who subbed as a fortuneteller for John Lennon, Paul McCartney and the Apple staff. His job was to read the stars daily and make a prediction: to move or not to move. Splitting his hours between his astral charts and the *I Ching*, he would make the daily rounds of the staff throwing three pennies and interpreting everyone's lines. After a while, having been asked for a chart prediction in *Billboard* one too many times, he decided it was time to go home forever.

The House Hippie was sitting in The Press Officer's room one afternoon, lazy as a lizard, lounging in the sunshine that flooded through the window when a slim, blonde American girl poked her head through the door and said, "Hi! My name's Chris. Some of the girls told me there was this really weird guy in here who's kind of freaked out and said I should come in and talk to him." Now The House Hippie *knew* he was the only one in that matchbox of a room but something made him turn his head first to the left and then to the right to confirm it before the thought occurred to him that this attractive country-woman of his had a come-on as subtle as an elephant. It was the beginning of a beautiful friendship.

The next day The House Hippie was again in The Press Officer's room when John Lennon walked in and asked him for a tanner. The House Hippie froze. It was the occasion of his first face-to-face meeting with his employer and he didn't know what a tanner was. He was reluctant to admit his ignorance. He knew what a "spanner" was and wondered if it was anything like a tanner when a voice said, "That's all right, John, I've got one." John Lennon thanked The House Hippie anyway and left. When The Press Officer came in a little while later The House Hippie asked him what a tanner was. "It's a sixpence, man."

The day after that The House Hippie was working on his press cuttings in the film room when who should come tearing into the cramped office but George Harrison. He was moving so fast that there seemed to be a cloud of dust in his wake. Neil Aspinall was right behind him.

He took one look at The House Hippie and jumped back as if he'd just seen the Gorgon's Head and knew it was all over. He almost knocked Neil Aspinall through the glass partition to the next office.

"Who is *that*?" he screamed.

The managing director came to The House Hippie's rescue with the *Good Housekeeping* Seal of Approval. "Aww, he's all right. He's Derek's mate, he's looking after the photees and the press cuttings."

George didn't say anything. He just looked at The House Hippie and slowly backed out of the room.

When he saw The Press Officer later that day, The House Hippie expressed his dismay at his first, rather unsuccessful encounter with his folk hero and Beatle boss, George Harrison.

"Quite frankly, Derek, I don't think he likes me."

"I wouldn't lose any sleep over it," said The Press Officer. "He'll get used to you. When we went to Haight-Ashbury last summer all those Hippies left a bad taste in his mouth with that, 'Hey man, play something on the guitar for us' stuff. Don't worry about it."

"But I wasn't even *in* Haight-Ashbury that day. Don't you remember? I was sitting on the curb in front of the Condor Club in North Beach when the limousine with you and George and Patti drove by. I started screaming, 'Hey Derek! Over here!' And all of you started to wave back. Don't you remember *that*?"

"No, man, we were so stoned we just waved at anything that moved."

THE DAY AFTER Paul McCartney left for the Capitol Records convention in Hollywood to announce that from August on all Beatles records were going to be released on a world-wide basis through Apple, The Press Officer announced to The House Hippie that he had found the partner he had been looking for over the past 36 years. His name was Jeremy Banks.

Derek Taylor first met Jeremy Banks on November 3, 1966, at the Arthur Howes Agency in London. He had accompanied his clients, the Beach Boys, on their British tour and Jeremy, who was handling special features for the *Daily Sketch*, was there with his star photographer, John Kelly, to get the story.

It was an extremely profitable meeting for everyone. Jeremy got his story and a photograph of the Beach Boys in a rowboat on the Serpentine that turned into an impressive seven-column spread. Jeremy and John Kelly went along with Derek and the Beach Boys for the remainder of their tour. It was a good beginning.

Derek said that Jeremy would be of invaluable assistance to Apple via his connections that spanned the entire city of Greater Glossy London. Jeremy, after years in Fleet Street as a photographic entrepreneur, was as thoroughly versed in the placing of visuals as Derek was in the art of dialogue. It appeared to be the ideal partnership.

The Press Officer told The House Hippie that Jeremy Banks was in the corner office and would like a drink. On entering the room The House Hippie saw two men in their early thirties with almost identical long salt-and-pepper hair. One was babyishly plump and the other aesthetically emaciated. The thinner of the two was Roman O'Rahilly, the founder of Pirate Radio in England.

Jeremy Banks motioned The House Hippie forward with a crooked, wagging finger. "My good man, would you be so kind as to get my very dear friend a glass of milk and I would like a vodka and Coke, very light on the Coke, please." The House Hippie nodded yes and returned five minutes later with the refreshments.

They were both sitting in identical office chairs opposite each other and Jeremy was weaving some obviously great story of intrigue in a guarded, hushed voice. Ronan was completely absorbed in Jeremy's tale. From the whispered intensity of the conversation The House Hippie was certain that they had just discovered the missing arms of the Venus de Milo.

He gave Jeremy his vodka and Coke – with the word "Coke" barely breathed over it so artfully had he mixed the drink – and Ronan O'Rahilly his glass of milk. They both thanked him at once. On his way out the door The House Hippie was called back by Jeremy Banks's voice.

"Young man!"

"Yes –"

"That was very, very kind of you. If there is *ever* anything I can do for you, *anything*, do not hesitate to let me know. Do you understand?"

"Yes, all right, thank you."

"Then, once again they both thanked The House Hippie and he thanked them again. He was going to thank them again for saying thanks but quickly decided it was best not to overdo it.

Outside in reception The House Hippie thought to himself, "All I did was get them a drink and he promises me the keys to the Kingdom of Heaven. I mean he was quite emphatic about me having *anything* I wanted. No wonder this is the guy Derek's been looking for for the past thirty-six years."

He came into The Press Officer's room one afternoon, a painfully thin fellow with shoulder-length brown hair and finely chiseled features. Together they talked about Liverpool, George Harrison, the dead old days and the shape of Apple to come. After he had left, The House Hippie asked The Press Officer, "Who was that?" The Press Officer looked surprised at his question. "Don't you know him? That's one of the great Liverpool rockers from back when. His name is Jackie Lomax and George is going to make him a star."

From playing in an unknown, getting-nowhere New York City rock band to being signed to The Beatles' new record label was a change of life-style that one had to ease into, like a new pair of shoes. When he wasn't over at Trident Studios putting the final touches to his first Apple album together with Peter Asher, James Taylor would pass through 95 Wigmore Street to reluctantly view the workings of the star-making publicity machinery that was bent on making *him* a star. The first time The House Hippie saw James Taylor he was in the same room with Derek Taylor and Alistair Taylor, rolling a cigarette with a glass of scotch in front of him, oblivious to all the dialogue bouncing off the walls.

The Press Officer made The House Hippie read a press release he had just written to Paul McCartney over the telephone to see how it sounded with an American accent. When he had finished he handed the receiver over to The Press Officer who asked Paul McCartney what he thought. Watching The Press Officer, The House Hippie turned over in his mind the question that his curiosity would oblige him to ask the minute The Press Officer was finished with Paul McCartney. Who was the Japanese lady with the very beautiful, fantastically thick waterfall of jet-black hair, always dressed in white, who kept coming in and out with John Lennon? "She's an artist from your part of the world, New York. Her name is Yoko Ono."

14

"BECAUSE I DON'T LOVE THE QUEEN BUT I DO LOVE YOKO."

THE REASON John Lennon was looking for a tanner that day was not because he needed the spare change to buy a hot meal but to try out one of those mechanical charity collection boxes that you feed a coin to and in return it gives you a 20-second display of monetary, digestive acrobatics. You drop a coin into the dog's paw, his eyes light up, his tail starts wagging, he says "Arf" and then pisses after consuming your sixpence.

John and Yoko were staging one of their first public happenings. It was the "You Are Here" show at the Robert Fraser Gallery off Oxford Street. It was their rapid-fire follow-up to a show in Covent Garden, where a handful of artists had been asked to donate a piece of their work. Time has obliterated the memory of what it was that John and Yoko contributed. It *might* have been a potted acorn or it could have been a chair with the legend, "Sit on this." Perhaps it was neither.

It was a very hot day towards the end of July when The House Hippie walked into the fifth-floor office at 95 Wigmore Street at two o'clock in the afternoon. The Press Officer approached him, handed over a card with the name and address of a nearby art gallery and told him that John Lennon had 500 white balloons that needed blowing up.

"Is he having a party?"

"No, he's having an exhibit and he and Yoko are going to release the balloons on the street later this evening."

"But I'm in no shape to blow up five hundred balloons –"

"You do it with the helium tanks."

"Ohh –"

When he arrived at the Robert Fraser Gallery there were a dozen people running around in the usual, pregallery-opening, last-minute panic. He looked around for the canvases but didn't see any.

There was a spiral staircase leading to the basement room. It was filled with charity collection boxes: boxes for the blind, for the spastic, for the Royal Society for the Protection of Birds, Donkeys, Lepers, dozens and dozens of boxes with a notice on the wall asking you to feed them. Behind a glassed-over partition was a movie camera on a tripod which was to film the comings and goings of everyone attending the opening.

John Lennon was there and took The House Hippie upstairs just as half a dozen helium tanks arrived together with the 500 white balloons. Yoko came in a few minutes later and she and John moved off to a corner to talk with Robert Fraser. The House Hippie got to work on the balloons. Looking around, he kept thinking that the day was getting on and still the canvases hadn't arrived – just the collection boxes downstairs and the balloons in progress upstairs.

Finally he asked Robert Fraser when the rest of the exhibit

would be arriving and he said curtly, "That's it," indicating with a nod towards the wall. The House Hippie looked behind him and there on the wall was a freshly painted stark white circular canvas that was six feet from top to bottom. When he moved up close he could read the minute, perfectly centered inscription: "You Are Here."

Two hundred balloons later The House Hippie handed over his task to Kevin Harrington, road manager for The Beatles, because it was time for him to baby-sit for The Press Officer so that he could attend the opening that evening.

When The Press Officer and his wife returned to their country home at two the next morning The House Hippie asked him how it had gone.

"Aside from the fact that there was nothing to drink except bottled water, it was fine. Those balloons you blew up had tags attached to them asking the finder to write to John. It looks like he's become the Rousseau of this generation."

15
THE LAMPS GO ON

THE WHITE BALLOONS eventually came down from the sky. In much the same way as a message found in a bottle washed up on a beach asking for a reply compels a response, so did John Lennon's helium-filled white bubbles. Some of the messages were lighthearted and well-wishing. Others asked for financial assistance, while a disturbing number hurled racial and sexual slurs at John Lennon's and Yoko Ono's relationship.

When Yoko Ono fell in love with John Lennon she also fell into the Biggest Goldfish Bowl in Town. From the very beginning Yoko was under public pressure. She was immediately aware that in the eyes of a certain portion of the show-business public, theirs was an unpopular liaison. There were few who publicly gave this partnership their blessing. With a beginning like that, the seeds of paranoia needed little tending.

There was already a lot going against Yoko Ono when she walked into the goldfish bowl. She was overeducated, spoke several languages, was highly proficient in the culinary arts and a writer of verse and creator of sculpture. She was well versed in history and a survivor of the New York avant-garde scrap race. She was also an older woman and Japanese. Somehow she managed to carry it all with ease, as she did her hair, as part of the terrain.

On the ground floor, closer to home, was a less threatening case of flu than the public's resentment of John Lennon's conversion to black hair from blonde, but one that none-theless needed getting used to. Apple was a very inbred scene. Everyone around John had been there for years. There were few new faces. They were mostly from the Liverpool days of NEMS and the Cavern and the touring years. The claustro-phobia of it all had a way of sometimes smelling a bit off but never evil, never truly evil. It didn't take long for John Lennon to catch a whiff of that breeze.

The press wasted no time. They would tell you, "That's our job." A statement difficult to refute but easy enough to have little sympathy with. The press chose the night of June 18, 1968, to launch the persecution of John Lennon and Yoko Ono.

Victor Spinetti had directed John's one-act play, *In His Own Write*, for the opening of the National Theater's season at the Old Vic in London. Lennon was expected to attend opening night with his newly rumored love, Yoko Ono.

When John, Yoko and Neil Aspinall arrived, Fleet Street was waiting. The story they were expected to bring back to the news desk had previously been worked out down to the column-inch. It was to be brief and to the point, including a captioned photograph of the couple. They had just one question to ask John, "Where's your wife?" The question was to carry a premeditated edge to it in order to goad John into snapping "I don't know!" It was important that he react in that way so the press could record his mood as well as the substance of the reply. They got what they went after.

Private Eye is the only publication in Britain that fears no world power, popular personality or resident government party. Because of its singular fearlessness it might well claim, along with a handful of selected devil's advocates, to have coined that pooped-out cliché, "No cow is sacred." Its strength lies in its pure viciousness, its ability to cut through every layer of socially accepted good taste and pompous public reform.

It seems to know everything that happens before it happens and will never hesitate to blab what its informants have come up with. Paid spies are the hemoglobin of many a successful organization and this one is no exception. *Private Eye's* most brilliant achievement, once one has acknowledged the importance of its social lampooning, is that hardly anyone bothers to sue them anymore.

Private Eye smiled when Yoko Ono walked into the world's headlines with John Lennon holding her hand. In the mythology of the times, Yoko Ono was miraculously transformed into Okay Yoni. Students of the *Kama Sutra* will appreciate this exercise of artistic license – seemingly the only license left in this age that cannot be revoked.

For years *Private Eye* has been running its continuing story of Spiggy Topes and the Turds. This is their flexible, cover-all putdown of pop moronics. Spiggy Topes is John Lennon, the Turds are The Beatles. When necessary, Spiggy Topes is Mick Jagger and the Rolling Stones the Turds. In the end we are all Spiggy Topes and without question, we are all Turds. *Private Eye's* ever-bouncing tennis-ball headline question is: "Is it all up for Spiggy Topes and the Turds?"

THE ADVANCE PARTY that had been sent ahead to blaze a trail at the new Beatle offices at 3 Savile Row in the next to last week in July 1968 had precious little to work with. The Press Officer had The House Hippie and a substitute secretary replacing his regular who was on vacation. The partner that Derek Taylor had been looking for over the past

16

LSD CONDITIONS AND BEAUTIFIES TROUBLED HAIR IN SECONDS

36 years had decided that the accommodations at the moment were a bit too primitive for his refined tastes. Jeremy Banks had informed Derek that he would be moving into Savile Row as soon as the interior decorators had "gotten it all together." In the meantime he would split his working days between Wigmore Street and his Chelsea studio in Pimlico Road.

A house always seems bigger than it is when it's new. As familiarity grows it shrinks and the proportions alter slightly. The front groundfloor office appeared very large that first day. It was very empty. The thick apple-green carpets had just been laid. Two telephone lines had been installed, three chairs had been brought in and a stepladder with a paint-encrusted plank strung between the ladder's rungs and the back of one of the chairs served adequately as a desk and kitchen counter. There was an electric kettle, a box of 72 Brooke Bond tea bags, one pint of Gold Top milk and a bag of white sugar. The cups were made of paper and the spoons were stainless steel.

The Press Officer knew a good room when he saw it. This one had come up for adoption immediately. It seemed only fitting after the deprivation he had been forced to bear in his shoe box at Wigmore Street. First come, first served seemed an appropriate epigram for the situation.

The furniture was on order. The walls had received their fourth coat of shock white paint and the carpets were down. The intricacies of the switchboard were being worked on full time and by now the major flaws had been ironed out. All that remained was for a glass and plywood alcove to be constructed over the red brick square of this major communications artery.

Those first days screamed by in a blur. All the press calls were gradually being transferred from Wigmore Street and the requests were being blurted out in what was to become the standard press office patter of *en garde* and *touché*, hit-and-run dialogue.

It didn't take the female rags long to spot Mary Hopkin as Certified Gold. The news that Paul McCartney had produced her first single was tantalizing copy fodder. The John Kelly photographs of Mary in her hometown of Pontardawe showed her as the epitome of the dew-drenched, Welsh daffodil cover girl. She was already a star before the release of her debut single. The calls for interviews and photo sessions kept coming in.

There was the very real chance that Mary's career could be killed by overexposure before she had even warbled her first note across the airwaves and jukeboxes of the world. And there was the danger of offending the important ladies and gentlemen of the press by a refusal to grant an interview, especially dangerous for a star not yet launched. This delicate refusal had to come from someone who could make it sound like a temporary postponement rather than a tentative no. There *was* a big difference between the two.

On this particular day there also lurked the details of the world premiere for the animated color cartoon fantasy, *Yellow Submarine*, that needed tending to. The world premiere on that warm night of July 17 at the London Pavilion in Piccadilly Circus was one of the last mass demonstrations of Beatlemania in Great Britain. The crowds were out in choking force. All four Beatles and their ladies would be attending.

Yellow Submarine was nothing if not devastatingly brilliant entertainment. On acid it is its own world, and any way you see it is a pleasure. The English press slaughtered it. The reviews on the following morning smeared themselves across the pulp of the page with enthusiastic abuse.

"Not bad, but not that good-can't see what all the fuss is about-seems old-fashioned already" was the national attitude. It was destined for failure before it was a week old.

The British Establishment conspiracy against The Beatles was back in full swing. This particular chapter was further kicked along when the distributors announced loudly to the press that due to poor attendance the film would only be released to half the theaters on the general provincial circuit. Laughably it was to go to America where it immediately earned itself four-star reviews and millions of dollars for Apple Films.

The lady from *Woman's Own* magazine sat on the chair and

accepted a cup of tea with just one lump of sugar from The House Hippie. She was waiting for The Press Officer to get off the phone so she might ask him when Mary Hopkin would be available for an in-depth cover story. Listening to him now filling in background information on the makers of *Yellow Submarine* she thought to herself how terribly efficient he was at his job. Shockingly efficient. What she didn't know was that The Press Officer was high on LSD. When he finished his telephone call he turned smartly on his heel and went immediately into his *Woman's Own* dialogue.

She left satisfied, with much arm-fluttering and many thank-yous; the promise had been made, the deal had been fixed. Peter Asher came in on his way to look at his new fourth-floor office to say "Hello" and leave news of James Taylor's musical progress with The Press Officer. The Press Officer informed him that he was pleasantly zonked out on acid and having a wonderful time. The A & R man took note of this fact. Two days later Paul McCartney informed his Press Officer that he did not want him artificially expanding his consciousness during working office hours.

Savile Row was getting itself together. The most constant sound was of banging hammers and muscle and bone stretching itself as the furniture arrived. Peter Brown's first-floor office seemed to sprout overnight from facelessness to blatant elegance. Neil's and The Beatles' offices were day by day gaining an identity. The Press Officer on the ground floor was still comparatively poverty-stricken.

Ron Kass was in America once again, so he hadn't been able to tell Derek Taylor the disappointing news. The unpleasant task was passed on to Alistair Taylor acting as office manager in addition to his ever-present chores as chief fixer. The disappointing news was that the office Derek Taylor was calling his own was actually promised to Ron Kass. It looked like The Press Officer would have to pick another one; he might even have to move back to Wigmore Street.

The House Hippie told The Press Officer that if he was forced back to the straitjacket of his former room he should, in all good faith, resign. The Press Officer dismissed this suggestion by pretending not to hear it and called for scotch and Coke. He had the good sense to know that a room is after all only a room. The rear second-floor office was chosen as the new Press Office.

BILL COLLINS wasn't always the Iveys' manager. Before he entered rock management he had built battleships and ocean-going liners with very complicated riggings and fores and afts and all the other related dialogue of that trade. At the same time he was playing piano in a jazz band in Liverpool. The Thirties became the Forties and his band played on. At the end of the war Bill Collins moved from the shipbuilding business into the motor trade, heading up a garage that specialized in the restoration and preservation of all four-wheeled vehicles. The motor trade was very profitable in those postwar days. And when he wasn't knocking the dents out of bruised fenders he was pounding out a dance beat on the ivories.

Mal Evans was the bouncer at the Cavern in Liverpool in the early Sixties before The Beatles left Liverpool forever and took Mal with them. It was during those days that Bill Collins met him. Bill's son, Lou, knew Paul McCartney's brother, Michael, so Bill consequently knew Paul in that shuffling, close, house-to-house trafficking of the Liverpool days. The first time Bill Collins heard the young Beatles at the Cavern he said, "I knew they were onto something good."

The Iveys were still playing semiprofessionally when Bill Collins heard them for the first time in April of 1966 at the Ammonford Ballroom in Swansea in south Wales. After their first set he introduced himself and in the same breath congratulated them on their performance. Bill Collins returned to Liverpool but over the coming months maintained a line of communications with the Iveys, always asking, after the fashion of a fan, how they were progressing. They were progressing.

43

Bill Collins landed the Iveys their first job as David Garrick's backing group on July 7, 1966, at the Seven Club, Shrewsbury, Shropshire. By now the Iveys had given up their daytime jobs and turned full-time professionals. In all, they worked seven engagements with Garrick up until December of 1966. In July of that year Bill Collins and the four Iveys – Pete Ham, Tom Evans, Mike Gibbons and Ron Griffiths – made the move from south Wales to London. They were playing at the Marquee Club in London's Wardour Street when Mal Evans brought Apple's A & R man along to have a listen. Peter Asher wasn't exactly inflamed with enthusiasm over the Iveys in concert but Evans became an instant devotee. Mal asked Bill for some tapes of the group to play to Paul McCartney.

When Paul heard their tapes he was sufficiently impressed to encourage the Iveys to continue their writing and make some more demo tapes. Mike Berry of Sparta Music had spotted the Iveys when they had first come to London. He tried to get them to sign with Sparta but Collins was in no hurry to rush their progress. He kept Mike Berry at an amiable distance.

And Sparta Music wasn't the only company interested in the Iveys. CBS had made several approaches and Mike Hurst, the man who discovered Cat Stevens, said he wouldn't mind a business association with this obviously talented, up-and-coming young group. Bill Collins was holding out. Then Mike Berry moved from Sparta Music to head the Publishing division at Apple, then working out of 94 Baker Street. He kept on at the Iveys to sign.

It was the third set of tapes that did it. Mal Evans played them to John Lennon, George Harrison and Derek Taylor. They said yes. The Iveys signed with Apple Publishing in April and with Apple Records in July of 1968. In spite of the enthusiasm over them, no one was really aware of what had come in under Mal Evans's arm that day, disguised as a group demo tape. Except, perhaps, their most devoted fan, Bill Collins.

18
BACK AT THE SANDBOX

THE THREE-CHAIR, two-telephone and stepladder arrangement that had passed as a Press Office was rapidly transformed into a glamorous showcase of a room for Ron Kass, head of Apple Records. Ron had the office built to his own tailored specifications.

A few Vasarelys on the smooth, white, white walls lit by subdued, adjustable spots with supplementary lighting coming from an invisible bank of indirect lights that hovered over an expensive sound system. The turntable and amplifier were built into a plastic and white formica cabinet that doubled as a record rack and liquor sideboard.

A quiet moment in the Apple Press Office.

45

There was very little clutter. A desk for Ron, one for his secretary Carol Chapman and a few chairs. The desks were space-age Danish brushed chrome and stained wood, the chairs were matching. Neither one smoked, leaving the white ashtrays gleamingly empty to increase the aura of brisk, efficient cleanliness and order. It was a lovely office to walk into on your way through life.

Peter Brown was runner-up for the best-looking office in Savile Row. The same white walls, deep plush carpet, same plastic and white formica shelving arrangement with the indirect lights spotting an assortment of hard-edge paintings in silver frames, with an enormous photograph of John and Paul in an ornately crusted gold frame. Peter had a dark mahogany round table that served for business conferences and opulent afternoon meals.

Neil Aspinall had retained a sense of humor when it came to outfitting The Beatles' office. Every week brought drastic interior changes. One week the carpets would be down and the next the floor would be gleaming, polished hard-wood. He had installed a ten-foot oak table with an inset gold hand-tooled leather top and four massively comfortable, un-related lounge chairs. A miscellaneous procession of nonsense objets d'art inflated and deflated the room at a stimulated clip.

The Press Office was astonishingly bleak in comparison. The furniture was standard office functional and hired from a large office supplier's. The filing cabinets were new but gray, unlike the sparkling white affairs in Peter Brown's and Ron Kass's glossy dens. Rock'n' roll posters filled the space of the white walls. The only hint of elegance was the enormously scalloped white wicker chair that held The Press Officer, and two white leather couches imported from 94 Baker Street. The room had a refrigerator and storage cupboard in dark stained wood that in no way resembled a refrigerator and everywhere was the thick apple-green carpet.

THE BEATLES, Mary Hopkin, Jackie Lomax and the Black Dyke Mills Brass Band launched the world debut of Apple Records. Since presentation is 50 percent of the sell, the advertising agency of Wolfe and Ollins had been called in by Apple to make the sell more pleasing to the eye.

The debut presentation package was a box made of plastic, 10 by 12 inches in matte black with a recessed lid carrying the Apple sticker that announced it as "Our First Four, 3 Savile Row, WI." There was a single colored folder containing the biographies and photographs of the artists with the record in a polyethylene sleeve. The name of the person to whom the box was going was printed on the outside Apple sticker.

This was primarily an interindustry gift presentation package for the benefit of Capitol Records and selected disk jockeys and journalists. If the package were to provoke ecstasy, then it would be considered on a larger scale for the general promotion field. Stanley Gorticov, president of Capitol Records, was coming to London the first week in August to look over Apple's progress and to be ceremoniously presented with "Our First Four." Nothing was too good for Stanley Gorticov – nothing short of being met at the airport by Ron Kass in a Rolls-Royce driven by a blonde English Beauty rose to a six-star hotel and from there to lunch at the Ritz with The Beatles. From the Ritz it was over to Savile Row where Derek Taylor was waiting to play him the four records and supply the presentation package with which he would be very impressed. Fortnum & Mason were there to serve a smashingly proper English tea, complete with scones, jam and double Devon cream.

It's important not to tire your visiting dignitaries unduly. So after the scones and double Devon cream (with jam) it was back to the hotel to sleep the whole affair off and recharge the batteries for the coming evening. The fun would include a taste of the English theater with a light drawing-room comedy, topped off by a meal at one of the Kings Road's more celebrated eating holes. The next day would bring more meetings, more dialogue and another lunch. Then it was back aboard a Los Angeles-bound jet with a slap on the back and a "Thanks for coming, hope you enjoyed yourself" farewell. Sometimes it's nice being the president.

The scheduled release date of "Our First Four" was August 26 in America and August 30 in Great Britain and Europe. The Beatles and Mary Hopkin were to be released simultaneously, with Jackie Lomax and The Black Dyke Mills Brass Band the following week. Everything was ready.

20

ONCE AROUND THE PIAZZA, DRIVER!

ON A WINDY morning in August Jeremy Banks told The House Hippie he had a *very* important mission for him to carry out. He wanted him to take Apple's "First Four" to the following people at the following places: the Queen Mother at St. James's Palace, Her Majesty Queen Elizabeth II at Buckingham Palace, Princess Margaret and Lord Snowdon at Kensington Palace, and Harold Wilson at 10 Downing Street.

"But I'm not dressed for it!" replied The House Hippie.

"Don't worry about that, you look fine," said Banks, attempting to soothe his obvious discomfort. "When you go to 10 Downing Street this afternoon two of my best photographers will be right behind you when you present the records to the Prime Minister."

The Prime Minister! Ten Downing Street! The House Hippie wondered if Jeremy was playing some gross gag on him. "Are you *sure* it's *me* you want to do this? Peter Brown sounds more like the man for this job." Jeremy was quite adamant about who he wanted to deliver the records and it wasn't Brown. Jeremy handed him the four packages. Sure enough: St. James's Palace, Buckingham Palace, Kensington Palace, and 10 Downing Street. All with the big green Apple sticker.

Jeremy Banks instructed The House Hippie to take his driver, Joe Marchini, and the white Mercedes and deliver the records to the palaces first. By then it would be lunchtime. Joe

Marchini and The House Hippie would then proceed to the Guinea, an Italian restaurant off Berkeley Square, where Jeremy and The Press Officer would join them for lunch. He would receive further instructions at that time. All through this dialogue The Press Officer sat at his desk, cigarette dangling from his mouth, pounding out a press release with two fingers, saying nothing. On his way out the door The House Hippie looked over his shoulder hoping to catch The Press Officer's eye. No chance. Derek Taylor sat crouched behind his Olympia upright, absorbed in his work and impervious to The House Hippie's pain.

St. James's Palace was a pushover. As the white Mercedes took a sharp left at the corner of St. James's Square and pulled up before the Tradesmen's Entrance, The House Hippie knew what he was going to say. Less than 30 seconds after pushing the service bell the upper half of the black door opened and a mouth asked him what it was he wanted.

"On behalf of The Beatles and Apple Corps Limited I would like to present these four recordings to the Queen Mother." He did it without fluffing one syllable. "The Queen Mother is not here at the moment but we will put them in the bag and send them up to her. Thank you very much," replied the mouth and a hand came through the upper half of the door to relieve him of his package. One down, three to go.

As the white Mercedes arrived at the back entrance to Buckingham Palace the keeper at the gate lumbered out and asked, "What's up, Mate?" Like a well-trained seal he knifed into his routine, "On behalf of The Beatles. . . ."

There was only Kensington Palace left to go before lunch. Joe Marchini handled the dialogue at Princess Margaret's residence while The House Hippie sat listening to the radio, looking at the sky.

"Well, so much for the palaces, eh, Rich?"

"Yeah, so much for the palaces, Joe."

Jeremy Banks and Derek Taylor were just going through the front door of The Guinea as the white Mercedes pulled up behind them. The arrival of Jeremy's party was met with a flurry of congenial greetings and general inquiries as to Mr.

Portrait of the author as photographer.

Banks's health by a headwaiter who, bowing and babbling, ushered them through the lunchtime crowd to a corner table. Before the waiter had completed the drinks order they were joined by John Kelly, Jeremy's first-string photographer.

Across the white linen and silver miasma of the table The Press Officer asked The House Hippie about his morning's progress. "Done!" Jeremy Banks gave him the thumbs-up sign of approval. "After lunch, my good man, you and John will proceed to my studio where you will telephone 10 Downing Street and ask to speak with Harold Wilson's press attaché. You will tell him who you are and that you will be coming down shortly to present him with a copy of The Beatles' latest recording on their new Apple label." He moved his gaze over to John Kelly. "John, you and Stephen will photograph Richard as he hands over the package, but make certain that the Apple is showing when you go in for your picture. I want that photograph in tomorrow's papers."

The House Hippie was still very apprehensive of the reception he might encounter at the Prime Minister's home. He suggested, quite seriously, that it would be a better idea to drive by Number 10 at high speed and simply *throw* the records out onto the steps. Seeing as they were unbreakable, he would be certain to get them in one piece. After all the thought behind the gift would still be there.

"Look man, you're not in America now, there's nothing to be afraid of. No one's going to break your head open for delivering a record to the Prime Minister. Don't forget you're representing The Beatles and a multimillion-pound organization," The Press Officer informed him. It was a heartening notion.

Half a bottle of wine and three Irish coffees later The House Hippie was quite prepared to deliver as many copies of *Hey Jude* as there were members of Parliament if only someone would tell him where they all lived.

Once they got to Jeremy's studio on Pimlico Road in Chelsea The House Hippie wasted no time. Three minutes later Harold Wilson's press attaché was on the telephone. He informed the press attaché that he would be down shortly with a package of records for the Prime Minister from The Beatles. As John Kelly finished loading the last of his four Nikons the other photographer for the expedition, Stephen Goldblatt, arrived.

John Kelly parked the white Cortina, with the empty film cans on the floor, two blocks away from Downing Street. "Listen Richard, Stephen and I will go ahead and get our light reading so it doesn't look like we're all together, and then you follow us up five minutes later, OK?" It was OK with him.

The House Hippie ignored the two photographers sunk in the middle of the small, gawking crowd opposite 10 Downing Street as he casually approached the bobby standing guard outside the door. He walked up to him and explained his mission. The bobby listened very politely and motioned for The House Hippie to follow him to the door.

It opened three seconds later and he was face to face with the press attaché. He went into his speech, very slowly this time, stretching it out while holding the envelope up for the benefit of the photographers. The only sound he was conscious of above the thunder of his own heart was the insanely incessant slap of the cameras' shutters going flat out. A brief tug of war ensued as The House Hippie and the press attaché struggled to retain possession of the package with the big green apple on it as the former stubbornly held onto one corner, drawing his speech out to the last syllable, while the press attaché quietly prayed for the whole business to end as soon as possible.

Back in the white Cortina with the empty film cans on the floor he asked the photographers if they had gotten their picture. "The bobby kept getting in the way and there was a lot of shadow around the door but I think we got it anyway," they both affirmed.

The first thing The Press Officer said when he came through the door was "George didn't think much of you going down to Harold's."

The House Hippie was shattered.

"Well, fuck, man! Didn't you tell him that this whole pipe dream was Jeremy's idea and not mine?!"

"No."

P

AUL SAID THAT he thought it would be a good idea if The Fabs did a concert soon, not Wembley Stadium but something small, so Neil's checking out the Round House."

"Yeah –"

"Jackie wanted to know why the release date on his record was put back a week 'cause he thought his was going to launch the label and I told him we figured he'd have a better chance if it waited a week 'cause it looked certain that Mary's and The Fabs' records would squash his chances, so now he knows but I still think he's a bit disappointed."

"Yeah –"

"And you know we've been having trouble over the question of who's going to be managing Mary's affairs –"

"I heard about that –"

"We've been trying to decide if it should be Terry Doran or Alistair Taylor or someone outside of Apple."

"We better take care of that one soon –"

"You're telling me! And Jeremy fixed it with Cecil Beaton to photograph The Fabs but now he's schized out of his brains 'cause they don't want to be photographed by him."

"Too bad –"

"Steve Miller's just been signed to Publishing –"

"Score!"

"And do you have any idea what's happening with the studio downstairs?"

"As far as I know Alexis and Apple Electronics are supposed to be getting it together. I mean it doesn't function at all right now but they tell me it's going to be ready in two months. They say it's going to be the best studio in town."

"Yeah –"

"Yeah and, oh I've got to tell you this one! I'm sitting in the Press Office the other day and Debbie says there's some chick in reception who claims she's been to more rock 'n' roll concerts than anyone in the world and she's in London for three days and wants to meet The Fabs so Derek tells Richard to go get rid of her –"

"Yeah –"

"So he gets rid of her and ten minutes later Debbie rings back and says an Adolf Hitler is in reception."

"And what did Derek say?"

"'Oh Christ, not that arsehole again! All right, send him up!'"

22
PROGRESS REPORT

AS EXPECTED, *Hey Jude* bounced into the number-one slot overnight with *Those Were the Days* panting heavily behind it and eventually getting there. The world debut of Apple Records had gotten off to a screamingly successful start with worldwide sales on those two records alone chalking up 13 million disks sold.

The proletarian contribution of the Black Dyke Mills Brass Band's version of Paul McCartney's *Thingumybob* hovered for a few weeks, more as a curiosity than as a serious chart contender. Jackie Lomax's *Sour Milk Sea* failed to make a chart placement either in Britain or the United States, despite heavy air play and a massive promotional shove. It was the one flaw in the system that no one could explain.

23
THE BLACK ROOM

THE LITTLE ROOM that measured no more than 12 by 15 feet joining the Press Office and the unoccupied front office was christened the Black Room sometime in September. It earned this monicker because of the role it played in the consciences of the occupants of the Press Office.

The influx of poetry manuscripts hadn't lessened any since April. They were still pouring in. If there was any noticeable decrease in volume it was only because the majority of it was still being mailed to Wigmore Street where it lingered for weeks before being sent to Savile Row. *None of it ever got read*. There was just no time in anyone's day to give it more than a cursory glance and eventually it was all relegated to the limbo of the Black Room.

It rested in mounds neatly stacked in cardboard boxes until the pile became so top heavy that it would capsize. Then it would get scrambled into an adjacent pile mixing the life work of the Haiku poet from Biloxi, Mississippi, inextricably with the abstract amphetamine mumblings of the girl from Newcastle-on-Tyne. It had a life force of its own.

The Black Room became the stash box for all the bits and pieces of life that one could accumulate and then found impossible to throw away. The pack-rat mentality at work reasoned that some of it might come in handy; someday it might be called for. The Press Officer had found it unbearable to dispose of a collection of old shoes he had brought with him from California. He had outgrown wearing any of them. So, like an old faithful horse who had put in his best days, they were put out to pasture in the Black Room. At night, when no one was listening, the dialogue between the shoes and the poetry was astounding.

The House Hippie had immediately turned the Black Room walls into a transient gallery of lust with a changing parade of girlie pictures; the gentle, the crude, the bizarre, the very beautiful, slapped on haphazardly, sometimes painstakingly, with adhesive tape, or sometimes just chewing gum.

The Black Room was the cloakroom for mufflers, wet umbrellas, topcoats, raincoats and scarves. The 35 collection boxes left over from John's "You Are Here" show had moved into the Black Room. There was no place else for them to die.

The weekly crates of Coca-Cola, the cases of beer, the bottles of scotch and gin and wine all waited patiently in the Black Room before being thrown into the arena of the Press Office for consumption. Excess artists' biographies, press photos and posters sat side by side with Tuborg, Pilsner and Gordon's Gin. The Black Room was the overflow drain of the soul.

24

THE PINEAPPLE ARCHIVES

THE PINEAPPLE ARCHIVES was The House Hippie's master plan for bringing order to the jangled asymmetry of the never-ending Banzai Pipeline of press cuttings that marked his daily existence and set the pattern for his morning routine.

History has a way of turning itself into an abnormal mosaic if it's not catalogued. It piles itself upon itself until, like the neglected poetry of the Black Room, there is nothing left but a disjointed ragbag of scraps of words. The Beatles had more press cuttings than anyone in the world.

With the addition of Apple and in anticipation of a thriving stable of artists it became necessary to turn all that paper into a readily accessible A to Z of Apple Rock History. It was likely that someday The Press Officer would ask The House Hippie what Paul McCartney had said to Alan Smith of the *New Musical Express* in an interview on August 24, 1968. Microfilm was the answer but for the moment manila folders with legible chapter headings (Mary Hopkin-Volume 1, Jackie Lomax, Beatles Apple, John and Yoko-Happenings-Volume 2), neatly stacked into a sliding accordion filing cabinet, would suffice.

The House Hippie loved his work. He loved the playground of the Press Office and the places it sent him. When he woke in the mornings he looked forward to the day stretching out before him. He liked the bus ride that took him there even if the sky was cold and flat. There was something about London that made up for the belligerent weather. For the most part he was punctual to the point of neurosis.

The day had its pattern. In at ten, lay the morning papers on the outer left-hand corner of the press table and the new magazines on the right-hand side. The weekly musical trade papers along the upper outer edge. Light a stick of incense. Check the pile of mail for any personal letters and look for the telltale green envelope that would contain the press cuttings sent by the agency.

Then take the silver serving tray and ice bucket to the upstairs kitchen and load with as many glasses as possible and fill the bucket to capacity. Return to the Press Office and lay the glasses and ice on the sideboard on the far right-hand wall. Into the liquor cabinet and check the level of all the bottles and replace what is necessary from the kitchen. Fill the fridge with beer and Cokes. Lay out the filing cards for the Pineapple Archives and begin to catalogue.

All of this to the accompaniment of a full-gale force of nonstop telephones – eight external lines and seven internal coupled with the cross-channel floating dialogue of casual conversation, shouted orders and dictation. The day had begun.

25

ART IS LONG, LIFE IS SHORT, JUDGMENT DIFFICULT, OPPORTUNITY FLEETING

*T*HAT GIRL IS *in reception."*
"What girl?"
"The one from Wigmore Street who wants financial backing to make nude sculptures out of patent leather covered in oil to simulate –"
"Tactile delight?"
"That's the one!"
"Send her up!"

26

FACT

*E*MPTY THE CONTENTS of one Benson and Hedges cigarette into a three-square cigarette paper, lace liberally with hashish, add a cardboard tip and roll. You now have a Benson and Hashish B-52 Bomber.

27

THERE HAS GOT TO BE MORE THAN LOVE TO THIS

'LL BALL YOU IF you introduce me to Paul McCartney.''

"All right.''

Two days later.

"Hey, I thought you said you were going to introduce me to Paul McCartney.''

"That's what I tell all the girls.''

"You bastard!''

28

DIALOGUE/ DIALOGUE/ DIALOGUE

HAT'S THE DEAL?''

"All four Beatles and Yoko Ono to pose with Mary Hopkin for Woman's Own *magazine at three o'clock in Ron Kass's office. And tell her to wash her hair.''*

"She doesn't have to be told''.

29

REPERTOIRE ENTENDRE

ELL, LET'S SEE. George was talking about getting The Band onto Apple but it doesn't look like we'll be able to swing it but we might as well keep trying. The jazz scene we'll leave up to Ron for the moment 'cause he's the only one that seems to know anything about it around here. There's a lot of bad jazz that sounds good to untrained ears. The Iveys are coming along fine. They've got a song called *Maybe Tomorrow* which just needs some overdubbing and remixing. Tony Visconti is going to start in on it with them right away, it could be their first single. Jon Isherwood? Well, on second thought there's nothing we can do with him, he's all right but he's not our bag. Kenny Everett has to be told that we can't use that song of his –''

"Who's going to tell him?"

"Let Derek do it. That guy Timon is OK but he needs a lot of working on and we can't spare the time but let's keep him in mind."

"Solomon Burke?"

"Well, you really can't tell from his latest stuff and there's no telling where he's going from here and it'd have to be on a record-to-record deal but we might as well give it a third listen."

"The Turtles?"

" 'Fraid not."

"MC5?"

"Too loud and sloopy. But the Easybeats are a strong possibility but we're going to have to make a deal with their label so I suggest you talk to Ron about them. The Black Dyke Mills Brass Band: For starters, get a shorter name but anyway if that single ever gets moving we'll have to do an album. Paul said he wouldn't mind producing one for them."

"It would be good for us if they did an album of Lennon and McCartney songs –"

"But let's wait and see what happens with *Thingumybob*."

"Classical music?"

"The same goes for classical music as jazz. If anything great comes up we'll take it. Now the idea of the spoken-word series has already been kicked around a few times and we could be onto a good thing with that one but we'd have to turn those records out at a very low price, say 12 shillings a copy. Derek has been on to Miles of IT and Miles says he'd like to produce some stuff for us if we decide to do it. He can get people like Ginsberg and Burroughs. By the way, whatever happened to that Lord Buckley record we were going to release?"

30

INTERMEZZO

O H YES!!! *That's beautiful!!! Jesus Christ!!!*
Please don't stop!!! That's lovely!!! Where
have you been all my life?!!!!?"
"*Living my own.*"

31

**LIKE BRINSLEY
SCHWARTZ OVER
TROUBLED WATERS**

O NE MONTH AFTER the release of *Hey Jude*,
Hunter Davies' authorized tapioca biography of The Beatles was published. Two
weeks later George Harrison took Jackie
Lomax to Los Angeles to record his debut
album. Since June The Beatles had been working on a new
album now near completion. Ringo Starr was on holiday in
Sardinia.

Jeremy Banks was quite fond of champagne, Panadeine,
Royalty and The Beatles. Every morning he would have The
House Hippie go out and buy half a bottle of Moët and
Chandon and a slim, red packet of Panadeine, a codeine-
compound pain killer. When The House Hippie returned with
these provisions Jeremy would uncork the champagne and
pop three Panadeines into his mouth and wash them down
with his warm, bubbling bottle of bliss. With breakfast out of
the way he could begin the marathon string of mysterious
phone calls that were his life's work.

The telephone only left his ear when he went to the toilet.
The hours he spent on the blower were shrouded in utter
secrecy. This was because Jeremy had the ability to conduct
hour-long conversations without anyone in the same room
ever hearing one single word of his dialogue apart from the
occasional "Mindbender" or "Blue Meanie" that escaped in a
spurt of animation. For the most part it was all very deadpan. It
sometimes forced one to think if the person at the other end
could hear him at all, so mumbled were the linguistics.

The House Hippie was profoundly grateful to Jeremy Banks
for educating him to a phrase that was hitherto unknown to
him. The addition of this phrase to his vocabulary enriched his

life. The phrase was "a knee trembler." A knee trembler is the vernacular for sexual intercourse hurriedly conducted in any number of awkward places, usually the toilet, a broom closet, a shower or under a desk. That expression was burned into The House Hippie's brain. He would conduct inner dialogues with himself and an imaginary companion, always working the conversation to a point where he could pose the apocalyptic question: "Excuse me, Madam. Would you care to retire to the bog for a quick knee trembler?"

This was not Jeremy's only verbal gem. Since the cartoon *Yellow Submarine*, Jeremy had popularized the use of the term "Blue Meanie." Its usage was constant. Generally speaking a Blue Meanie is a particularly unpleasant experience. Being arrested is a Blue Meanie. The arresting officer is likewise a Blue Meanie for having performed a Blue Meanie. "Mindbender" was his other contribution to the popular semantic flow. A mindbender is any situation or experience that derails a person's train of thought, causing a traumatic jolt to the nervous system. However, it need not always be an unpleasant experience, as compared to a Blue Meanie which most certainly always is most unpleasant.

Jeremy took great pleasure in cultivating friendships with the famous, the gifted, the beautiful and the titled. In addition to being photographic coordinator of Apple he was also Diana Rigg's manager. Jeremy was fully aware of the benefits that associations of this sort can produce. It was no fool that sent The House Hippie to the royal palaces and 10 Downing Street that day.

One morning he said to The House Hippie, "I want to show you something, my good man." The House Hippie crossed the room with his curiosity inflamed.

"What's that, Jeremy?"

"I want you to read this out loud to Derek."

He read.

"Dear Sir: I am commanded by Queen Elizabeth the Queen Mother to send Her Majesty's thanks for so kindly sending the four new records recently made by the Apple Corps. Her Majesty is greatly touched by this kind thought from The

Beatles and their new company and has much enjoyed listening to these recordings. Yours faithfully, Jean Rankin, Lady-in-waiting, Birkhall, Ballater."

It was a moment of great personal triumph for Jeremy Banks. The results of his tenacious PR-ing were there to be seen on Royal Family stationery with its searing red coat of arms with the Queen Mother's Lady-in-waiting's own signature. Visions of the Queen Mother foot-tapping to *Sour Milk Sea* and the grating guitar of John Lennon's *Revolution* swelled the Apple Press Office to bursting with pride.

32
DIALOGUE/ DIALOGUE/ DIALOGUE

CHRIST, THAT Press Office is a regular nuthouse. I mean it *never* stops. I walked in this morning and Derek had just finished a session with Paul and he looked like he had been stepped on. I said, 'What's the matter?' and he says, 'What's the matter? Oh nothing! Nothing at all except that McCartney is *so* charming! He calls me a cunt, ya know, "Ya coont!" He told me I always was more clever with words than he was and then he tells me I should take a vacation and then he pokes me in the ribs and starts pulling all those cute chipmunk faces that he's got and then you can't help but *like* him." And then someone screams, 'Hey it's *Disc* on the phone and they want you to say something about Apple's first few months, and he says, 'All right, tell them we've sold four million records in five weeks and we are what we appear to be which is successful though we aren't always what we are –' "

"Huh?"

"That's what I thought but it doesn't stop there. Someone else shouts, 'Hey, they want you to say something about John!' and without hesitating he says, 'He was what he was then but he is what he is now and shall be what he's meant to be when the time comes for him to be what he is going to be, got that?' "

"It's a little hard to follow –"

"And the phones just keep going, Beatles, Beatles, Beatles. He screams, 'Isn't there anything else in this world beside these damn Beatles?!?' but you can see he really loves it and then he starts telling Jeremy, 'Look man, we need some pictures immediately,' and Jeremy says, 'Don't worry, I've got that one together –' and Derek says, 'But I *am* worried. I'm worried about that last session with the Iveys. What's Mal doing putting them in those fucking suits? Suits!!! It's 1968, man!' and it goes on. 'Derek, the Doors are in reception for you!' 'Send them up!' 'Derek, it's the *Evening Standard* on thirteen for you!' 'Pass it over!' and then Neil comes in and tells him he's been to the Round House and it's all wrong for the concert we want to put on and to forget it and then someone screams, 'Hey, Yoko wrote down the name of an art critic they want you to get in touch with about those films. She says you probably haven't heard of him but he's very important.' Which really flips Derek out. 'O right! We're all such fucking ignoramuses, all of us! We've never heard of anything but The Beatles, I suppose. I forgot we're working for that eminent Oxford scholar, John Lennon! Excuse me! 'Derek, *Daily Mirror* in reception!' 'Derek, Paul says he wants a garden on the roof –' "

"Does he?"

"I guess so. Anyway Neil finishes with the Round House rundown and turns to Jeremy and starts shouting, 'No, man, I keep telling you it's a mistake to have a resident art department! All you have to do is look at the shit that comes out of those other record-company art-department factories. It all looks the same. It's much better to keep it on a loose, free-lance basis, otherwise we're going to get involved in all the wrong things. One time you use John Kosh, the next time Alan Aldridge, the next Gene Mahon. You know, farm it out! You have different designers with different styles and in the end it looks better, you'll see 'cause all those guys are very good at what they do and all it takes is a phone call. So forget about the live-in art department!' and Jeremy nods at him, 'Right!' and then someone screams, 'Hey it's *Melody Maker*, they want you to talk about The Beatles!' And he's on one phone, cups the mouthpiece and says, 'Tell them there are four of them, they come from Liverpool, they've got long hair and they've had a few hits.'"

"Good answer –"

"But never mind all *that* dialogue. You know, no matter how you look at it, Mary's our baby and there's no way we can cop out on her. So we're not equipped to act as a booking agent, right? So she goes over to Colin Berlin. Fine! Paul says he's going to produce her next single and album, that is if he doesn't lose interest beforehand. Fine! Even if he doesn't we can fix something with someone and come up with a monster. But it's still the same fucking story! Who is going to manage her? Her old man is putting the screws on us and we don't know what to do. Alistair Taylor wants to manage her but that's out of the question. Terry Doran is doing the job for a while but the old man figures he's too far out. He's probably got a knockout drop fantasy going and *she* would believe it. Christ sake! Derek's tried explaining to her that she's got to stop telling the papers that she thinks everyone in show business is shallow, degenerate and phony! Her mother told her not to talk to strangers on train rides down from Wales and, brother, she never got over it. But anyway the old man has solved the problem for us."

"Yeah –"

"Yeah! He's keeping it in the family. You know who's managing her from now on? Her sister! That's who! Now Carol Hopkin is a nice girl but come on! Own up! What does she know about artist management?? I mean she's not much older than Mary, now is she? Anyway we've got two new guys coming in this week to work with John Hewlitt and Jean Griffiths in Publishing. The guy who is covering America is Mike O'Connor and the guy who's looking after Europe is Wim Schut, so Publishing is taken care of."

"You sure?"

"Well, we're getting there."

33
THE WOMEN IN
BLACK

THE HOUSE HIPPIE saw them standing in quiet knots of two and threes all through that first Wigmore Street summer and thought to himself, "They'll go away when the weather gets bad." He was wrong.

After seeing them day after day for month after month he started *looking* at them. He noticed a handful of faces that were permanent pavement fixtures. When he went to deliver a parcel to Paul McCartney's house they would be there. When he had to go to Abbey Road they were there. When a shorter journey was involved to Trident Studios where one of them might be working *they* were there.

They would be standing by the cast-iron white picket fence outside Number 3 when he went in at ten and some nights leaving at eight they would *still* be there. The faces would remind him that he had seen them at least half a dozen times that day as he had exited on half a dozen separate missions.

There are Beatle fans and there are Beatle fans; that much he knew. It was becoming clearer to The House Hippie that these girls were not just any old Beatle fans. They were always positioned on opposite sides of the steps when the obvious, one-day-wonder fans from America and Europe were out in force for an unimpressive two-hour vigil. They retained an aloofness from these hysterical screamers that bordered on supreme dignity.

It never mattered what the weather was doing. They stood there and allowed the rain to soak them and the wind to cut through their young-girl clothes. At last it dawned on him. He knew they would be there longer than anyone else; after everyone else had left, *they* would still be there.

34

DOUBLE WHITE

THE PRESS OFFICER figured it out. Only one person in every hundred buys a Beatles record. He said that wasn't good enough. Paul McCartney agreed. In the third week in October Paul McCartney told Derek Taylor that he wanted a high-powered publicity and advertising campaign for The Beatles' new album. It had to be the best there was. The Press Officer agreed.

The Press Officer phoned that octopus of the advertising world, J. Walter Thompson, who immediately dispatched a senior director and his younger underassistant to 3 Savile Row.

"It would help us if we had some idea of your anticipated budget on this project, Mr. Taylor."

"We have no budget."

"Well, would it be closer to six thousand pounds or sixty thousand pounds?"

"Closer to sixty thousand pounds."

"I see –"

"But of course with a budget like that we'd have to sell over a hundred thousand albums to justify that kind of expenditure."

"No problem. In a successful campaign we can easily double a number like that."

The Press Officer suggested constructing an enormous billboard heralding the arrival of the new album. The men from J. Walter Thompson reminded him that if the album was to be released in October they would have to count on a delay owing to the necessity of getting ministry planning permission for a project of that nature. And time was the enemy.

The Press Officer was also in favor of a huge wind sock flown from the Post Office Tower that would say The Beatles. They said they would check that out straightaway. The Press Officer was also in favor of skywriting but knew that the success of that depended on who was looking at the sky at that moment. They said nothing.

"Of course in a campaign of this nature we will need the complete trust and cooperation of The Beatles themselves. In the event of a television commercial being made, I think it would be appropriate if Paul McCartney would take part because, quite frankly, without a Beatle participating visually, the whole thing would be a waste of time and money. We ourselves spend somewhere in the region of thirty-six million pounds a year on advertising. About fourteen million pounds of that goes on television and seven million pounds to the newspapers and the remainder on posters."

Prime television time is becoming more and more of a rarity in this age of the tube but owing to their considerable power and influence in this medium the men from J. Walter Thompson said they would be able to swing the choice spots during prime time. Of course the damage would come to about £13,000 a minute. The Press Officer reasoned that if you were to do a medley of song snatches you would be able to include at least 12 recognizable songs.

The men from J. Walter Thompson said that it would be necessary for an already established director to do the commercial when the time came. When The Press Officer informed them that there were 30 tracks on the album they were flabbergasted. When he went on to tell them that the 30 songs were all new compositions they came close to a coronary. The Press Officer said he would send them the album-cover artwork so they could see what it was they had to sell. The men from J. Walter Thompson left to come up with a figure for The Beatles' campaign.

The double white album cover had been put together by a conglomerate. Neil and Mal had collected all the old Beatle snapshots that were to make up the collage poster to be included inside, Jeremy was to act as chief coordinator and got John Kelly to take the four beautiful portraits, a designer named Gordon Howes had put the finished mechanical together. The minimal concept had been talked over by all four Beatles with Neil, Mal, Derek and Apple Records.

The Press Officer remarked that 30 new songs in one album from The Beatles was an unheard-of feast; more than 30 would be grotesque.

35

**DOUBLE WHITE
AGAIN**

A WEEK AFTER the opening talks between J. Walter Thompson and Apple a second meeting was held attended by Paul McCartney, Derek Taylor, Ron Kass, Jeremy Banks, Peter Asher, Neil Aspinall and Jack Oliver. Plus half a dozen men from J. Walter Thompson.

Derek Taylor started the ball rolling by playing a few tracks from the album. The man from J. Walter Thompson picked it up and began the dialogue.

He told everyone that J. Walter Thompson could produce a complete advertising package deal that would cover both press and television. However, his strong opinion was that Paul McCartney should appear in the commercial.

"As our objective we have selected three dominant target groups. These are completely separate from those which any accomplished editorial publicist could get at. They include the already existing consumers of Beatle records, those people on the fringes of the recordbuying public who wouldn't normally buy a Beatle record and the enormous Christmas market. Seeing as time is our biggest contender – you've said that your release date is the fifteenth of November – we suggest commencing our press campaign on the previous Monday. The TV spot should take place on the Sunday after the fifteenth."

Everyone was listening.

"The newspaper ads will be short and to the point. For instance: Saturday morning at nine o'clock a new issue of one million Beatle records comes on the market. While the price of each album, two records in each, is expected to open at about four pounds, experts predict that heavy speculation will soon cause the price on certain of the albums to be marked up five pounds, ten pounds and even one hundred pounds. Each album has a different number and low numbers will irrationally gain a certain mystique. A spokesman has been quoted as saying, 'Heh, heh, heh!'"

Everyone was still listening.

"Next. It's eight o'clock. You're eating breakfast and exactly forty-nine hours from now you could be the proud owner of

Beatles album number 1. Or, of course, you might get number 3972 but that's pretty good, too. It is the exact height in millimeters of Ringo Starr standing on John Lennon's shoulders."

Mild applause.

"Well, gentlemen, that's a sampler. These teasers would be featured daily leading up to the release date, along with a separate ad for the *Financial Times* and most of the Sunday papers. The TV commercial is a fixed spot following right after the news on Sunday and will be ninety seconds long. It will feature Paul McCartney reading an imaginary music critic's article on the new album, spliced with five-second snatches from the songs. It's going to cost you fifty-six thousand pounds."

Screams of disbelief.

Ron Kass said that if this were the States it might be worthwhile, but monetarily speaking that amount would be squandered in England.

"I mean we can approximate total sales of five hundred thousand dollars but our advertising budget should only be two percent. Fifty-six thousand pounds is too much."

Paul thought that the presentation was nice but that the 90-second TV spot was too expensive. He suggested that something shorter be worked out. He added that Ringo would be better on TV than himself. He also wanted to talk to the other Beatles about it.

The man from J. Walter Thompson then took out six miniature London buses painted white with "Beatle Bus" written along the side with pictures of well-known personalities staring out the windows.

"We propose to buy six buses from London Transport at five hundred pounds each and outfit them like this."

Paul appreciated the idea but added that it was too much of a gimmick for The Beatles. He said that he preferred not to overadvertise on The Beatles, that in fact they were already a presold commodity; at this point in their career they didn't have to steel to sell The Beatles to the masses. It was also important to avoid any kind of glossy, self-indulgent advertising approach. Paul said that Ringo would definitely do the commercial when he got back from his holiday. He added that 45 seconds seemed more reasonable a running time.

"Well, as far as underplaying the campaign goes, say that if seven hundred thousand copies of *Hey Jude* were sold without advertising, that still leaves you with almost sixty million people who didn't buy the record and *that* is a very considerable market."

With that the meeting ended.

Three days later it was decided that if one person out of every hundred bought a Beatles record it would be quite enough.

36
POPULAR PHOTOGRAPHY FOR FUN AND PROFIT

IN THOSE DAYS seven people occupied the Press Office full time: Derek Taylor, Jeremy Banks, their shared secretary, Carol Paddon, Terry Doran, Jack Oliver and their secretary, Dee Meehan, and The House Hippie.

Therefore it wasn't the number of people that caught his attention when The House Hippie, returning to the Press Office late that afternoon from Fleet Street, realized something had happened. In fact there were less than half the usual staff and *no* guests. In comparison with most days the place was barren.

Before The House Hippie had taken his coat off The Press Officer called for a drink. Jeremy Banks followed suit. As he mixed the drinks he watched The Press Officer open his top desk drawer, look inside, half smile, shake his head, slam it shut, stand up placing both hands in his back pockets, sprint to the bog, return two minutes later and reopen the desk drawer to look again at some object which absorbed his complete attention.

Jeremy appeared to be unusually hypertense. He kept putting a finger up to his lips in a gesture that suggested to Carol Paddon that she too must remain tight-lipped. He kept running his fingers nervously through his hair.

At that moment Neil Aspinall walked into the room visibly shaken. He walked up to The Press Officer almost fiercely, pointing a finger at him. "Well, *I* don't like it and Paul doesn't like it and none of the others are going to like it, and I don't care what the fuck *he* says, I don't want it coming out."

"Well, look," The Press Officer replied, "I didn't take the picture and it wasn't my idea so don't get uptight with me! I'm only the publicist."

"We'll sort something out," quipped Jeremy. Neil looked at him with cold contempt, completely ignoring his contribution to the crackling dialogue. Shaking his head in disgust he left the room.

"What's up, chief?" The House Hippie asked.

"Come here."

He opened his desk drawer and pointed to a 12-by-15 black-and-white photograph of John Lennon and Yoko Ono looking out at the world on a cold day, stark naked.

37
DIALOGUE/ DIALOGUE/ DIALOGUE/

THE RELEASE DATE on James's album has been put back three weeks but that doesn't depress him as much as the feeling that no one is interested in him. That nothing is being done."

"Not *doing* anything for him! We've had photo sessions, we've written biographies, he's been interviewed by the papers. All right, granted nothing has come of the interviews, but you know the story. If you don't have a single or an album in the charts nobody wants to know, *nobody*! You can take a flying fuck at a galloping goose, move heaven and hell from here to eternity back and forth between the devil and the deep blue sea till hell freezes over and Lucifer comes skating out but Jesus Christ Almighty we've all been on this scene up to our noses long enough to have learned one thing and that is if you're not in the charts you're not going to be number one in any of these journalists' hearts no matter how fucking good you are and he's great! He's also very impatient. So what can we do? Bend their arms behind their backs and say, 'You give us a front page on James Taylor or else we gouge your eyes out?' He's going to take time to break. We can't push things. I can't even get anyone to come to a decision to release *Carolina in My Mind*. I think it's a sure winner but try and get anyone around here to make a decision. Everyone is scared shiftless to take step one. And there's no one to be afraid of except The Fabs."

"That's just it. You see he feels The Fabs have lost interest in him."

"Well, as his friend I suggest you tell him that's one hang-up he's got to get over right away because that thought will stop him from getting *anything* done. It doesn't matter if they *have* lost interest in him. You don't expect *them* to be James Taylor maniacs. Look, he's made an excellent album that's going to be released in a month's time with all the enthusiasm we can get up. We're doing the best we can with what we've got and I fucking well wish we could do better."

38

PLAY THE ALBUM COVER AND THROW THE RECORD AWAY; BEATLE DEMYSTIFICATION

"THAT," SAID The Press Officer with a smile, "is Apple's next album cover."

"I want you to be very careful with that photograph, Derek," Jeremy Banks said, shaking his finger at The Press Officer.

"Piss off, Jeremy!"

"I won't have you talking to me that way."

"And I won't have you whining at me like some possessive spoiled little brat just because your fucking lab developed the film! These pictures have nothing to do with *you* or *me*, so take that enormous ego of yours in the bog and flush it! If Lennon says this is the cover for his debut album with Yoko, then it is and it doesn't matter what the fuck *he* says!" said The Press Officer, pointing to the door that had just slammed behind Neil Aspinall.

"What's the record like?"

"What a cover like that, who needs a record?"

"What's it called?"

" 'Two Virgins.' "

A week later.

"It's the most revolutionary album cover of the decade. You might not *like* it, but because it's John's the implications are going to be profound. Just watch what happens to the market, to the trends in the industry. He's sticking his cock out a long way on this one and now they've really got an excuse for going after him *and* her. We've got a scheduled release date for November 20 but it looks like it might be put back another week. We can't get EMI to distribute it. They said they won't have anything to do with it, so Ron's fixing a deal with Tetragramaton to handle it in America and Track in England and no one, I mean no one, will take any ads for it in any of the trades. *Disc's* advertising manager, Peter Wilkinson, says he won't accept any advertising from John and Yoko because most of his readers fall into the twelve-to-fourteen-year-old bracket. Morally he says he doesn't think it's right for 'youngsters,' as he calls them, to be encouraged to go out and buy that kind of a record. The mothers are the ones who pay for the subscriptions and if they find out that their kids heard about the record through *Disc* that would be the end of the subscription. Ray Coleman, the editor of *Disc*, and Jack Hutton, the editor of *Melody Maker*, shook their fingers and said, 'No thanks, we're not having anything to do with it.' Percy Dickens at the *New Musical Express* said their ad man washes his hands of it, and in the same breath all these people are asking us when they can expect the artwork for the ads for the new Beatles album."

"It's a shitty business –"

"Anyway, we're pressing a hundred thousand copies of 'Wonder-wall' for release on the first of the month and the Iveys' debut single is *Maybe Tomorrow*. The new Beatles album is out on the twenty-first and James and the Modern Jazz Quartet on the sixth. By the end of December we'll have released six LPs: 'The Beatles,' 'Yellow Submarine,' 'Wonder-wall,' 'Two Virgins,' 'James Taylor' and 'Under the Jasmine

Tree.' We've had five singles, *Hey Jude, Those Were the Days, Sour Milk Sea, Thingumybob* and *Maybe Tomorrow*. Oh by the way, have you heard about the Apple Foundation for the Arts?''

"I've seen it on paper –''

"But you'll believe it when you see it, right?''

"Right.''

39
THE PROCESSION OF THE PAPPARAZZI

AS PHOTOGRAPHIC coordinator for Apple, Jeremy Banks was in a position of some considerable power. On the London photographic grapevine it was common knowledge that if you wanted to land a gig photographing any of the Apple artists, Jeremy Banks was the man to see.

If your work got his nod of approval, there was always the faint hope that you might get to photograph The Beatles, something no photographer would sneer at. Of all the London record companies, Apple was the highest-paying and the most prestigious to work for.

They never stopped coming in with their portfolios. On the average Jeremy would see three photographers a day. "Send him up." And up they'd come, each to perform the degrading ritual that all photographers must go through, turning over print after print of his life's work. "Very nice." It was always very nice. And out they would go. "We'll call you as soon as something is going." Jeremy had seen it all.

But what none of the photographers knew was that it was a dead end. The call would never come. It happened that way because in his photographic empire, Jeremy had a handful of selected photographers – and one in particular, John Kelly – that were used time and time again. The auditioning of new talent was merely a reflex action that could not be shaken.

A photographic coordinator's job does not end at finding the right photographer for a specific job. That is difficult enough. The eye must have a conceptual brain behind it. Jeremy's eye had that brain. But there's more to it. Once the photograph is taken and in hand the picture must be placed. Jeremy had worked a deal with one of the London photo syndication agencies that gave Apple a 65 percent slice of all photographs sold. An intelligently placed photograph of The Beatles could earn up to £500 per print.

T HE PRESS OFFICER looked at his room through the cigarette smoke and clanging of ringing telephones and went into his rap, calling his staff to attention. "All right, this afternoon we've got a press conference for John and Yoko. We've got Ray Connolly of the *Standard*, David Wigg of the *Express*, Dougie Marlborough of the *Mail* and Mike Ledgerwood of *Disc* coming in. Ringo's in at three to tele-phone ten radio stations in America to talk about Apple, which is something he volunteered for. I didn't ask him to do it. And Mary is coming in for that *Petticoat* interview which has already been cancelled twice. When she gets here, Carol, take her upstairs to the guest lounge because I don't want her doing it here with all this madness going on.

"It looks like we've got Moya Hutt to take all that poetry off our backs. She says she wants to turn it into a book and all I can say is, thank Christ for that! We've got one-fifth of the Jefferson Airplane in, plus Dean Stockwell and Jeremy Clyde. I want revised biographies on Mary, Jackie and James by next Friday lunchtime, which means we need to get one a day done so that we don't get stuck at the last minute.

"Alan Aldridge is coming in at four to see if we'll go halves on a book he's doing of illustrated Beatles' lyrics. Justin and Twiggy are in with Peter Brown so someone in this room might have to give them a guided tour of the building if they should ask. Peter Asher's found an American group called Mortimer who are in this afternoon, which means another biography. I want to keep Ringo away from the press because I don't want him Beatled today because he's got enough to contend with. And let's make sure we've got enough glasses and ice."

He said it all in one long breath with hardly a pause between conjunctions and was just about to pick up the dialogue when the secretary handed him a telephone. "It's Neil for you." In a few seconds the expression on his face registered a cold horror.

"What? When? Where? I'll be right down!" Without looking he handed the telephone back to the secretary. "Call off that press conference," he said in a half whisper.

"What's the matter?"

"They've just busted John and Yoko!"

41
NEWS ITEMS

HE TIMES. Saturday, October 19, 1968.

LENNON ON DRUG CHARGE
John Lennon, aged 28, of The Beatles pop group, will appear at Marylebone Magistrates Court today charged with being in possession of Cannabis and with obstructing the police in the execution of a search warrant.

To appear with him on similar charges is Mrs. Yoko Ono Cox, aged 34, film director and friend of Mr. Lennon.

The Times, Friday, November 22, 1968.

Yoko Ono Cox, the Japanese artist and friend of John Lennon of The Beatles, has had a miscarriage in Queen Charlotte's Maternity Hospital W. Mr. Lennon has said he was the father.

End of news items.

If you really want to meet John Lennon to get his autograph or perhaps just to see how he moves and you set your mind to it, you'll find a way. The Blue Meanies decided it would be easiest just to arrest him. They had been waiting a long time.

When the drug squad arrived at the flat in Montagu Square in the heart of better-heeled London they brought a police-woman for Yoko and dogs for the hashish. The dogs were more intrigued by old socks then the search for Cannabis but they had their work to do. It wasn't very difficult; it was all over the place. They allowed John Lennon to make a phone call and he telephoned Neil.

"Imagine your worst paranoia, Neil, because it's here right now!"

It wasn't really the hashish they were after and they probably could have done without the autographs. A year earlier this arrest would have been unthinkable. It would have been a monumentally unpopular move in the wake of the Rolling Stones's purge that had somehow unexpectedly back-fired in sentiment.

It was *that* picture that did it. It was the one slap in the face that could not go unanswered. In that one single act of unadulterated exhibitionism, John Lennon had stepped on the hypersensitive big toe of his fickle public. Arresting John and Yoko was a wasted motion. Being John Lennon, nothing would really happen to him. It was only the loss of a few hours, the drudgery of that gray wait as police protocol cleared itself. Any fine, no matter how out of proportion to the deed, could in no way dent his bank account. But the gesture had to be made.

The flat they were arrested in at the time had been rented out to Ringo. The landlords immediately demanded the court slap a series of restraining injunctions that prohibited John and Yoko from using it under any circumstances, that no one except Ringo and his family were to make use of it, that no immoral practices should take place, that no business be carried out on the premises and no music or musical instru-ments were to be played at any time.

The case was heard by a judge in chambers. Peter Brown represented Ringo and agreed that no one else would live there except Ringo and that no business was going to be conducted from there. He refused to accept the remaining injunctions as totally disgraceful. His refusal was accepted.

Follow-up to News Item One
The Times, Friday, November 29, 1968
JOHN LENNON FINED £150 ON DRUG CHARGE

John Winston Lennon, aged 28, of The Beatles, was fined £150 with 20 guineas cost at Marylebone Magistrates Court yesterday when he pleaded guilty to the unauthorized possession of 219 grains of Cannabis resin found when detectives accompanied by dogs searched his flat at Montagu Square, Marylebone, on October 18.

Appearing with him on remand was Mrs. Yoko Ono Cox, aged 34, artist, of the same address, who denied charges of unauthorized possession of the drug and willfully obstructing detective sergeant Norman Pilcher when he was exercising his powers under the Dangerous Drugs Act.

She was discharged and Mr. Lennon was also discharged on a similar charge of obstructing the officer, which he denied. The prosecution offered no evidence on those three counts.

Mr. Roger Frisby for the prosecution told Mr. John Phipps, the Magistrate, that although the flat appeared to be in the joint occupation of the couple, Mr. Lennon had taken full responsibility for the drugs and said Mrs. Cox had nothing to do with it.

Mr. Frisby said that when the officers got into the flat and told Mr. Lennon that they had a search warrant they found a large quantity of drugs properly prescribed by Mr. Lennon's doctor. When asked if he had any he should not have, such as Cannabis, Mr. Lennon shook his head.

Mr. Frisby said a cigarette-rolling machine found on top of a bathroom mirror, a tin originally containing film found in a bedroom and a cigarette case all bore traces of Cannabis resin. In an envelope in a suitcase was found 27.3 grains of the drug and 19.8 grains were in a binocular case nosed out by a dog, on the mantleshelf in the living room.

End of news item.

In his summing up for the defense, Martin Polden pleaded for leniency from the court for a man who had given so much pleasure to so many untold millions of people through his music. An ounce and a half of compassion was not too much to ask.

42
SAMANTHA

I T'S A VERY NICE donkey, Jeremy, it really is. If the children were here they'd thank you loudly I'm sure but as they're not I'll thank you for them," said The Press Officer.

"Think nothing of it, Derek, but remember it shouldn't be ridden until next spring, its back isn't strong enough and by the way, its name is Samantha."

The House Hippie, the secretary, the two Cordon Blue cooks always kept on the premises, The Press Officer and the photographic coordinator stood in the center of the Press Office admiring the young donkey named Samantha.

"Lovely ears –"

"Intelligent eyes –"

"Fantastic tail –"

"I hope it doesn't shit on the floor –"

"Oh, Richard!"

"How did you get it up here in the first place?"

"In the lift –"

The gray quadruped swished its tail, bobbed its head and rolled its eyes. If it could have talked it probably would have asked for a scotch and Coke.

"Well!" said The Press Officer, "I think it's time for Samantha to make an about-face into the lift and downstairs into the trailer so that she can get on her way to Sunningdale because it's 11:30 and we've got Beatles and Taylors and Lomaxes and Hopkins and Iveys and a thousand and one other projects to get working on. Thank you, Jeremy. It's a beautiful gift, it really is."

They all stood and watched as the donkey with the lovely ears, intelligent eyes and fantastic tail named Samantha was about-faced, led out the door into the lift and out of their early morning lives.

"Enough assing around," said The Press Officer, "Richard! Roll a joint!"

43

A WELL-STOCKED CUPBOARD

ACCORDING TO THIS drinks list the Press Office in the past fifteen days has consumed six hundred Benson and Hedges, eight dozen Cokes, eight bottles of J & B scotch, four bottles of Courvoisier brandy, three bottles of vodka, two dozen ginger ales, one dozen tonic waters, two dozen bitter lemons, one dozen tomato juices, three bottles of lime and four dozen lagers –"

"Is that all?"

"Seems to be –"

"Hmm, I guess they're cutting down, because according to last month's drinks list . . ."

44

AND DON'T FORGET TO LIGHT A CANDLE FOR ME WHEN I'M GONE

WELL, WHAT DID Derek say when you told him?"

"He told me I was a twat and I had no right to assassinate him and it was unfair and he didn't want to be around when it happened. But it's already happened! I told Jeremy, 'I don't want you around here anymore because you're not doing anything and I want you to leave *right now*!' And you know what he said to me?"

"What?"

"Give me six weeks –"

"What did you say?"

"I told him, 'You better be out of this building by three o'clock –' "

"What did he say to that?"

"He's gone!"

45

A GHOST FROM THE PAST

A DOLF HITLER? The name rings a bell," said The House Hippie.

"It should."

"Was he a client of yours in LA?"

"No, man!" snapped The Press Officer impatiently, "I didn't want that arsehole's account. It was more aggro than it was worth. But didn't you ever meet him up at my office?"

"I can't remember –"

"He was also at Monterey –"

"What does he do?"

"Do! He doesn't do anything these days. Listen, when he comes up here get him a drink but cut out the dialogue. I don't want him hanging around this place all day."

Two minutes later Adolf Hitler walked into the Apple Press Office and belted a warm greeting at The Press Officer who managed to muster a "Hello, how have you been, how's Eva?" before nervously introducing the secretary and The House Hippie to his guest.

The House Hippie served The Press Officer and Mr. Hitler with two scotch and Cokes and then remembered all the things he was supposed to do and hadn't. He got on with it. Half an hour later he looked up from his pile of cuttings and saw The Press Officer walk Mr. Hitler to the door, shake his hand and bow a curt farewell.

"Christ! I'm glad *that's* over!" he said.

"He seemed nice enough," observed The House Hippie.

"Oh sure –"

And then it all came back to him!

"*Now* I remember him! Of course! He looks pretty good

81

with that mustache and his hair is a lot longer but I *do* remember him. Didn't he used to be a real *creep* a few years back?"

"The *biggest*, but you've got to admit it's much more far out to say 'I'd like you to meet my friend Adolf Hitler' than it is to say, 'I'd like you to meet my friend John Lennon –''

"Yeah, that *is* pretty far out."

46

"WHEN WE DO RIGHT NO ONE REMEMBERS, WHEN WE DO WRONG NO ONE FORGETS"

FROM GEORGE HARRISON to all Apple staff: "Hell's Angles will be in London within the next week on the way to straighten out Czechoslovakia. There will be 12 in number, complete with black leather jackets and motorcycles. They will undoubtedly arrive at Apple and I have heard they may try to make full use of Apple's facilities. They may look as though they are going to do you in but are very straight and do good things, so don't fear them or uptight them. Try to assist them without neglecting your Apple business and without letting them take control of Savile Row. December 4, 1968."

"I hear those Hell's Angels are pretty tough characters."

"The toughest."

"Well, if there's a siege what do you think we'll need?"

"Oranges, chocolate, tobacco, cigarette papers –"

"Don't forget matches –"

"Matches, brass knuckles, lead pipes –"

"Brass knuckles! Lead pipes!"

"Well, what are you going to hit them with? A rolled-up comic book?"

"No, but from what I've heard if you hit one of those guys with a lead pipe you break the pipe."

"Well, in that case I hope we can settle this thing peacefully. But maybe we're jumping the gun. Like George says, they just look like they're going to do you in but they're not."

"Yeah, well I hope you're right and he knows what he's talking about."

"Besides, if they're on the way to Czechoslovakia they're going to have to save their energy and anyway I can't see any reason for them to start pulling this place apart."

"Yeah, you're probably right –"

"So we can forget about the brass knuckles and the lead pipes."

"But what about some hashish?"

"What about it?"

"It would be nice to have some around, wouldn't it? I mean, even if the siege is peaceful –"

"That might be a big mistake because you'd probably smoke yourself soft and pass out in some corner and then you'd miss the whole show."

"That's a point. Anyway, I heard the alert signal is three long and two short blasts of the fire-alarm bell."

"That should do it."

"And you know if we don't want to we don't *have* to stay around for this thing. We can walk out of this building the minute that bell goes but if we stay around and anything bad happens all injuries are covered by the workers' compensation clause of the company's policies and procedures."

"But what if you get knocked off?"

"Well, then that's it."

"Yeah, but somehow I think this thing is going to do this place some good."

"How's that?"

"Well, everybody around here has become kind of jaded from all our day-to-day encounters with the exotic and the bizarre and something like this could actually inject some adrenalin into the place. You know, shake things up a bit."

"Yeah, I see what you mean."

Two days later, on December 6, Derek Taylor, The Beatles'

Press Officer and Apple's publicist, sent an interoffice memo to four of the Apple hierarchy: Neil Aspinall, Alistair Taylor, Peter Brown and Peter Asher.

"Here is a list of George's friends, Hell's Angels. I am giving them your home phone numbers so that if they get into Shit Creek, as seems likely, they have friends to help them. They have my number and many others."

Shit Creek runs from the tarmac at Heathrow Airport through Passport Control and Immigration to Customs and on through those swinging, one-way doors. If you manage to avoid a refusal of entry or a Customs declaration seizure then you have done far better than if you had run with the bulls at Pamplona and made it. You have just shot the rapids at Shit Creek.

Alistair Taylor, one of the four mentioned in Derek Taylor's memo, was the first to actively involve himself on behalf of Hell's Angles and Company. His even years' devoted service to The Beatles as chief fixer had not passed without his having acquired a no-nonsense, working education in the ways of the world.

A chief fixer must be acquainted with people in all walks of life. From diversified high-ranking public officials on down to the shoeless little girl selling lavender soap on Old Bond Street. His job had carried him through the dusty passageways of the Egyptian wing of the British Museum on through the gilded drawing rooms of Belgravia, down motorways and into and out of many different airports, harbors and train stations.

He was able to fix on half a day's notice a complete holiday with transportation, hotel accommodations and safari particulars through Tanganyika when any or all of his employers might snap two fingers. He was familiar with the going market price of jade and the best shops to acquire the most Nikons in Japan. He could introduce his employers to the best art dealer in town who in turn would make his recommendation on what surrealist painting would make the best investment of the season.

Alistair Taylor was an ace chief fixer. He gracefully side-stepped the hurdles of red tape that cut off the common man from those people in the seats of power. A few minutes of dialogue, the right words to the right people in the right places and the affair was settled. The ballet of the exchange of a favor for a favor had been danced out to perfection. Providing any of George's friends weren't in possession of unauthorized drugs or firearms or smitten with hoof and mouth disease, it seemed certain that they would pass untroubled and with a minimum of static through Customs and Immigration. The deed was as good as done.

Twelve noon. On the second floor of the Apple building in the Press Office, Carol Paddon was on the telephone in deep conversation describing the delights of a dinner party attended the night before. A London girl with one of those sparkling English peaches-and-cream complexions. She had on an impossibly long pair of eyelashes. In the midst of this conversation she adjusted those eyelashes for the fourth time that day.

Sitting opposite her on the other side of the room with his feet resting comfortably on the desk sat The House Hippie. He was having a daydream. Beside him on the sideboard in readiness for the afternoon's invariable influx of people, bottles of liquor, soft drinks, ice and glasses were arranged in a perfectly symmetrical row. It was a bar as well stocked as Napoleon's Chateau Malmaison.

The House Hippie's fragile, introverted dreaming was suddenly shattered by the noise that seeped through from the guest lounge directly above the Press Office. The sound of dancing feet, the wailing of guitars and the pounding of drums suddenly dominated the momentary dull hush of the lunch-hour break. "What the fuck is going on up there?" he thought to himself.

The only way to find out was to explore. Swinging his legs off the desk and onto the floor he casually made his way out of the office and up the thick, green carpeted staircase, an easy two at a time. At the top of the landing he met the two female Cordon Blue cooks struggling under the massive, gluttonous trays of food that were this and every afternoon's fare.

Peter Brown, The Beatles' personal assistant and social coordinator, was entertaining and one could imagine what illustrious persons were his guests today. Many company deals and problems had to be worked out. The intricate social engagements created by The Beatles had to be fixed. peter brown, a man of refined tastes and untouchable panache, chose to do this social trafficking over a succulent roast beef and a bottle of Château d'If.

The music grew lounder the closer. The House Hippie got to the room. When he opened the door he was slapped with the odor of California patchouli oil. He immediately noticed that the harsh, fluorescent office lights of the guest lounge had been mercifully exchanged for homemade candlelight. A hail of cheers greeted his entrance. Of course! How could he have forgotten them? Emily's Family!

Emily's Family was the original Shoot-'Em-Up-Head-'Em-Off-At-The-Pass-Pardner-Psychedelic-Traveling-Family-Medicine Show. They had left California on their way to the Fiji Islands to establish their own alternative universe. A stopover had been made in London so that she and the brood could pick up John and Yoko to take them off to a better life. The purpose of their mission had manifested itself in an acid vision.

Emily was comfortably into her thirties but still as compact as most girls in their twenties with her thick, red hair and neat, little-girl torso. She was pacing the room unable to contain her energy, nude, breast-feeding the youngest of the crew. She had two boys, aged nine and twelve, quick and precocious. Then there was Jenie. She was the oldest at fifteen, with the same beautiful hair but two shades darker into the red. The thread of their mother-daughter relationship was a pitched sexual competition that was in a constant flow of abrasive motion.

Frank, Emily's husband by a second marriage and ten years younger, removed himself from the turmoils of these conflicts and the frenzy of large family coexistence by a comfortable retreat into detached silence. His natural grace was topped by a constant, beatific smile.

They were the complete innocents. No shadow of doubt ever fell on the walls of their minds that this mission with its final objective of kidnap by consent of John and Yoko to an as yet unspecified island in the Fijis would meet with anything but a thumping, resounding success. Their proposition had been placed through all the formal channels of approach to John and Yoko. They were awaiting the reply.

They hadn't been laughed at and they weren't told that their dream was unworkable. They were politely informed that at the moment John and Yoko were heavily committed to numerous projects and the running of a record company. They were given the daytime run of the building and use of the guest lounge with a quiet, cautious hint to kindly stay out of the way of the workings of the office machinery.

Jennie leaned on The House Hippie playfully and whispered huskily into his ear.

"You know, I'd really love to ball George."

"I'm afraid I can't help you right now, kid."

"I'm not a *kid*! I'm fifteen and a *half* years old! So stop calling me kid!"

"Jenny, tell me something."

"What!"

"Does *every* woman *need* a second deodorant?"

"Huh??"

One of Emily's boys, unable to keep in check his youthful curiosity, bounded into this engrossing dialogue.

"Hey, Richard, have John and Yoko been in today?"

"I don't think so but –"

The other one shrieked, "When are the Hell's Angels getting here?"

"I don't know. Their time of arrival is unknown to us all."

"Can you get us something to eat from the kitchen, honey?" Emily asked.

"If you'll just put on some clothes so you don't freak the chicks in the kitchen out and ask them as sweetly as you just asked me, I'm sure they'll knock out a dose of sandwiches for you."

"All right."

"I'll see you all a bit later."

The House Hippie departed amidst screams and squeals and the familiar cry of "Say hi to George and Derek!" ringing in his ear.

Back in the Press Office, the door closed behind him, the room went very quiet. The roar from the guest lounge had subsided and only the faint shuffle of feet reached through the ceiling. The phones were peacefully slippered in their cradles. A rarity really. The House Hippie picked up one of the internal phones.

"Laurie, please put all calls through on thirteen. I'm here alone."

"All right, pet, will do. There's one for you right now."

"Thanks –"

"Press Office?"

"Yes –"

"Air Freight Arrivals, Heathrow Airport here, sir. We have two Harley-Davidson motorcycles which are ready for collection. However, the shipping costs must be paid before we can release them."

"Just a minute please, who are they for?"

"Well, all it says here is Hell's Angels care of Apple, 3 Savile Row. Are they a group of yours?"

"Not exactly but how much are the shipping costs?"

"Two hundred and fifty pounds."

"I see. Well, what I think has happened is that the motorcycles have preceded their owners but they're expected soon, sometime this week, probably tomorrow. But are you sure there are only two?"

"Yes, sir, quite sure."

"Hmm. Well, hold onto them until someone comes to claim them and please, I beg you, make sure nothing happens to them. No scratches, *please*."

"Yes, sir."

The Apple Press Office. Same time only twenty-four hours later. The setup is a carbon copy of the previous afternoon. The House Hippie is again alone in the deserted lunchtime office. The internal phone rings and the cool, fresh-water voice of the receptionist comes bubbling through the blower.

"Richard –"

"Yes, Debbie –"

"The Hell's Angels are here!"

A shiver of excitement ran down The House Hippie's spine. The Hell's Angels! Downstairs in reception! He remembered George's memo. ". . . They may look as though they are going to do you in but are very straight and do good things, so don't fear them or uptight them."

The House Hippie walked across the hall into the unoccupied office and looked out the window down into the street. On the corner opposite the Apple building, gleaming in the December sunshine were two outstandingly gorgeous, Harley-Davidson motorcycles. Their singular presence dominated the block.

Everyone that passed stopped short to gawk open-mouthed at these two-wheeled, eccentric marvels. The jutting monkey bars, the mirrorlike chrome work, the erotically curved gas tanks and the outsized twin exhaust pipes were a cause for wonder. In the entire history of British motoring nothing like them had ever been seen. History was sitting peacefully that day on a busy corner in the heart of London's West End.

The House Hippie thought it odd though that there were only *two* of them. Hadn't George said there were going to be twelve? But then when the Air Freight Arrivals had telephoned the other day they had said the same thing. Only two motorcycles on receipt, positively.

He found them in all their splendor sprawled across the reception lounge; laughing, smoking and reeking of patchouli oil. There were men and women and babes in arms; leather, suede, headbands, cowboy hats, bells, sleeping bags, backpacks, beads, mountain boots, sticks of incense, flutes and guitars.

"Hey, where are The Beatles?"

"How much is ten shillings in American money?"

"Where's a laundromat?"

"I've gotta take a piss!"

89

"Who's got Mick Jagger's phone number?"

In actual fact the anticipated, twelve-strong army of leather and chains that was on its way to Czechoslovakia to straighten out the explosive and highly degenerate political situation had somehow been watered down to *two* genuine, dyed-in-the-Levis Hell's Angels and sixteen California freaks: zonked, wired and suffering from massive time displacement and cultural shock. The two Hell's Angels were Billy Tumbleweed and Frisco Pete of the San Francisco chapter of the Hell's Angels Motorcycle Club, California, USA.

The House Hippie took two baby steps forward.

"Hey, man, you work here?"

"Yeah –"

"Well, look can you fix us up or tell us where we can get something to eat and crash for awhile?"

"Uhh, well, uhh, we'll try and figure something out, uhh, did you have any trouble getting through Customs?"

"Naah! It was so fuckin' easy. We just walked right through wearin' our colors and no one said shit to us –"

"That's good –"

"Where's that cat George Harrison? They tell me he's an OK dude –"

"Oh you'll like George all right, but he's not here this afternoon but he told us you were coming here before you went to Czechoslovakia but he said there would be *twelve* Angels and –"

"Yeah, well, we thought it over and decided it would be smarter if just me and Billy, by the way my name's Frisco Pete and this is Billy Tumbleweed –"

"M-m-my name's R-R-Richard –"

"Yeah well, where was I? Oh yeah, anyway it's just the two of us at the moment –"

"The papers all know you're coming –"

"The fuckin' papers, huh? What else did they say?"

"Oh just that you'd be visiting Apple and –"

"Well, we'll give 'em a fuckin' mouthful if they wanna ask us any questions. Say, this is a pretty nice joint you got here and that's a good-lookin' broad behind that desk. Hello, sweetheart!"

"That's Debbie –"

"Yeah, well, dig it. I think we're all gonna split for a while and have a look around but we'll be back later and if ya come up with someplace for us to crash keep it in mind and where can we dump all our shit?"

"Oh just leave it here; Debbie'll look after it –"

"Yeah, well, catch you later –"

And then just like *that* they all piled out into the street, breaking up into groups, looking in every direction with the overeager anticipation of the newly arrived, not knowing which way to go first. Frisco Pete and Billy Tumbleweed crossed the street to their magnificent chrome steeds, joined by two of the ladies from the crew. They kicked their motorcycles to life and roared off into the London lunch-hour traffic leaving a sudden vacuum in the reception lounge and a hanging cloud of patchouli oil as a reminder that you can take a wildflower out of the woods but you can't take . . .

Watching them now all going their separate ways, The House Hippie thought he recognized Ken Kesey somewhere in the middle of that 16 strong, zonked and wired contingent of flapping, jangling California freaks.

47
OUR MOTTO: PLEASURE BEFORE BUSINESS

THE PRESS OFFICER had accepted the responsibility of organizing the Apple Christmas party. He danced with the concept in the morning and by that afternoon he was ready to dictate to his secretary the polished proclamation. He dictated.

"The Apple Christmas party will be held on December 23 at 2:30 in the afternoon and will go on until evening. In the middle of the party we will be visited by Ernest Castro and April, entertainers to the Queen and Duke of Cornwall and the late Sir Winston Churchill, MacDonald Hobley and others. Mr. Castro is a conjuror, ventriloquist and children's entertainer. April is his assistant and also his wife and she plays guitar. So the idea is that all of us at Apple will bring our children and those of us who have no children are invited to bring a couple unless they can arrange to have one of their own in the meantime. Immaculate conceptions will not be accepted. There will be a party with food and wine and children and a Christmas tree and it will be very good. I would be glad if today you will write your name on this memorandum together with the number of children you will be bringing and hand it to Carol Paddon. It goes without saying that wives, husbands, boy and girl friends are welcome but no more than one per person unless bigamists wish to plead a special case."

"Got it? Read it back to me –"

48

LOST A SON BUT GAINED A DAUGHTER

THE PRESS OFFICE in the early weeks of December 1968 lost some weight and gained a little elbow room. The sudden departure of Jeremy Banks left one desk empty. Then Terry Doran and Jack Oliver moved downstairs to the Record Department, taking their secretary, Dee Meehan, with them. This left The Press Officer, his secretary and The House Hippie.

The Press Officer announced one morning that the desk which Banks had occupied would not be vacant for long.

"I need someone else in to help me because this new year is going to be frantic and the lunacy is just beginning. She starts work on December 16 and I want you to make her feel welcome and at home. Her name is Mavis Smith."

In her girlhood before the world of public relations snatched her up, Mavis Smith studied dance with the Ballet Rambert for three years, finishing off her fourth and final year as a featured dancer on a six-month continental tour with that illustrious company. From the world of classical dance Mavis Smith moved into PR where she worked with Les Perrin, a top London publicist on a Phillips Record account. After a year she grew restless with the job.

Mavis is married to Alan Smith, a respected journalist with the *New Musical Express*. On several occasions Alan had talked to Derek Taylor at various Beatle functions and mentioned that his wife was in publicity and looking around for another job that would prove more stimulating than the one she was doing.

Mavis met Derek at a London concert. A week later Derek phoned Alan and asked him if his wife would like to work at Apple with him in the Press Office. The answer came back, "Yes!"

Mavis Smith walked into the Apple Press Office at 10 a.m. on the morning of December 16 before anyone else had arrived; an attractive, petite, dark-haired young woman with her whole life stretching out before her.

49
100 EASY STREET

T HE ARRIVAL OF Frisco Pete and Billy Tumbleweed with the California Pleasure Crew at Apple in the London December of 1968 was the mescaline icing on the hashish cake that climaxed the year. No one at Apple knew quite what to expect. George Harrison's memo had sent shock waves through the organization, sparking off lurid fantasies nurtured on countless motorcycle movies and dime-novel hallucinations. The fact that there were only *two* Hell's Angels mattered very little to anyone.

That first night no one had to sleep in Hyde Park or in a cardboard box in a doorway on Oxford Street. The bulk of the Pleasure Crew were immediately dispatched to a large ground-floor flat on Prince of Wales Drive in Battersea, belonging to a friend of a friend of someone. Frisco Pete and a tall, blonde girl named Paula stayed with The House Hippie in

Ladbroke Grove. They were all thoroughly versed in urban survival tactics.

After a refreshing night's sleep and nutritious breakfast topped off by a two-hour drive around London on a day blessed by the absence of rain and severe winds, Frisco Pete and Billy Tumbleweed returned to 3 Savile Row.

Derek Taylor and Peter Brown were in the Press Office when the door opened and in walked Pete and Billy, full of confidence and good cheer. They were instantaneously recognizable as thoroughbred Hell's Angels.

"Hello, everybody!" boomed Frisco Pete to The Press Officer and the Ambassador of the Apple diplomatic corps. They froze. For the first time in his experience The House Hippie saw Derek Taylor and Peter Brown at an absolute loss for words. The moment stretched into long seconds. A newly recruited secretary, Sally Burgess, who sat where Terry Doran's secretary had once been stationed, looked up over her IBM golfball and blanched, crystallized with fright. Frisco Pete caught her look and felt the waves of fear.

"What's the matter, sweetheart?" he asked her.

"Uh, n-n-n-nothing's the m-m-matter –"

"Good, I'm glad to hear it –"

"Hi, Pete and Billy!" The House Hippie leaped into the silence.

"How's it going?"

"OK! Hey, that's Derek and Peter and that's Frisco Pete and Billy Tumbleweed –"

And then a set of fumbled handshakes and mumbled greetings. Slowly but still fast enough to be comfortable everyone's composure returned. The tension level dropped. "Well, see you later," said Peter Brown making for the door but not before telling Pete and Billy that it was a pleasure to make their acquaintance. "And I do hope you enjoy your stay in London." Exit Peter Brown.

And then The Press Officer uncoiled.

"Well!" he boomed, "You are here and so are we and this is Sally who has just joined us and that is Carol who has always been with us and Richard you know and if you would like a cup of tea then a cup of tea it is but if you would rather have a glass of beer or a bottle of wine or a scotch and Coke or a gin and tonic or a vodka and lime then that it is because it is all here and if it is not then we will come up with something but have a seat or have cigarette or have a joint and I will be back in three minutes so please don't go away because there is a lot to talk about and more to find out and stranger days to come!" Exit Derek Taylor, who was not the world's highest paid Press Officer for nothing. That avalanche of monologue had riveted Frisco Pete and Billy Tumbleweed to the thick apple-green carpet.

"Beer?" bellowed The House Hippie.

"Beer –"

"Beer –"

The promised three minutes had turned into 30 when Derek Taylor made his reentry but no one had noticed the time discrepancy. He continued with his stream of consciousness, now completely warmed up and keenly honed.

"Well, it's almost Christmas and this is Apple and today is today and tomorrow is tomorrow and George said you were coming and so you have and how is London treating you?"

"Well, what we've seen we like –"

"How many of you are there?"

"Well there's me and Billy and about sixteen jokers in the Pleasure Crew –"

"Fantastic –"

"We're over here to check out the English Angels and have a look around –"

"Did you have any aggravation at Customs?"

"Nahh, they didn't even check our bags –"

"They can be real twats when they want to and gentlemen when it strikes their fancy –"

"Well, we're not lookin' to have any shit thrown at us and anyway the club paid for Billy and me and the bikes to come over 'cause if we couldn't bring them there wouldn't be any reason for comin' 'cause I don't walk anywhere and I hate cars. If this place makes it, we'll be bringin' back the rest of our brothers in the spring."

"You know that the newspapers are curious and want to talk with you and if you'd like this office will fix all that but if you'd rather pass then that's fine too –"

"No, man, we'll talk to all of those dudes 'cause I gotta lot to talk about and we need to do some explainin' because we're always getting bum-rapped and we don't need any more bad shit than we've got 'cause I've *had* it up to *here*!"

"Well, I must warn you that the English press isn't the most sympathetic in the world but they will listen and they will let you talk."

"Look, man, we're not askin' for any fuckin' favors. Just as long as they give us a fair shake –"

"We've got a room upstairs that you can use as you see fit during the day and come and go as you please and keep in touch with this office and we'll do everything we can. There's a family from California up there right now but there should be plenty of room for all of you and right next door is the kitchen and it's full of tea and coffee and sandwiches and we've got a record company to run but that doesn't stand in the way of making our friends feel like friends and warm and welcome –"

"Good enough. We're gonna go and look around some more and we'd dig to meet The Beatles if they come in but don't get the idea we're pushin' it and well I guess we'll see ya later. Oh yeah, Ken Kesey's with us and he'll probably come in and see you soon, what's your name again? I didn't catch it –"

"Taylor, Derek –"

"Yeah, well later –"

Ken Kesey became the first tangible candidate for Apple's Spoken Word series, which had been under consideration since the late spring. In a joint decision that included Taylor and Asher, Kesey was supplied with a portable tape recorder and the use of an electric typewriter; the record was to be an informal street diary of his London visit.

The Press Officer warned Kesey about the press.

"Watch out for them –"

"Why?" he wanted to know.

"Because they're straights –"

Ken Kesey and his Cadillac at Savile Row.

"Well, you're sitting behind a straight desk –"

"True, true. I forget about that sometimes –"

The guest lounge was transformed into a second-string Press Office and Club House. The Press Officer had fixed a run of interviews for the Hell's Angels and Company with the dailies, the musicals and the underground press. A stack of Beatle albums was brought up to feed the record player and two cases of beer sent in to quench the Big Thirst. Within two days the room had been transformed into a California Free-Form Freakout. The smell of hashish and grass, mixed with the insistent odor of patchouli and sweat, produced a scent that could have been bottled as a worldwide original.

Amidst all this there were four Beatles that had to be spoken for and Jackie Lomax, James Taylor, the Modern Jazz Quartet, the Iveys, the Black Dyke Mills Brass Band and Mary Hopkin who needed attention, love and no small amount of back-patting. There was a Christmas party to arrange and a Christmas card to be designed to Paul McCartney's specifications. And a new auxiliary Press Officer to initiate into the Beatles' empire.

Mavis Smith looked at the musical paper on her desk in complete disbelief.

"But *why*, Derek?" she intoned. "This stuff in *Alley Cat* about John and Yoko is utterly foul!"

"You're telling me!" The Press Officer boiled. "I'm fucking fed up with it. I'm sick of that smutty, racist prose slime of theirs. And I'll tell you something, if it goes on, the Press Council is going to be hearing from us and at the next threshold of a hint of a whisper of libel that dirty cat will be dragged from his filthy alley and sued to hell and back and that's not just *dialogue!!!*"

50

THE BATTLE FOR THE LARGEST TURKEY IN GREAT BRITAIN

NOT ONLY WAS THERE going to be a conjuror, a Yuletide tree, acres of food and oceans of drink, but John and Yoko agreed to dress up as Father and Mother Christmas and hand out presents to all the children. The crowning glory of the elaborate, stand-up buffet dinner was a 43-pound turkey billed by the supplying butchers as the Largest Turkey in Great Britain.

December 23. Preparations had begun at nine that morning. The children's party was scheduled for 2:30 in Peter Brown's office. At six o'clock the adults' version of the children's party would begin in Neil's office. By 11 o'clock the Press Office was filled to overload with the Christmas-season glut of good-time Charlies on their record-company-to-record-company marathon sprint for alcohol, inside talk and free LPs. Of all the record companies in London, Apple was number one on the list for abandoned cordiality and excessive generosity.

By 11:30 the Black Room was swollen to standing-room-only proportions with hashish smokers puffing their brains out while the front office catered to the scotch and Coke brigade. By noon all pretense had been dropped and the hash heads were indistinguishable from the juicers. The telephones that refused to quit were barely audible above the record player turned to three-quarter volume.

By three o'clock Peter Brown's office was a scene of un-paralleled frenzy as more than a hundred children screamed and smashed their way through a mountain of ice cream, cake and sausage rolls, impatiently clamoring to be entertained by the ventriloquist and conjuror they had been promised.

At last Ernest Castro and April, entertainers to the Queen and Duke of Cornwall and the late Sir Winston Churchill, made their entrance. The roar of recognition from a hundred pint-sized Frankensteins must have been honeyed music to their ears. In the greatest tradition of English garden-party entertainers, they lanced into their live-wire routine of silvered voice projections, sleight-of-hand wonders and barnyard-beast imitations. The eardrum-shattering squeals of delight from the youngsters did not decrease one decibel the entire length of their performance. They closed the show with a sizzling rendition of Lettuce Leaf Hop.

John and Yoko in full Christmas drag were waiting for them in the Press Office when the show let out. Mary Hopkin had joined them to lend an additional two paws to the distribution of gifts. Unrattled by the greedy stampede for toys, John Lennon stood calmly in the middle of the room, deadpan, muttering through the false beard on top of his own beard, "Ho, ho, ho."

From the reception lounge to the Press Office the party-goers lined the walls and the landings, filling the building with roof-lifting talk, blue smoke and the rumble of several

Celebrities, non-celebrities, would-be-celebrities, assorted hangers-on, wives, mistresses, children and visiting Hell's Angels types met during the Apple Christmas Party on December 23, 1968. Ernest Castro, a professional children's entertainer, sought to give structure to an otherwise Chaotic Encounter Group with pine trimmings, plus the Battle for The Largest Turkey in Great Britain.

hundred churning, empty stomachs. The Largest Turkey in Great Britain was locked safely behind the kitchen door away from an increasingly restless crowd. The kitchen counter and sideboard were barely holding up under the weight of a thousand assorted hors d'oeuvres, platters of cold meat and jellied fish. Salads, cakes, bowls of fruit and boiled sweets, biscuits and cheese lined the floor.

John and Yoko, freed from the burden of their costumes, sat on the Press Office floor surrounded by Emily's family. The Press Officer hovered nearby, glass in hand, cigarette in mouth, hoping that his employer would not be Beatled unmercifully on this day of all days. The noise level in the room was more suitable for lip reading than conversational audibility.

It took only three seconds for this atmosphere of intense gaiety to turn radically and almost irrevocably sour. Frisco Pete, elbows pumping him energetically through the crowd, covered the length of the room in four enormous strides. He poised menacingly over the slight figures of John Lennon and Yoko Ono.

"What the fuck is goin' on in this place!?!" he screamed at them. The room dropped into a clammy, itchy silence. No one moved.

"We wanna eat! What's all this shit about havin' to wait until seven?!"

Mavis' husband, Alan, gallantly interrupted Frisco Pete with a request for a little consideration for the situation. His efforts were rewarded with a single closed-fist punch, carefully measured by a man who knew full well the power of his own strength. The room darkened. Frisco Pete returned his attention to John Lennon.

"You got more fuckin' food in that kitchen than there are people and it's all locked up and those two fuckin' broads upstairs tell me I've gotta wait until seven o'clock just like everybody else! There's a forty-three-pound turkey in that fuckin' kitchen and I fuckin' want some of it now!!!"

John Lennon, at this moment in his life a squeamish vegetarian, looked up at the frightening figure of Frisco Pete

in total bewilderment. He knew nothing of the release schedule on the Largest Turkey in Great Britain. The Press Officer
turned to The House Hippie and told him to fetch Peter Brown
without any further delay. With relief he found him outside in
the hall talking to Ron Kass. "Peter, you'd better come inside
right away—" and The House Hippie pulled him by the arm,
fearing the loss of precious seconds.

"I don't know where those fuckin' heads of yours are at but
where *I* come from when we got food we feed people, not
starve them!" Peter Brown glimpsed in two blinks what was
happening. The House Hippie gulped and closed his eyes as
Peter walked calmly up to the San Francisco chapter of the
Hell's Angels Motorcycle Club.

Tapping him lightly on the shoulder, Peter Brown moved
between John Lennon and Frisco Pete just as a fresh flow of
verbal punches was about to begin. An audible intake of
breaths circled the room.

"Now listen, Pete, we have every intention of feeding you
and I apologize for the delay but I was hoping you could
appreciate that the kitchen staff have been working since nine
o'clock and they've been under considerable pressure. We're
waiting for the caterers to finish laying the tables and it
shouldn't take more than another ten minutes and then
we can all go downstairs and gorge ourselves to death but
please, I beg you, be patient."

That did it! An up-front answer to an up-front question.
Frisco Pete shook his head once, turned and left the room. In
the course of 60 seconds Peter Brown had become the hero of
the Battle for the Largest Turkey in Great Britain.

When the door to Neil's office was thrown open ten
minutes later everyone could see it was going to be a sump-
tuous feast The massive catering tables buckling to support
food and drink ran the length of three walls. Frisco Pete was
the first to reach the main table where the Largest Turkey in
Great Britain sat. Before the waiter had a chance to work up
his best carving voice to say, "And would you like *white* or
dark meat, sir?" Pete grabbed a firm hold on the poor dead
bird's body and without any further ceremony ripped the

turkey's left leg from its torso. It easily weighed four pounds and more closely resembled a caveman's hunting club than a turkey leg.

The hordes were right behind him in full force.

By midnight there was nothing left but the washing up.

It was a very fine party, just as The Press Officer had said it would be.

Nineteen sixty-eight was over.

PART TWO

1969

"HEY, MAN, HOW DO I GET IN TOUCH WITH RINGO STARR?"

John Lennon at the Amsterdam Bed-In.

I T'S A NEW YEAR and this office is dedicating itself to developing and promoting a massive public following for Mary Hopkin, James Taylor, Jackie Lomax, the Iveys and the Modern Jazz Quartet in addition to all newly requisitioned talent plus all specific product promotion such as J and Y's "Two Virgins" and George's "Wonderwall" score."

"How are we going to go about it?"

"We'll begin with a new singles release campaign and carry it out on the following lines: Every six weeks we'll rewrite our handout biographies and rephotograph every artist. We'll have a new interview conducted by this office if nothing worthwhile has appeared in the trades that we can reprint in order to accompany and fill out our bio. We've got to keep all management and agency details up to date. Every *five* weeks our comprehensive press kit should go out on our overseas mailing list plus. *Woman, Woman's Own, Photoplay, Weekend, Rave, 19, Fabulous, Valentine, Honey, Mirabelle, Tit Bits* and *Showguide*. As regards the dailies and the trades, full information must be kept going at all times. Singles promotion must never be covered less than two weeks before release and needless to say immediately on all rush releases. We're going to draw up a new master mailing list of *all* our press contacts, with a second, selective list of record reviewers which will take in only the dailies, trades and major provincial papers. It wouldn't be a bad idea to introduce a weekly newsletter on a specially designed paper which will include personal press contacts for our artists with agency and management links with the day and night record-company telephone numbers –"

"Is that everything?"

"For the moment."

52

WILL YOU LOVE ME IN WALLA WALLA LIKE YOU DID IN SING SING?

WHAT'S THIS ABOUT a new Beatles film?"

"It's starting soon –''

"What's it about?"

"It's about *them* at work recording an album. Neil wants to shoot it for television."

"Any specifics?"

"Very specific. The staff call is for 8:30 A.M., Thursday, January 2, at International Recording Studio. The cast includes John Lennon, Paul McCartney, George Harrison and Ringo Starr, our own dear boys, The Fabs. They're on call at 10 A.M. sharp. Neil is the producer, Michael Lindsay Hogg is the director, Ray Freeborn is assistant director and Tony Richmond is the cameraman. The camera requirements include two complete sixteen-millimeter Beaulieu outfits. The sound recording for the moment is two Nagras with two neck microphones and a single rifle microphone. Mal Evans and Kevin Harrington are road-managing the whole setup."

"Anything else?"

"We're making a book at the same time to go out with the album as a super deluxe package. The whole thing is being photographed by Ethan Russell and the text written by David Dalton and Jonathan Cott."

"Sounds good –''

"Should be *great*!"

53

GOOD-BYE MY FIJI ISLAND BABY

WASN'T IT A GREAT PARTY?"

"Yes, Jenny."

"Brian Jones was there and I followed him around for an hour and when he wasn't looking I pinched his ass. He was *real* cute."

"When are you going to the Fiji Islands?"

"As soon as Mom says so. We went out to see John and Yoko last week."

"What was it like?"

"Well, they were real nice and everything but they said they were too busy to go with us to the Fijis but John said we could go stay on his island in Ireland."

"Are you going to?"

"Well, if he pays for us to get there and gets a well dug because there isn't any water on the island, then we might go."

"Why should he pay for you to go stay on his island?"

"Because –"

"Because *why*? Because he's John Lennon and has all the money in the world?"

"Well, we don't have it and it wouldn't hurt him to give us some and besides we're so groovy we *deserve* it."

W HAT ARE THEY on about?"

"What are they on about? They want what's coming to them, that's all. They're making a bid for a complete takeover so they can control their own finances."

"How does Triumph Investment come into all this?"

"Triumph, on behalf of The Beatles, is attempting to buy out NEMS which is getting twenty-five percent of The Beatles' income. When Brian Epstein died he left his seventy percent share in NEMS to his mother, Queenie; Clive, Brian's brother, is the central man in these talks."

"Very complicated, isn't it?"

"Very –"

"What's Ron Kass gone to LA for this month?"

"He's there to set up an Apple office in Hollywood that'll work independent of and at the same time with Capitol Records because what we've been afraid of has started to happen."

"What's that?"

"You know! They're only too happy to be pushing a Beatle product but when it has anything to do with an Apple artist like Jackie or James they get very relaxed about the whole thing and we can't afford to let that happen. We need equal enthusiasm on every level. Flogging a Beatles album is no hard shakes but building a new star takes work."

"What's Peter Asher doing?"

"When Ron gets back Peter is going out to the Coast on a talent hunt."

"Who's that guy George brought into the sessions?"

"Billy Preston, but we're to keep it quiet."

"Do you think he'll be signed to Apple?"

"Well, if George has anything to say about it he will."

"Do you know how the sessions at Twickenham have been going?"

"From what I hear it's very tense. That film studio doesn't help any either. It's too big, too cold and is the worst place to try and get an album together in. They turn the cameras on the minute they arrive and keep them going until they leave. Everyone is getting very uptight with everyone else."

"Why don't they move the setup to the basement here? After all, this is their building and they built the studios so they could work here after all those years at EMI."

"Well, that's what's *going* to happen. They've already said, "Move it to Apple,' but that's going to take another week because the downstairs studio, as you should know, is a *mess*. I mean it looks beautiful but *nothing* works."

"What's wrong with it?"

"Everything's wrong with it. Only half of the eight tracks work and sometimes the whole thing packs up. The studio isn't even soundproof. You can hear people walking across the floor upstairs and you can even pick up the bass vibrations from loud conversations. Sometimes when there are a lot of people running around up there it sounds like the ceiling is falling in."

"Doesn't sound very encouraging. Whose fault is it?"

"Well, Apple Electronics was supposed to be overseeing the whole thing but there doesn't seem to be any one person in charge of the whole setup. Magic Alex spends all his time over at Boston Place and no one ever sees him and has no idea what inventions he's inventing, but every once in a while you get the word that he's working on something big and about to make a breakthrough. Who knows? If you'll remember, his lab was going to be in the basement with the recording studio but that doesn't look like it's going to materialize."

"Wouldn't it save more time if an outside team of engineers was called in and told, 'Here, design a functioning studio for us!'?"

"Well, there's been some dialogue about that but nothing ever came of it. And another big booboo is that the damn boiler that heats the building is located right in the studio so you can't record when it's on which means you have to turn it off which means you have a building full of cold people and musicians with blue fingers."

"So what's going to happen now that they've said they want to finish the album here?"

"Everyone's freaked out of course, running around in a blind sweat trying to get the control room working but nothing seems to be making any sense there. So Glyn Johns isn't going to have the easiest time either."

"Whatever happened to Francie Schwartz? She doesn't seem to come around anymore."

"I thought you knew. She took off very fast and mysteriously about a week after Jeremy got it."

"And who's that other guy in the Press Office these days?"

"He's another one of those kids that came here with a book of poems and drawings he wanted the Apple Press to publish and when he found out there wasn't an Apple Press and there was no chance of getting *anything* published *ever* he asked Derek if he could just hang around. And you know Derek, heart of gold, can't say no so he says sure stay around for a while. And on top of that I think Derek is giving him money to stay alive but that's Derek for you. The other day he took all the photographs off his wall, all those ones of the different colored Apples and gave them to this disk jockey plus all the LPs he had and when I asked him why he did it he said,

111

'Because he's ugly and unloved and no one has ever given him anything in his life except abuse and hard times.' So what can you say to that? In answer to your question, that kid's name is Stocky and all he does is sit around, he never talks, just stares straight ahead. I think Richard has tried to get him to do all the shit he doesn't want to do but it's useless. Last time I saw him he was in the lotus position on top of the filing cabinets in the Press Office and the really weird thing about it was that it looked perfectly normal."

55

CHOPPED LIVER, WHEREVER YOU'RE GOING I'M GOING YOUR WAY

S END HIM UP," said The Press Officer before sprinting to the bog.

"Send him up," said the secretary, relaying his message to the receptionist. The fluorescent lights were burning through the ceiling of cigarette smoke and the wall of ringing telephones on an afternoon indistinguishable from any other afternoon of the working week.

The Beatles were in the basement of their Savile Row recording studios going through what looked from the control room like a tortuous grind of forced creativity. The complicated and bulky paraphernalia of the film unit recording their agony littered the entire basement with its tentacles of cable and massive arc lights. Film cans, dead cups of tea with cigarette ends floating in them and trays of half-eaten sandwiches covered the control room and spilled out into the corridor.

The crackerjack stills photographer, Ethan Russell, assigned to the documentation of the event moved with the grace of a panther on benzedrine amidst the jam of wires, cables and amplifiers, staying out of camera range, working on getting his best shot. Encrusted with five Nikons and an assortment of light meters he had long ago given up trying to be inconspicuous.

Linda Eastman and her daughter Heather kept passing

between the studio and the control room while Yoko Ono sat quietly, absently passing her thumb over her fingernails, looking over at Billy Preston, watching John and then the others and always returning her gaze to John.

Mal Evans and Kevin Harrington were absorbed full time handling the flow from control room, studio, kitchen and the Shaftsbury Avenue string of music stores, all supplying them with anything their bosses might need to keep them running smoothly through their twelfth album.

In the small rectangular area between the tiny rehearsal room and the back wall of the control room sat four technicians assigned to the film crew with nothing to do but drink cups of tea and pass half-hearted, derogatory remarks about the music coming in jerky stops and starts from the studio.

Outside, the number of girls clustered around the door had quadrupled. The Beatles were inside recording an album and this was going to be *the* vigil. Occasionally one of them would reluctantly break off and run around the corner to the Wimpy bar for coffee, hamburgers and cigarettes to supplement the diet of January winds and sporadic high-velocity showers.

The seats running the walls of the reception lounge were all occupied and had been since ten o'clock that morning. As soon as the man from toronto with the three-o'clock appointment to see Derek Taylor had left his seat to go upstairs, someone took his place.

That afternoon the Press Office had seen the Iveys and their manager about the direction their career was headed, one-quarter of the California Pleasure Crew, one half of the Hell's Angels, 12 journalists between one o'clock and 2:30, the film crew from French television working on a documentary about Apple and the London music scene, and one very inebriated Indian gentleman in search of financial backing for a proposed Apple magazine.

When the man from Toronto walked through the Press Office door the secretary greeted him with a smile and asked him if he would like a cup of tea or an alcoholic beverage. He settled for a vodka and tonic.

The Press Officer emerged two minutes later in a gush of speed with an unlit cigarette in his mouth.

"Match?" he asked The House Hippie.

"No but I'll go out and get some –"

"You don't have to leave the building for a match, do you?"

"Well, we also need some cigarette papers."

The House Hippie was out the door before he could catch the expression on The Press Officer's face that conveyed nothing if not a deep understanding. "That boy has the attention span of a three-year-old and the concentration of a grasshopper," he quietly remarked to his secretary. The House Hippie returned four and a half minutes later with enough matches and cigarette papers to get them through the month.

"My name is Davidian," said the man from Toronto. "Someone gave me you name and said you were the one to see when I got to London." The Press Officer stiffened. Something was wrong. "Well, bring that chair over here and let's see what we can do for you. Scotch and Coke please, Richard." Mr. Davidian sat himself next to The Press Officer and rested his slim, black attaché case on his knees. Everything about him was in place. He was dressed all in black save for a white shirt. His black-rimmed glasses rested on a pallid face framed in tame, neatly trimmed sideburns.

"Nice setup you got here," he observed.

"Umm, not bad," answered The Press Officer, moving restlessly in his chair.

"Any of The Beatles around?"

"In and out."

"I was told you could get me to them."

"Well, tell me what's on your mind before you start asking questions like that."

"You see, it's like this. I've got this furniture business in Canada, very hip furniture, not like this stuff you've got here, no offense –"

"No, no offense –"

"It's just that it's all custom designed for very hip people."

"And if they're not very hip people then they don't get the furniture, is that it?"

114

"Well, if they're not our kind of people we don't want to know –"

"Sounds very selective –"

"Well, we can't afford not to be. Now maybe we can do some business together."

"Before we go any further I must explain that we are a record company primarily, and that while Apple from tiem to time finances projects that take our fancy, I have the feeling that the furniture business is something that's not quite in our line."

"That doesn't matter, this is different. I'll take care of that side of it so don't worry."

"I'm not really worried but I have a feeling – and you must understand that it's just a feeling, not a judgment – that the twain won't meet –"

"Look," the man from Toronto was beginning to crack, "I want to talk to one of The Beatles! I don't want to go through all this shit with you. You're only their PR man and I'm not into your game –"

"I'll tell you something right now, you're not going to have any more success with The Beatles than you're having with me at this moment if your attitude and your tone of voice don't change and I just might be forced to ask you to leave this room if this conversation continues as it is –"

And then he *cracked*.

"Look, I don't have to take any more of this horseshit from you, just get me to the people I want to see! All right!?!"

"Never! And if I were on an acid trip and this conversation we've just had took place, with the vibrations that *you're* sending off I'd throw you right off that trip but seeing as we're not on an acid trip I'm throwing you off anyway! Now I'm going into the bog and when I come out I don't want you to still be sitting here!"

The Press Officer rose from his chair and retired to the bog. Davidian sat, unmoved. The House Hippie looked at him. "Hey, man, you just blew it! In the course of three minutes, due to some personality defect, you've managed to alienate *him* beyond repair so why don't you just leave before it gets any uglier –"

The man from Toronto sat there with his hands clasped, looking through The House Hippie, wordless. The Press Officer emerged from his momentary exile.

"You're still here, I see. Well, I'm going to ask you again to please leave. I can see we have nothing in common that will benefit either you or this company and now will you please *leave*!"

"No!"

The Press Officer picked up the receiver of his intercom system. The two secretaries and The House Hippie sat in the silence of the moment, strangely impassive to the psychological turmoil about them, waiting quietly for the man from Toronto to leave.

"Debbie, would you please ask Jimmy Clark to come up here and remove a piece of unwanted *human* furniture from this office –"

At that moment the door opened. It was Mavis Smith and Stocky, the Office Zombie. Mavis whiffed the bad feeling at once, sat at her desk and lit a cigarette, not saying anything. Stocky, standing in the middle of the room, blurted, "Hi there, everybody! Who wants some bread and cheese?" innocently looking into everyone's face. The gross silence answered his question. No one wanted any bread and cheese.

The arrival of Jimmy Clark broke the tension. The Apple doorman, who doubled as Apple bouncer at moments like this, walked towards The Press Officer. His eyes asked the question, "What am I supposed to do?"

"Now I'm going to ask you for the third and final time to leave this building and if you still refuse to do so then Jimmy here is going to *help* you to leave."

Jimmy Clark quietly rippled his back muscles and slowly pumped his arms in a gesture of impatience, threatening and mute. The man from Toronto looked at him and then silently, without a backward glance, left the room.

"A right fucking arsehole he was!" said The Press Officer to the walls.

"What was that all about, Derek?" Mavis Smith questioned.
"Oh just another aggressive Beatlemaniac, that's all—"
"Derek, about that Ringo interview—"

56
JACK THE RIPPER-OFFER STRIKES AGAIN

WE'VE GOT TO DO something about the crime wave that's hit the building or we're not going to have a building left—"

"Is it that bad?"

"Fucking hell, you're joking! Do you want me to show you the figures? In the last two months we've lost thousands in thefts alone and I can't figure how the hell it's all getting out of here but one thing is for sure and that is it's all going out the front door because we don't have a back door, as you very well know!"

"But how? What's missing?"

"Well for starters someone's nicked all the lead off the roof which in turn has caused leaks that are going to cost thousands to repair. That entire wall next to George's office is going to have to be built up and that lead replaced! Television sets! Gone! Just like that! Imagine a fucking television set! It wouldn't be so bad if it was just one, but no, three! Those cartridges in the record players that cost thirty pounds each, gone! Electric typewriters! Gone! Those things cost a few hundred quid each and even though we only hire them we've still got to cover them. Adding machines! Gone! Cases of wine from the kitchen gone! You know that load of "Two Virgins" albums that was sitting in the basement waiting to be picked up by Track Records? Well, over three hundred copies have suddenly just walked off! Three of the secretaries on one Thursday had their pay packets pinched and *they* can't afford to have that happen. A movie camera that was locked up in the Press Office was taken and more than half a dozen speaker cones out of the Telefunken monitors in the studio just vanished! Someone unscrewed the back panel, took the

Ringo Starr, bearing quadruple awards.

speakers they needed, and then refitted the panel nice and neat like it had never happened. Six of those fan heaters at thirteen pounds a throw have walked off plus an electric skillet from the kitchen! It's got to stop!!!"

U HH, EXCUSE ME, Chris, but what did Peter say was happening when he called you from LA?"

"He said that Capitol was very excited about the Iveys' single and they've said that they're going to give it a massive shove. Their promo man had some acetates cut last week and sent them to all the major radio stations, and the program directors liked it so much they started playing the acetates on the air. Peter says it's getting played in Philadelphia, New York, Chicago and San Francisco and Capitol is rush-releasing it with an initial pressing of two hundred and fifty thousand this week. He says that Mary's album in the States is going to include *Those Were The Days* so they're going to have to leave one of the other tracks off it. He says that James Taylor should be getting into LA any day now and he'll be going into the studio with Peter to do a few more tracks. They're releasing James's album in the middle of February and there's a chance he might get him a *Smothers Brothers Show*. EMI in France wants to release a James single with *Knocking Round the Zoo* as the B side and *Something's Wrong* as the A side. James is going to try and make it back to England by March. And George told Peter there was a group in New York called the Raven that he should look up when he's there—"

"Did he sound like he was having a good time?"

"Oh yes. Capitol's given him an office to work out of and he says they really seem flipped about having someone from Apple in the building, especially a real Englishman from London. At least that's what it sounds like. He says that Buffy Saint Marie said she wanted to be on Apple and that he's going to San Francisco this weekend to see Grace Slick of the

119

Airplane. She says that contractually she's free and would dig to do an album with us—"

"Anything else?"

"He just sends his love—"

58

WHERE?

J ACK?"

"Yes, Derek?"

"About the press reception for Mary's album, have you come up with anything? All we've thought of is the Ritz or a barge on the Thames and neither one sounds very exciting—"

"I've been thinking about the Post Office Tower. The whole restaurant rotates three hundred and sixty degrees in something like an hour and—"

"Yes, yes, why not?"

"You know we're doing a tie-up with Valentine's Postcards, you know the firm, and the album is called 'Postcard' and we could have it on Valentine's Day and well what do you think?"

"I think that's fine—"

"So it's the Post Office Tower?"

"Yes, all right. You get on to them and see if it's free that day and I'll ask Paul if he'll put in an appearance and give Mary away to the press. Yes, all right—"

"Talk to you later—"

59

CAN YOU SPARE A SIXPENCE FOR A STEAK DINNER?

W HAT DID HE WANT?"

"Christ, he was really in bad shape. He said he was at the end of his rope and Apple was the last place he could think of coming because he knew we'd help him out and that if he didn't get a grant from the Apple Foundation of the Arts he was going to commit suicide. Commit suicide!"

"What did you tell him?"

"What could I tell him? I told him there was no such thing even though we'd been talking about it and maybe he should reconsider before he did himself in and I gave him two pounds and told him to call back in a few days."

"Then what did he say?"

" 'What's the telephone number?' "

THE PRESS OFFICER put down the telephone receiver, lit a cigarette and pushed the white switch on his intercom system marked P. Brown. Three and a half bleeps later the voice of P. Brown answered.

"Hello—"

"Peter, I've just had a call from Allen Klein, yes the Stones' manager, and he asked me if I could fix a meeting between him and The Fabs so I just thought I'd pass it on to you so you could pass it on to them and that way we're both covered—"

"What does he want?"

"Fuck knows, man, fuck knows—"

60
WHILE YOU WERE OUT . . .

WELL?"

"He said he had a vision while meditating –"

"What kind of vision?"

"He said he saw the British Isles as the last place on earth to be hit by the Apocalypse. The Mongol hordes were sweeping the world in a blaze of destruction and he saw John sitting at the Master Control Board that played every instrument in the world and there was only twenty minutes left before the hordes reached the shoreline and it was all up to John to find the Lost Chord that would stop them from overrunning what was left of the world. He said, 'I've got to see him!' "

61
IN THE NAME OF THE FATHER (JOHN LENNON) AND OF THE SON (JOHN LENNON) AND OF THE HOLY GHOST (JOHN LENNON) AMEN

Peter Brown. The Beatles' Personal Assistant, presents Ringo Starr with "The Kimmy" Award for The World's Best Group of 1969.

GEORGE TELLS ME that we've signed a new group who have just made a fantastic record that's being rush-released as soon as we can get it out," The Press Officer told his staff.

"They'll be coming in this afternoon so, Richard, I want you to get all the dialogue from them for a bio and as soon as he's done that, Carol, I want you to have five hundred copies printed and we'll need some pictures so, Richard, you can do that as well as the bio. I saw you with that Nikon at the Christmas party—"

"Well, it was my first time and not much came out that was any good so you better get a real photographer 'cause I'd hate to blow it, Chief," amended The House Hippie.

"Well, do you know anyone?"

"It just so happens that there's this photographer staying at my place for a few days and—"

"Call him and tell him to be here at three—"

"OK, chief."

"Oh shit, just another group," thought The House Hippie when they walked into the Press Office at three o'clock that afternoon.

"Where's that photographer!?!" asked The Press Officer impatiently.

"He's on his way—"

At that moment the photographer walked in and The House Hippie introduced him to The Press Officer.

"Just let me tell you what we need," he said. "It's very simple. Just a few head shots, half moody, half laughing, half *anything*, close together, far apart, just a *group* picture. Richard will show you upstairs to the roof where you can shoot a quick two rolls and then he'll take you down to Ron Kass's office and do one more there and when you're finished come back here."

The House Hippie, the photographer and the new group left the office in the direction of the fourth floor leading to the roof, leaving The Press Officer in deep conversation with the group's manager who looked much younger than any of the group.

62

THE LAUGHTER, THE HEARTACHE AND THE PULSE-POUNDING EXCITEMENT OF THE GOLDEN AGE OF SCOTTISH GORBALS ROCK– WHITE TROUT– FRESH DAILY!

In the basement, The Beatles were moving through the motions of take after take. The arc lights, on since early that morning, had turned the studio into a sweat box.

In the Record Department on the ground floor, Jack Oliver had just hung up the telephone with a sigh, having finalized the date for Mary Hopkin's press reception at the Post Office Tower. Tony Bramwell walked over to his desk, sat on the corner and lit a cigarette.

"Well, how was the BBC Brambles?" his sidekick asked.

"Same—" he replied, looking out on the blackening sky.

The photographer was halfway through his second roll when The House Hippie noticed a man in overalls with bad skin and red hair coming through the roof hatch of the adjoining building that the new group and the photographer had stepped over onto. "Go on now, get off this roof, you're not supposed to be here so stay on your own side," he whined at everyone and no one in particular.

"Aww get thee fuck ya fuckin' mug," muttered the new group in unison.

"The light's going anyway," said the photographer.

"Let's go down to Ron's office, it's warmer and the company's better," added The House Hippie, leaving the man in the overalls with the red hair and bad skin on the roof feeling like King Shit on Piss Island.

"How soon can we see the contact sheets?" asked The Press Officer.

"Tomorrow."

"Fine and thank you and please have a drink if you like because you don't have to go and where's Richard?"

"Here."

"Go over there and get everything from them that you need but come here first and meet their manager." The House Hippie was introduced to the new group's manager, Tony Meehan. "Tony, tell him everything he should need to know for their bio and something about yourself and the record," The Press Officer said, sealing the pact.

"Well where should I begin?" asked Tony Meehan.

"Anywhere."

"Well, this songwriter I know from Glasgow, George Gallagher, brought me some tapes of his songs and this group was playing on them and they sounded very interesting and I asked him who they were and he said they were called the Pathfinders and they were from Glasgow and were also the biggest group in Scotland. So I went up to Glasgow that following weekend and met them and one thing led to another and I brought them down to London and we decided to make a record of this Goffin-King song they'd been doing in their stage act, it's called *Road to Nowhere*, and I financed and produced it and then brought it around and played it to George and Paul who liked it and said 'Let's put it out.' We didn't think we'd have to move so fast on it but Carole King is releasing her version of it so that's why all the panic. We want to change their name though. I think the Pathfinders is a little old-fashioned –"

"You said it, I didn't, but I think we can come up with a better one than that. OK, I think that should do it. I'll get the rest of the bumf from them."

"All right, boys, names, dates and places of birth, instruments played, musical backgrounds, likes, dislikes, all the schluff and I'll fill in the rest."

Ian Crawford Clews, Vocalist.

Fraser Watson, Lead Guitar.

Colin Hunter-Morrison, Bass.

Ronald Leahy, Organ.

Timi Donald, Percussionist.

"Do you have it all?" asked The Press Officer.

"I think so."

"Are you sure now, because I need that bio right away and I hope you're not giving me one of your casual hippie job answers, otherwise –"

"Nahh, don't worry about it, chief. I've got It all covered. You'll have your bio on time and top-notch."

When the five group members and their manager left the office 40 minutes later, the room was at the height of the 5:30 panic. Mal Evans was up for a five-minute break from road-managing the album in progress in the basement. Ron Kass was in to talk about where the newly signed Scottish group stood in relation to the record company and John Hewlitt was down from the fourth floor reporting on the songwriters newly signed by Apple. Mavis Smith was seeing a French pop-magazine writer about the possibility of an interview with Mary Hopkin and if at all convenient a quick 20 minutes with Paul McCartney. It had been decided that Mavis would handle all the foreign journalists, not because of any multilingual talents, but simply because Derek Taylor thought she should.

The Press Officer had just said good-bye for the third time to the English photographer who had photographed the Scottish group and was now asking the American photographer, Ethan Russell, how soon the Press Office could have some Beatle stills from his camera for the files and a desperately needed new handout. Stocky sat on top of the filing cabinet containing the Pineapple Archives with eyes not focused on anything or anyone, lost in a private vision.

Screamed questions from across a crowded room.

"Derek, the *Sketch* wants to know what Billy Preston is doing playing with The Fabs."

"He's rehearsing with them, that's all and leave it at that."

George Harrison stuck his head in the door for a quick look at a portion of his empire just as Emily's Family en masse, with three of the California Pleasure Crew, descended from the third-floor guest lounge. At the sudden, violently unexpected sight of a Beatle in the flesh all pulses instantly quickened. George, having picked up on their excitement, said a quick hello and did a graceful Beatle run down the stairs to the more restrained and less congested atmosphere of Peter Brown's office.

"Did you see him?"

"Gosh, wasn't he beautiful?"

"Maybe he'd dig to get high with us."

"You should have said something."

"Maybe Derek's got Mick Jagger's phone number."

John Kosh, the designer of the Beatle book, working with Ethan Russell, came in to sit down on the white leather couch but finding all seats occupied settled for a corner on the House

Hippie's desk and a cold lager. The writers of the book, Jonathan Cott and David Dalton with his wife, Andy, followed John Kosh by three minutes. David and Andy were immediately surrounded by Emily's Family with outstretched arms and groping questions, while Jonathan Cott broke away to say hello to The Press Officer holding a telephone conversation with *Bravo* magazine who were demanding that he pin down a time and a place for a photo session with George and when George was over with, Ringo was to be next, and just for curiosity how about Ringo's wife Maureen?

White Trash. Left to right: Ronald Leahy. Timi Donald, Ian Clews, Colin Hunter-Morrison and Fraser Watson.

Sally Burgess, the new temporary secretary who had just become a permanent secretary, was talking to Frankie Hart who The House Hippie thought was extremely healthy-looking for a Hell's Angels mama. Carol Pardon was chatting at the entrance to the bog with Dee Meehan, who had just informed her that Jack Oliver was no longer working as assistant to Terry Doran but just somewhere to the left of Tony Bramwell who was lower down to the right of Ron Kass.

Neil Aspinall had brought an acetate of Jackie Lomax's newly recorded album into the office and proceeded to put it on the turntable at three-quarter volume but The Press Officer signaled for him to turn it down because he was trying to catch the tail end of *The Times* reporter's question asking for clarification on the Triumph Investment-NEMS talks in progress *and* arrange a luncheon appointment with himself, Peter Brown and The Press Officer to talk about Apple and the climate at Savile Row.

Mavis Smith had no sooner finished with the French pop-magazine writer when an Italian journalist from Milano walked in to see if he could interview any of The Beatles for his magazine *and* a radio show from Rome on which he had 20 minutes air time every Thursday. He was very curious about progress on Magic Alex's inventions, especially the transistorized radio shaped like an Apple that was going on the market at the unbelievably low price of ten shillings.

David Dalton, with flawless timing, popped his request to The Press Officer for a tape recorder so that he and his cowriter could get on with the transcribing of The Beatles' tapes. The Press Officer told the House Hippie to take care of that detail immediately.

The House Hippie was on to Kafetz Rentals of Baker Street within three seconds of the command but the continual ringing told him that everyone had gone home. It had just gone 6:05. "Tomorrow," he told David Dalton. "How about a Uher?" A Uher would do.

What could be heard of Jackie Lomax's album above the racket of cross-room dialogue and ringing telephones sounded absolutely luscious. "Bring it in tomorrow, Neil, when it's a little quieter, will you?" requested The Press Officer. "And Richard, do an interview with Jackie about the album for the States after you've done the other bio."

Upstairs in the Accounts office Allen Lewis and Brain Capocciama, tending petty-cash vouchers and balancing the company's books, were talking to Alistair Taylor about his desire to take a crash course in French so that in the future whenever he traveled abroad on Apple business he would not be handicapped by the knowledge of only one language. It would only cost £140 and was well worth that paltry sum.

Chris O'Dell interrupted their conversation with a request for 18 shillings for a cab ride she had incurred in the line of Apple duty, signed the petty-cash voucher, lit her thirtieth cigarette of the day and headed for the Press Office and a scotch and Coke. On the way down she passed the two kitchen girls who had just exited from the Press Office after having delivered one dozen cups of tea and were contemplating the task of serving up another dozen, plus eight cheese and tomato sandwiches that had just been ordered from the basement. But that order could not be filled until they had cleared all the dirty plates, cups and saucers from the guest lounge that had been left behind by the California Pleasure Crew and Emily's Family.

While no one was paying him any attention amidst the rush of getting six sacks of mail out to the Trafalgar Square Post Office before seven o'clock, an office boy quickly slipped the remaining lead off the roof into one of the red mailbags and dragged his treasure down the spiral staircase into the lift, through the lobby and out the door.

Jimmy Clark, the Apple bouncer, looking out the third-floor window of the Accounts office, spotted the office boy struggling down the street with a suspiciously overloaded mailbag. Twenty feet before he reached the corner the office boy heard Jimmy Clark's voice screaming for him to stop right there. He paid no attention and increased his pace, his heart pounding dangerously in his chest.

Just around that corner sat his partner in crime in a red Mini waiting for the late afternoon's delivery of lead. If it wasn't

129

lead today, then likely it would be another 100 copies of the banned "Two Virgins" LP.

Jimmy Clark had reached the first-floor landing on the last stage of his descent to satisfy his aroused curiosity when suddenly Peter Brown emerged from his office. Over his shoulder Jimmy could see John Lennon talking with Paul McCartney with Yoko Ono in profile reading a magazine.

"Jimmy, please get me my car from the garage right now," said Peter Brown. As he opened his mouth to protest, George Harrison and Neil Aspinall walked out of the opposite office.

"Hello, Jimmy," George said.

"Hello, George," Jimmy said, his attention shot now and irrevocably diverted.

"Well, don't just stand there, Jimmy," Peter cut in, "get my car and when you've done that go see Barbara. She has a list of things you're to get for Paul tomorrow."

The office boy, sweating with fear, collapsed in a mental heap in the front seat of his friend's Mini.

"Cor fuck me, let's get out of here quick!"

"Did you get it?!?"

"Yeah," he said, looking fearfully over his shoulder trying to pick the face of Jimmy Clark out of the crowd of pub-crawling, going-home masses that overflowed into the gutters of London on an early winter's night.

"Quite a day we've had," said The Press Officer, calling for another scotch and Coke. The room had cleared, leaving only a few stragglers behind.

"Sure was," added The House Hippie, serving up The Press Officer's drink.

"By the way, how do you spell that guy's name?" he queried.

"What guy?"

"You know, that guy that manages that group that was in this afternoon."

"M double e h-a-n. Don't you know him?"

"No."

"Of course being American you wouldn't."

"What do you mean by that?"

"He was the drummer with Cliff Richard and the Shadows. They never made it very big in the States but before. The Fabs came along they were *it*. He was the hottest little drummer in the business and the first to have words like 'brilliant' thrown at him long before Ringo and Ginger and Mitch Mitchell came along. He was an idol at the age of fifteen. Quite a story behind that one."

"Doesn't he play anymore?"

"No, no I don't think he's played for years. He's managing that lot now and was doing a lot of producing but he's out of the game now. I did his career a lot of harm in the old days. It was a nasty piece of business, that."

"What do you mean?"

"Well, after he left the Shadows he formed his own group which was very successful for a while, and then he teamed up with Jet Harris, another ex-Shadow, and they had a hit record and then suddenly Tony stopped being a drummer and went into record production. He was very young and precocious and successful, I think he was only seventeen at the time. Anyway it must have been late '62, before *Love Me Do*. He was working at Decca as a free-lance producer on assignment to the record company and he was in the studio one day when a man named Brian Epstein walked in and asked him if he could arrange an audition for a group he was managing from Liverpool called The Beatles. Tony explained to him that he was only a free-lance producer and in no position to audition groups but if Brian would leave his name with his secretary he would gladly try and book a studio for them. By this time Brian had been to about every record company in London and wasn't getting anywhere and when he heard that from Tony he figured, 'Right!! This fucker's giving me the runaround just like the rest of them!' Which wasn't true but that's the way it looked to him. Well eventually, as you know, they did land a contract and they did *make it*. When it came time for me to ghost *A Cellar Full of Noise*, Brian decided he was going to assassinate Tony Meehan. He had to put the finger on someone and that's who he wanted to do it to. I think it was on page fifty-three that it happened. He *made* me write it into the book that Tony Meehan was the man who turned The Beatles down and all the while we were doing it, we both knew it was a lie. I had a very hard time living with *that* one and you can imagine what that did to Tony in *this* business—"

"Why didn't he punch you in the mouth?"

"Because he's too civilized and because it wouldn't undo the harm done to him and because he knew Brian had me over a barrel and—"

"He didn't seem uptight today?"

"Of course not! It's over and I've apologized a thousand times and he knows what the score is—"

"Blood under the bridge, huh?"

"Gallons of it!"

63

THE BRIGHT LIGHTS OF SAVILE ROW

"FRISCO PETE couldn't believe John and Yoko crawling around in that bag last night at the Albert Hall," The House Hippie told The Press Officer a few minutes later. "It really threw him for a loop. He asked me what the fuck it was all about—"

"Hey listen, that reminds me," The Press Officer said, "What are we going to do about all those people upstairs?"

"What people?"

"Emily and all those bats out of Haight-Ashbury, Spider and Billy Tumbleweed and the rest of them. George says he doesn't want them around the building anymore."

"Don't look at me, man! I'm not telling anyone they've got to get out of here; besides I like all those freaks—"

"Well, I like them too and *I* don't want to tell anybody they have to leave but he says to me, 'When are they leaving?' What the fuck am I supposed to say?"

"Tell him, 'Hey look, man, it's your house so you tell them to leave," or get Peter Brown to do it because he's good at that kind of shit. I really thought he and John were going to get their asses kicked at the Christmas party. It was very tense—"

"Fuck, man, don't remind me of that one!"

Linda Eastman before her marriage to Paul McCartney.

"Derek, *Woman* magazine and *Disc* have been on about Linda Eastman and they want to know if she's going out with Paul and there was a call from the States while you were out with Neil and they asked the same thing and they're all asking if she's Eastman of Eastman Kodak—"

"Let me talk to them next time they call but don't say anything more to them. Paul's life is Paul's life and when we have anything to add to that we will and not before and *no* she is not Eastman of Eastman Kodak!"

The Press Officer sat on the white leather couch and looked out the window, silent for half a minute. Then he leaped up and said to The House Hippie, "I'm also getting a lot of feedback on Kesey. They said, 'What the fuck is he doing for us?' and I said, 'He's making a record, that's all' and now they want to know where he got the tape recorder from and who gave him permission to use the back room and who said he could take that typewriter out of the building and *we* did of course! No one around here has even heard of *One Flew Over the Cuckoo's Nest!*"

The secretary interrupted his tirade to ask The Press Officer if he would like to have lunch with Peter Brown and Lionel Bart. "I've already told him *yes!*" was the reply.

"We've got to get to work on Mary's reception and I've asked Paul if he'll be there to give her away to the press and he said yes and by the way have you been downstairs lately?"

"Ahh, every once in a while I go down for a few minutes but there's so much going on I just get the jitters but I think the whole thing is almost over and I heard someone say that The Fabs were going to give a concert on the roof in about a week and that should wrap it up—"

"What about Jackie's album?"

"What about it?"

"What's it *called*?"

"Is This What You Want?" and George wants us to get to work on it so that's what *he* wants. They're almost done but for the final mix and it's out at the end of February."

"Peter Asher says that James's album and the MJQ's are going to be released in the States in the second week in

White Trash at the American Hotel, Amsterdam, March 1969.

February. He's pushing the Iveys to finish their album and they've started work on the cover and their single is moving along very nicely according to the cable we got from Capitol this morning. Mary and Jackie have a split release schedule on

135

their albums and it looks like if they meet the deadlines we've set, the artwork on those covers has to be done and sent to Capitol by the end of this week at the latest. We should check with Ron Kass on that—"

And at that moment The House Hippie received a divine flash.

"Wait a minute, Derek, I've got it!" he howled.

"Got what?" The Press Officer wondered. "The clap?"

"No no no I've got the name for that Scottish group!"

"What?"

"White Trash!"

"White Trash?" said The Press Officer.

"White Trash?" said Mavis Smith.

"Yes White Trash!"

"Well that sounds all right to me and I can't think of anything better. What about you, Mavis?"

"Well."

"It always comes in flashes!" The House Hippie instructed.

"Well done! OK, White Trash it is! Get me Tony Meehan and tell Ron Kass we've got the name and how about a drink?"

64
FACT

BOTH BRIGITTE BARDOT and The Beatles wash their hair every day.

65
THE TITANIC PASSING THE ANDREA DORIA IN THE NIGHT

WELL, WE KEEP SEEING each other around but we never seem to say hello properly," said The House Hippie to the young lady.

"My name's Frankie Hart and you're The House Hippie, right?"

"Right."

"Well, I'm gonna be workin' in this office with you guys for awhile. Derek said it was all right."

"But what's your old man going to say?"

"What old man?"

"Aren't you one of the Angels' old ladies?"

"Who, me? You're putting me on."

"No really, I thought you were a real live Hell's Angels mama!"

"That's gotta be the funniest fuckin' thing I've heard all month!"

"And that other chick, Paula?"

"Nahh, she's not a mama either, she's just hangin' out with 'em."

"Well, in that case welcome to the Apple Press Office and uhh, in any case, welcome to the world!"

HAVE YOU DONE that White Trash biography yet?" The Press Officer asked The House Hippie.

"Nahh. I'm not very good at writing those things. In fact I *hate* it."

"I know what you mean and I realize it's pain in the ass but we've got to get it *done.*"

"What should we say?"

"What *can* you say nowadays? A group with a great future? It's all been said."

"I know!"

"What?"

" 'They begin where the Cream left off!' " said The House Hippie.

"No!" said The Press Officer emphatically.

66

AND NOW IT IS OUR PLEASURE TO ANNOUNCE THIS YEAR'S WINNER OF THE NOBEL PRIZE FOR LITERATURE

67
SHOWDOWN!

I T WAS SIX O'CLOCK. Most of the California Pleasure Crew were in the guest lounge. Kesey wasn't there and Frisco Pete and Billy Tumble-weed weren't there but Spider was, and he was the unofficial brigadier general of the Patchouli Platoon. He had three of his girls and three of the guys and at least four of Emily's Family were also around when George Harrison walked in.

"Hello, everyone!" he said.

Everyone stopped in his tracks. George Harrison! Alive and in person right before their eyes in the guest lounge.

"Well, are you moving all of your stuff out of here tonight?" George asked rhetorically.

There was a hush so deep it seemed as if the molecules in the air had stopped moving. All eyes turned on George. An intense seesaw struggle to maintain a psychological cool bounced from one end of the room to the other in a duel of eyeballs. The silence seemed to stretch out forever.

Spider broke the spell. Very slowly he removed his shades with his right hand and in the same movement very gently nudged the girl standing in front of him to one side with his left, leaving nothing between him and George Harrison but vibrations. He took four steps forward, which placed him six inches from George's nose. Neither one of them blinked.

"Hey, man," Spider said," I just wanna ask you one question. Do you dig us or don't you?"

"Yin and yang, heads and tails, yes and no," replied George Harrison.

This answer to that question completely *fucked* everyone's mind. No one knew quite what to say or how to say it. No one except Spider.

"All right man, I can dig it. We'll be outta here in ten minutes."

George turned and left the room. "Good-bye, everyone!" he hurled over his shoulder.

One of the micro boppers, still shattered by the aura of this charismatic young man who had just dazzled them all, finally found her vocal chords.

"Gosh, he sure is beautiful," she moaned.

"Shut the fuck up, you asshole!" snapped one of the Pleasure Crew, having found not one thread of beauty in the last seven and a half agonizing minutes in the guest lounge of 3 Savile Row, London W1.

68
SOME PEOPLE WILL BELIEVE ANYTHING

JACK OLIVER TOLD The Press Officer he had received a cable from Larry Delaney at Capitol Records saying that the TV and newspapers in the States were announcing that Paul McCartney and Linda Eastman were being married on February 16 in either New York or London.

"All right, thanks, I'll take care of it," he said, motioning for his secretary to send a telegram. "To Larry Delaney, Capitol Records, Hollywood, California. The message reads, 'They are not being married.' Derek."

69
WHERE PROGRESS IS NEVER OUR MOST IMPORTANT PRODUCT

INITIAL ACCEPTANCE PATTERN. IAP for short.

Your Initial Acceptance Pattern is selling enough records within a specified time period to justify a continued promotional push from the record company to make that record a hit.

From the Underassistant West Coast Moron comes the following message:

"There is a need to establish a framework for scheduling Apple album releases in the United States. This will facilitate the Apple people in visualizing when their product will be released based on the time the final artwork and tapes are received. Without going into abundant detail we should think in terms of sixty-day cycles for a consistent product release. This sixty-day schedule begins with your shipping the last completed components up through delivery of product to consumer level. Should we get into a rush-release situation, figure thirty to forty-five days dependent upon quantity and the intricacies of packaging. Needless to say, with any given product we will want to discuss the most appropriate release date to insure its best exposure to the American public."

Well, it's all in the mouth.

70
BUSINESS AS USUAL

GEORGE HAS FOUND this singer from New York called Brute Force who's recorded a song called *The King of Fuh*."

"The King of?"

"Fuh. The King of Fuh. It's song that tells about a beautiful land called Fuh and in this land is a King. He's the Fuh King. You dig?"

"Yeah. Well?"

"Well Jack Oliver phoned Rand at EMI to ask for the DJ copies of *The King of Fuh* and he was told that Ken East said that under no circumstances were they going to press the record. We planned to release it on February 14 but it doesn't look like we're going to be able to do that until we sort out this mess with them."

"How long will that take?"

"Fuck knows! Maybe never but George says that if they don't press them then we'll do it ourselves and the distribution as well. Do you have anything going on this week?"

"American *TV Guide* is photographing us this week but I don't have a time on it yet and oh by the way, what's the story on Mary's follow-up single?"

"It's a very short one. It's impossible. Paul says we'll never get anywhere near the sales of *Those Were the Days* and if we try we'll just hit under the mark and that's going to have a negative effect on the market psychologically. So it's best if we just let it ride for the moment. What we're doing is releasing her album and then if everyone starts screaming for any one song in particular we'll pull it off the album and release it. I mean I'm sure there's single on it but no one can figure out what it is. What did Stigwood's office want?"

"They want Paul to write the liner notes for the Marbles' album but he's not going to do it. Fucking' liner notes! *Almost!*"

"By the way, White Trash's single is out on the twenty-fourth—"

"All right. Later—"

R ON KASS SAYS we're giving away too many free records."

"Is that true or is that paranoia?"

"No, I think that's what's really happening. Apparently hundreds of pounds of free re-cords are being handed out to anyone who asks for them. The staff, friends of the staff, anyone who comes in and says he's a disk jockey or has a music column, the usual scive. A lot of the really legitimate people are getting two copies of the same record also."

"Two?"

"Yes, two. Like the Press Office has its master mailing list that they have to cover with each release and the Record Department has its own mailing list but no one has bothered to compare the two lists so there are quite a few repetitions on each list and if there are three hundred names on a list with a new mailing every six weeks, well it mounts up, doesn't it? Ron's started a policy for staff sales of records. Everyone is entitled to one free copy of each new release and then after that you're allowed to buy up to three of any one single catalogue number which you get at the wholesale selling price plus purchase tax. It has to be done that way because it costs about twenty-two shillings every time you hand a record over to someone and needless to say you've seen this morning's papers—"

"No."

"Front-page story with John Lennon quoted as saying, 'If we let Apple go on the way it is we'll be broke in six months' time.' How about that?"

"Well, that's a load of bullshit! I mean that can't possibly be true. Can it?"

"I'm not so sure it's a load of bullshit. You're here every day so you can see what's going on. Since it's not our money we never really think about it and therefore everyone just treats the place like a bottomless well. It's almost like working for General Motors. I mean that's the way we all relate to the place. You never say to yourself, 'Well, after all they're only four wealthy musicians.' Do you realize that the liquor bill alone is now up to six hundred pounds a month! Just on booze! And The Beatles never get any of that. And how much food do you think that kitchen turns out a month? I'd say their bill is pretty close to what we spend on liquor and that's just in-the-office entertaining. What about all that wining and dining expense-account scene that goes on after hours outside? All those television producers, journalists and BBC DJs that get taken to the Speakeasy every night for drinks and dinner. It's common knowledge in the business that this is one place that will treat you well on that score. The Speakeasy! It's just a nightclub with a mediocre kitchen but what prices they charge! And the traveling expenses! I'm not talking about taxis from Savile Row to EMI, or The Fabs personal holiday expenses. Who's taking all those flights to Paris and London and America – and who the fuck knows where else – that get booked through our travel agents? The phone bill! Fuck sake! Sometimes it's four thousand pounds a quarter! No one around here has *that* much to say. Every time you turn around there are at least half a dozen people on the phone who don't even work in the building and I've got a feeling they're not just calling someone in Hampstead either. A string of phone calls to Nepal? Since when is there an Apple office in Katmandu? or in Sausalito? or Acapulco? Now I know we've got a floral arranger who comes in once a week to bring fresh plants and flowers for the offices and replenish the window boxes but who are all those corsages and long-stem roses going to?"

"But haven't they been looking for someone to straighten the place out for months? What about Lord Beeching?"

"Beeching didn't want to touch this job with a twenty-foot pole from across the street! And he was probably the only person in England that could have done it. Everyone else that's been in to see them has reeked of greed and incompetence."

"So what's going to happen?"

"We'll just have to wait and see."

P AUL IS VERY concerned about Apple."

"What, that we're spending too much money?"

"No, no. Just that it become a success. That we do what we set out to do."

"Save the world?"

"No, I think they've all given up on that idea by now. It sounded good back then but fuck it, look what's happened. It was too ambitious. No, what I think what he's concerned about is that we just make it as a record company with the occasional romp into whatever catches our artistic fancy. It was Paul's idea to have that meeting the other day and he hardly blinked when he heard that we were spending six hundred pounds a month on liquor. No, he just wants the place to be more together. He's sending around a letter to all the staff and artists."

"A letter?"

"Yeah. Let me read it to you. 'In case you are ever worried about anything at Apple, something which you don't feel able to sort out yourself or maybe something you can't get answered, please feel free to write me a letter telling me about the problem. There's no need to be formal about it. Just say it. The main thing is to keep the lines of communication open. Incidentally, things are going well – so thanks – love, Paul.'"

"And everyone's getting one of those?"

"Yeah. We're typing up a batch and he'll fill in the name of the person it's going to and sign it."

"Not a bad idea. It's about time one of them made some contact with the people in the building because that's the big hang-up around here. No one knows what he's supposed to be or what this place is supposed to do. I mean everyone knows out front that it's a record company and that we said we were going to help the artistically needy but the actual mental climate of the building is one of total uncertainty. Even Derek doesn't know where he stands. He's always walking on ice. Sure, he knows he's their mouthpiece but he's also the reflection glass of the place and he needs to know what, if any, our ideology is. I mean own up, Derek's the only one in this whole fucking organization that is articulate enough to translate what is happening but he's kept on a shelf half the time. Everyone else just moves through the motions of doing what he has to do and quite a few do it very well, too, but that's not enough, that's not the idea. This identity crisis has to be faced up to. Who are we? What are we supposed to do? Where do we go from here?"

"The age-old question, huh?"

"Yes, the age-old question and if we don't find the answer to it soon we're going to end up like the man who had all his clothes taken away, got locked in a rock garden and had the key thrown away on him."

"What happened to him?"

"He was in *bad* shape."

73

IN WHICH THE TRUTH IS REVEALED IN THE HARD LIGHT OF DAY

THE HOUSE HIPPIE moved along the street in the direction of 3 Savile Row, his early-morning mind occupied with thoughts of the previous day's leftover chores. There were the four photographs of The Beatles and the David Bailey picture of Mary Hopkin that had to be taken to the framers on Earlham Street; there were the back issues of *Black Dwarf* to be picked up from Tariq Ali for John and Yoko; the

White Trash biographies were waiting for collection from the printers on Bond Street; there was – when suddenly a voice from behind him roared, "Get yer 'air cut!" There was something so nasty in the delivery of that order that his adrenalin instantly boiled out of all proportion to the taunt. "Go fuck yourself!" he screamed back.

Turning to see where his retaliatory abuse had landed he saw, only 12 feet behind him and smiling with childish pleasure at the success of his put-on, his boss, Derek Taylor, The Beatles' Press Officer.

"Well, well," he chuckled, "*so that's* the real Richard. Not a smiling, fuzzy-haired hippie from California at all but just a foulmouthed, nasty guy from Queens."

"Ahh, take a long walk off a short pier, Derek!"

"You see what I mean?"

H

OW MUCH LONGER are they going to be filming downstairs?"

"Today's the last day. They're doing a concert on the roof this afternoon which closes the film."

"And then it's over?"

"No they've still got another three or four days' recording to do but the film crew is ready to pack up and go home."

"How long have they been at it now?"

"A month at least. They're happy as fuck that it's over too. It was a real grind if ever there was one."

"Does Neil still think it's a film for television?"

"I think so. Anyway he's going to be talking with the television people this week about it. And the press knows about Billy Preston huh?"

"There are *no* secrets in this building."

"So we've got another Apple artist. By the end of this year I predict that financially Apple will be the most successful new record company in the world and artistically the same can be expected. I mean *everyone* wants to be on Apple. We can't really lose, can we? In a way it's kind of a drag that it's going to be so easy but why fight it?"

75
INTRODUCING

PRESS OFFICE RELEASE to UPI, AP, Reuters, PA: The Beatles have asked Mr. Allen Klein of New York to look into all their affairs and he has agreed to do so, it was announced from their headquarters at Apple, 3 Savile Row, London W1, today Monday, February 3, 1969.

76
MARY HOPKIN AT
THE GENERAL POST
OFFICE TOWER AND
A BARREL FOR
BEATLE JOHN

BARREL?"

"Yes, a barrel!"

"Where the fuck am I going to get a barrel from?" The House Hippie asked.

"Use your head, man. Figure it out. There has to be someplace in the city of Greater London where one can get a barrel. It's not like I'm asking you to paint the Sistine Chapel, just find a barrel by one o'clock. Try Covent Garden!"

"Derek, the last time I went to Covent Garden to return that tuxedo you rented from Moss Brothers some asshole threw a tomato at me. Besides, what do you want a barrel for?"

"To fill with apples, you twat! We've got a press reception at three o'clock this afternoon at the Post Office Tower for Mary Hopkin, who I might remind you is a major Apple artist, and a barrel of apples placed at the door will be a very nice touch. I also want you to get two dozen album posters and a dozen record sleeves from Jack Oliver and then go upstairs to Accounts and get twenty pounds and go out and get enough apples, green ones if you can, to fill the barrel. I want the place completely decorated forty-five minutes before the press starts to arrive."

Mary Hopkin, who wore her popularity like a halo of innocence.

Donovan and Mary Hopkin.

George

"Oh brother," The House Hippie moaned.

"Look, if I told you this barrel was for John Lennon, would you move any faster?"

"A hell of a lot faster than I'm moving now."

"Well then, just *pretend* it's for John Lennon. Get Stocky to give you a hand. Come on now, get a move on, you lazy bastard! It's already 11:30!"

"All right. Come on, Stocky, let's go get a barrel for John."

The House Hippie and the Office Zombie put on their coats and left The Press Officer, the two secretaries and Mavis Smith behind to cope with the less important details of the press reception for Mary Hopkin at the General Post Office Tower, two souls in search of a barrel. On the stairs they met Frankie Hart.

"Where are you guys off to?" she asked perkily.

Jimi Hendrix at the reception for Mary Hopkin.

"To find a barrel—"

"A barrel for John Len – I mean Mary Hopkin, I mean—"

"Boy are you stoned! Fuckin' far out! Well see you later!"

"Yeah, see you later, Frankie."

In reception Debbie asked them, "Where are you going?"

"To look for a barrel. Do you have any idea where you can get one at this time of day?"

She thought about it for a moment.

"Wait a minute! A friend of mine is in the theatrical supply business and maybe she can come up with one."

The House Hippie brightened a bit.

"Fantastic! Give her a blast and tell her it's for John Lennon's reception at the Post Office Tower."

"John's reception? I thought—"

"Yeah, I know, but just tell her, well tell her anything but we've got to have it by three."

Debbie got on the blower and called through to her friend in the theatrical supply business.

"Hello, Cecilia, it's Debbie. Look, love, do you know where I can get a barrel? Yes a barrel. It's for a reception we're having this afternoon for John, uhh, Mary Hopkin and, oh how wonderful, yes, yes, just a minute, she's got one! She says it's an enormous wine barrel, big enough to climb into."

"Just like Jim Hawkins in *Treasure Island*, huh?"

"What?"

"Never mind, just ask her if she can have it delivered toot sweet."

"Cecilia love, how soon can you get it over here? Wonderful! Yes 3 Savile Row and send an invoice with it. Bye now, love." Debbie hung up and smiled. "It'll be here in forty-five minutes!"

"Debbie?"

"Yes, love."

"You're the greatest!"

Derek Taylor, Mavis Smith, Frankie Hart, Carol Paddon and Sally Burgess were putting up the last of the Mary Hopkin "Postcard" posters and record sleeves when The House Hippie and the Office Zombie arrived in the stomach-churning ex-

151

press lift at the top floor of the restaurant of the General Post Office Tower with their cargo: one gigantic wine barrel and half a dozen crates of Granny Smith apples.

"You made it!" said The Press Officer in surprise.

"Did you think we wouldn't?"

"Just put it over there and fill it up without any dialogue," said The Press Officer and walked away to oversee the catering facilities.

"You take that end, Stocky," dictated The House Hippie, "and, ouch! Hey watch it, man, those are my fingers! And let's roll this goddamn thing! I'm not going to rupture myself on this friggin' barrel."

The Press Officer surveyed the scene. Everything was perfect. The buffet table was a glutton's delight and a drunkard's joy. There was a lot of open floor space for the 300 invited guests to circulate and there was still plenty of light left in the sky. There was all of London for a view. The perfect circle of the tower restaurant was conducive to strolling when one got impatient for it to turn, and the microphone was in flawless pitch for the announcements. Press receptions are thrown in the hope that – given enough food, alcohol and the opportunity to talk with the artist – some mention of the event will find its way into the paper and though never a great deal of space is expected, it's felt that even a brief mention has somehow justified the expense. The more lavish the catering the better the chance of finding yourself in print the next morning.

This one was a smashing reception. The Press Officer set the rhythm the moment the first elevator load of guests had arrived. In the first ten minutes he corraled Mary Hopkin, her mother, father and relatives and briefed Mary on the running order, what to expect, and filled her with confidence. At the same time he turned to her relatives, who were painfully uncomfortable, and made their uneasiness secondary to having a good time; here is your little girl and this is something to be very proud of and after all, these people have come to see her and who better than yourselves know her so well?

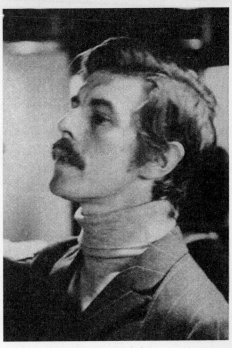

ndrix, before his tragic death, in a huddle with Paul ·ney.

Derek Taylor, the Beatles' embattled Press Officer, at a reception in the General Post Office Building, February 1969.

Then all the familiar Fleet Street faces started to appear and he had to momentarily abandon the Hopkin contingent. Doubling as a record-company spokesman and an ultrasophisticated maitre d', he made his cursory greetings, diverting all the boys – to whom this was just another press reception that would soon fade into a brandy blur – to the buffet table.

The arrival of Paul McCartney and a handsome blonde American girl, Linda Eastman, formed a natural focal point for the photographers' attentions and the journalists' questions. The Press Officer now had more front to cover.

Paul was there to give Mary away to the press. He did it gracefully and without the slightest touch of show-business artificiality. On the one hand he satisfied the photographers scrambling for the obligatory picture of him and Linda, and at the same time politely reminded them that this was Mary's reception and neither the time nor place for resurgent Beatlemania. He posed with Mary, hamming and hugging his way through a back file of camera faces and postures guaranteed to please the boys from the Street of Ink.

"A little closer, Paul!"

"Mary, over this way and down a little more!"

Mary Hopkin, accepting plastic-encased bouquet from Paul McCartney.

"Give us a smile, love!"

"Go on, kiss her!"

The Post Office Tower did rotate just like they said it would. If you stand at the bar looking at the floor, you can see the break between the outer rotating circle of the restaurant and the stationery control anchor at its center. Standing at the window you can feel the movement as your whole world turns ever so gently in a clockwise direction.

One of Mary's chores was to present an enormous bouquet of flowers to a postman retiring that day after having dedicated a lifetime of service to the English postal system.

Midway through the reception, The Press Officer announced that Donovan – who had contributed three songs to Mary's album – was present and was going to sing a few songs. He peeled through half a dozen numbers, mercifully taking the alcoholic edge off the gathering that by six o'clock was totally unbuttoned.

Mary was holding up well. Beseeched for autographs, chased by questions, asked again and again for just one more smile for the camera, fending off advances, she carried the whole thing with a surprising expertise for a girl who had had to make the transition from knee socks to world stardom in less than a year.

The first four hours had been devoted to a soft-sell-meet-the-press-campaign-mission but as night moved in, everyone dropped the front and fell into sloppy abandon. Paul and Linda's presence was not simply a token guest appearance. They held out until the very last hour, giving an air of confirmation to the reception which said, "This is a record company that is also a family." Jimi Hendrix turned up as the party was on the last lap for a drink and some talk with Paul, and good-naturedly fenced with the journalists and photographers grown bored with taking Mary's picture.

The final announcement from The Press Officer was that regrettably the time had come to call it a day and kiss all your friends good night with a reminder to dress sensibly against the elements because outside an English rain had begun that was to last for the next three days.

77

**IN ORDER TO
COMPLY WITH
ACCEPTED
COMMUNITY
STANDARDS**

TROUBLE!"

"What kind of trouble?"

"Bramwell just got back from the BBC and he says they're not going to play White Trash's single because they find the name offensive."

"What!"

"He says that Ron Kass told Peter Asher that if that's the way they're going to react to it in England then sales will probably be disastrously affected in the southern United States."

"So what are we supposed to do?"

"Change their name—"

"To what?"

"Trash."

"Trash?"

"Yes just plain Trash."

"Trash! What kind of a fucking name for a group is *that!?* Trash! Come on, man, I mean White Trash has got a lot of *class* but Trash! Uggh!"

"We've got to do it if that record's going to get any air play."

"Goddam the BBC! And what are we going to do about all the handout pictures and bios that say White Trash?"

"Put a label reading, 'Censored' over the offensive word 'White.'"

"Ohh, that's real clever! And what about the poster Mouse has designed for the record?"

"Who?"

"Stanley Mouse, America's most beloved artist. He's the guy from San Francisco who did all those acid posters. He's been in here half a dozen times and he always wears that big black hat and like his name he's quiet as a mouse."

"So that's the famous Mouse—"

"Yup—"

"Well, he's just going to have to redesign it!"

"And the record labels?"

"They'll have to be reprinted."

"And the revolution?"

156

"The revolution?"

"Yes the revolution! What kind of a fucking revolution is this when a rock 'n' roll band has to change its name just because the British Broadcasting Corporation doesn't *like* it! What kind of a record company is this that bows so easily to a fascist demand like that! Yes, what *about* the revolution?!"

"The revolution will have to wait. We have our Initial Acceptance Pattern to think of!"

Two days later The House Hippie was still psychotically depressed over the shattering implications of the White Trash mandatory name change. Somehow it didn't seem right. Somehow he was the only one that was bugged by it. The group and their manager had only mildly objected; if that's what it takes to get the record across to the public, well then, that's the way they would have to go. Besides, what's in a name? Trash, White Trash, it's all the same isn't it?

No, somehow it wasn't quite the same. There was just something about Trash that didn't sound right. Besides, whether the group knew it or not, they deserved better. They were a good group! And they did have a great future even if they didn't begin where the Cream left off.

The House Hippie had decided his first impression on that first day when they'd all walked into The Press Office was wrong; this wasn't just another group. They had been booked to play at the Bingo Hall on Lancaster Road in Ladbroke Grove and he had gone to see them.

Within the first three minutes of their opening set they had managed to convert an audience of insipid, zonked-out zombies into a totally disoriented version of the Bolshoi Ballet, quadrupled on an overdose of pure methedrine. When they had finished their 45 blistering minutes on stage the audience had been left limp but still screaming for more.

Turning to Stanley Mouse, America's most beloved artist, The House Hippie asked for a confirmation of opinion.

"Well what do you think, Mouse? Are they as great as they seem to be or what?"

"Well, man, I'm not sure. I mean one minute they have you thinking, 'Holy shit! What a group!' and then the next minute

Out and about in Amsterdam. Left to right: Ronald Leahy, White Trash organist (partially concealed); Gene Mahon; Richard DiLello; Ian Clews, lead singer of White Trash.

you're asking yourself, 'Are they or aren't they?' They're weird, that's for sure."

"But would you say they generate *raw excitement?*"

"Yeah, man, I suppose you could say that."

Potentially a group with a great future. A lead singer who was as good as any Joe Cocker, an incredibly aggressive drummer, an organist who made three-quarters of the organists in rock look like butter left out in the sun, a bass player who could hold his own with his fellow countryman, Jack Bruce, and a crackling guitarist who handled his 1945 Les Paul Gibson like – well, it was all there, especially the raw excitement.

"Hey, Derek, how about 'A group with a great future who generate raw excitement beginning where the Cream left off'?"

"Are you still on with that 'They begin where the Cream left off' shit?"

"What about 'They *leave off* where the Cream *began*'?"

"No no no, we can do better than that. I like that 'generating raw excitement' bit though. And I was only kidding about 'A group with a great future.' We could never say that now, *could* we?"

"Well, I guess not but I think you're a little jaded after all these years with the Greatest Group in the History of Show Business."

"Jaded? Yes, I suppose I am—"

"But don't worry, man, you've got a great future—"

Sitting there at his desk with a pile of White Trash handout photos and a stack of stickers that read, "Censored," The House Hippie methodically executed his distasteful duty. On one photograph he had blotted out the words "White Trash" and had inserted in huge capital letters the word "Fuck" with a "Censored" sticker preceding it. Mal Evans walked into the room at that moment. They greeted each other with a nod. Approaching the desk Mal noticed the group photograph and the word "Fuck" with the inserted sticker, "Censored."

"What's *this?*" he asked in startled tones.

"Oh, haven't you heard, Mal? That well-known Apple

group, White Fuck, in order to comply with accepted community standards, has decided to drop the offensive 'White' in their name and are now known simply as 'Fuck.' "

"Richard!" he protested. "I'm really surprised at you! I didn't think you were like that at all."

"Well, surprise, surprise!"

78

BAD TIMING AND WHO'S BEEN READING OLIVER TWIST?

OF ALL THE Goddamn luck! One of England's best-known comedians has to drop dead the day Mary Hopkin has her press reception and of course the nationals don't run one fucking word about our reception! And the musicals! All they do is feature one frigging picture of Paul and Linda and ask the cryptic question: 'Is it wedding bells for Beatle Paul and his mystery blonde?' Christ, what a business!"

"Well, I'm sure if it was up to that comedian he would have made other arrangements but since it wasn't—"

"Ahh fuck! And what do we have? We have James Taylor sitting around here wondering what's happening to his career and Bill Collins, the Father Christmas of rock management, is in here every day asking us what we're doing for the Iveys and he keeps telling me when they make it he's going to see us straight for all our help and what do we know about the Iveys? Has anyone ever *heard* them?

"I hear all they ever do is stay in their house and write songs and rehearse day and night. They never stop! So if manic devotion to their craft is any indication of impending success then they should make it sometime within the next ten years. After that, though, if they haven't made it they probably won't care anymore. Can't say as I'd blame them—"

"And Jackie? Jackie's in here asking everybody, 'What are you doing for me?' What are we doing for him? We've only spent twenty-five thousand pounds on him, that's all! And who's heard his album?"

160

"I have and it's a real gem at that. George did an ace job on the production and Jackie's sounding very good and every song's a winner so this one has *got* to be the one that's going to make him a star."

"Well, I'm glad to hear it but that good news is cancelled by this memo—"

"What memo?"

"This memo from Alistair Taylor! 'As from Monday, lunchtime sandwiches will cease to be automatically supplied as at present. If anyone is genuinely staying to work over their lunch period would they please advise the kitchen before 12:15 and order their sandwich.' Maybe you haven't heard but we have a new boss now. His name is Allen Klein. This memo didn't come from Alistair's head. It comes from someone who's working under pressure. He's been told to start cutting down on expenses. So what's his first irrational act, inspired by fear? Stop giving sandwiches to the *slaves!* Make them beg for it! Of course this has no effect on Peter Brown or Neil or Derek, just the slaves, the office boys, the secretaries, all the minions! Mark my words, this is the beginning of *The Fall of the House of Asher!*"

79
NO, NO, A THOUSAND TIMES NO!

I T'S THE *SKETCH!* They want to know if Paul and Linda are engaged—"

"Rumors! Tell them as soon as we find out about Paul McCartney's matrimonial plans they'll be the first to know."

"It's the *Evening Standard!* They want to know when Paul and Linda are getting married—"

"Never!"

"It's the *Express!* They want to know if Linda is the heiress to the Eastman Kodak fortune and if so what are Paul's thoughts on marrying a millionairess, speaking strictly as a millionaire—"

"Eastman Kodak! Christ, how many times are they going to

ask us that? At this moment all I'm glad for is that Yoko's last name is Ono and not Nikon. No, they are *not* getting married!"

"Talking about John and Yoko did you hear about their concert last night?"

"What concert?"

"It was Yoko's concert at Lady Mitchell Hall in Cambridge and she just wailed and screamed and moaned and John accompanied her on feedback guitar."

"Wailing, screaming and moaning? Well it makes sense doesn't it? I mean after all she isn't your average, everyday girl-next-door now is she? If you ask me this is just the beginning of John and Yoko. They're getting quite far out—"

"Peter Brown says that Ringo has started work on a film with Peter Sellers called *The Magic Christian* and he's not going to be giving any interviews for a while—"

And then someone screamed at The Press Officer.

"Triumph Investment has just obtained control of NEMS!"

The Press Officer careened into action.

"Get me John right now and be ready to talk to the *Financial Times after* we've got the official statement from Allen Klein! You can say one thing for these Americans, they don't waste any time once they get going—"

80

THERE IS STILL NO TRUTH TO THE RUMOR THAT PAUL McCARTNEY OF THE BEATLES WILL . . .

T*HE TIMES.* Wednesday, March 12, 1969

BEATLE PAUL TO MARRY

Paul McCartney, aged 26, is to marry Miss Linda Eastman today at Marylebone Register Office W1. They first met two years ago when Miss Eastman, a professional photographer, took photographs of the Beatles in America.

Mr. McCartney is the only unmarried member of The Beatles group. Miss Eastman, who is 27 is a member of the Eastman Kodak family. She has a daughter, Heather, by her first marriage.

Last night a group of teenage girls waited outside Mr. McCartney's home in Cavendish Avenue N.W. When he arrived in his car three police cars accompanied him. A policeman said they had been asked to clear the pavement but there was no trouble.

A

ND ONLY A FEW hours later, on the very same day that Paul McCartney got married, the police moved in and busted George and Patti Harrison.

81

A TRIPLE-DECKER ACE BLUE MEANIE

The Times. Thursday, March 13, 1969

DRUGS RAID ON BEATLE

Scotland Yard drug squad detectives last night arrested George Harrison of The Beatles and his wife Patti Boyd at their £40,000 bungalow at Esher, Surrey.

Police said later that they would appear at Esher and Walton Court on Tuesday on charges involving alleged possession of Cannabis.

Patti Boyd was alone in the bungalow when detectives with two Labrador dogs arrived shortly before 8 P.M. She telephoned her husband in London and he arrived shortly before 10 P.M. They spent about an hour at the police station.

Follow-up

From the Press Association Staff Reporter

Walton-on-Thames, Monday. Beatle George Harrison and his wife, twenty-four-year-old model Patti Boyd, pleaded guilty today to illegally possessing Cannabis Resin.

They appeared at Esher and Walton Magistrates' Court here, charged with having in their possession a quantity of Cannabis Resin without being duly authorized. Patti Boyd was charged in her married name of Patricia Anne Harrison.

They walked into court hand in hand, Harrison wearing a dark blue suit, blue shirt and black tie, his wife in light gray trousers and a mulberry velvet jacket.

There were extra police on duty outside the court when they arrived in a chauffeur-driven white Mercedes, but few people were about. Only a dozen, most of them teenagers, were in the public gallery.

Mr. Michael West, Prosecuting, said that both had been of impeccable character hitherto. Their appearance resulted from the execution of a search warrant at their home in Claremont Drive, Esher, where officers went at 7:30 P.M. on March 12.

Harrison was not at home but his wife spoke to him on the telephone while the police officers were there. A police officer also spoke to him and asked him if he had any drugs on the premises and told him he had a warrant.

Harrison told him, "No, there is nothing there. There is only the stuff I got on prescription on top of the fridge."

His wife told the officers that there were no drugs other than those to which he was entitled. It became apparent that the two people had spoken of drugs during the telephone conversation, he claimed, because at one point, Mrs. Harrison said: "Where in the living room?"

Later a box containing Cannabis Resin was found in that room.

When the police officers made it abundantly clear that they were going to search, there was no obstruction of any kind put in their way and indeed Mrs. Harrison cooperated with them fully.

She showed them pills to which she was entitled but in her handbag was a phial which was later found to contain four grains of Cannabis Resin. She said someone had left it in the car.

In a cabinet some other items, including a home-made metal pipe in which Cannabis could be smoked, were found and another pipe was found later.

Mrs. Harrison then told police about drugs in the living room and agreed that they were the ones mentioned on the telephone.

In a box were 217 grains of Cannabis and 228 grains of Herbal Cannabis and in another box in another room there were 36 grains. There were also traces of the drug in a cigarette roller.

A police dog trained specifically to trace drugs by scent found another 304 grains in a wardrobe in their bedroom.

Mr. West told the magistrates: "It is infrequent to find quite as much of the drug as one found in this case, there is something like 570 grains which would result, when used, in a large number of cigarettes. It would be wrong to draw the inference that there was any intention to sell them. It is quite clear on the evidence that this was for personal consumption and no more than a private supply."

Mr. West asked if he should call a police witness, but both the bench and Mr. Martin Polden, representing the couple, said it was not necessary. Mr. Polden said that when police arrived, Mrs. Harrison was alone. "It is not surprising that with the sudden arrival of the police with two dogs that she was initially shocked and this explains why she was not coopera-tive."

Her husband told her when they were talking on the phone to give police any help they wanted. After the initial shock, said Mr. Polden, Mrs. Harrison did not try to hide anything and police went everywhere they wanted without obstruction.

The phial found in Mrs. Harrison's handbag was given to her, as she said, by a stranger in Chelsea. The long pipe was a gift from a friend in San Francisco. But it was a gift that had turned against them. They did not know that it contained traces of Cannabis.

Mrs. Harrison made no attempt to hide the white box containing Cannabis which was on the table. Police saw, and indeed took an interest in, the many oriental items in which the house abounds, he said. They found powders and crystals and joss sticks which were all quite harmless and all emphasized Harrison's interest in Yoga, said Mr. Polden.

Of the drugs found in the wardrobe he said, "The couple cannot explain this find. They know nothing about it to this day. The large amount of Cannabis found does not indicate that theirs is a household of corruption and debauchery. There is no question of addiction."

Mr. Polden said that the case could affect Harrison's traveling abroad in the future, particularly to the United States. This was of great concern to himself and Britain as the Beatles were always being asked to represent Britain abroad.

Mr. Polden emphasized Mrs. Harrison's hospitality after the initial shock. "When her husband arrived, police were watching television and playing Beatle records. She had been very hospitable."

When the magistrates returned after a fifteen-minute retirement the chairman, Mr. Eric Causton, said that Harrison and his wife would each be fined £250 and there would be 10 guineas costs against each of them.

Mr. Polden referred the magistrates to the ornamental pipe in which the traces of the drug had been found and said it was an ornament and nothing more. In reply to him Mr. Causton said they would permit the Harrison to keep the pipe.

As he left court, George Harrison told press men, "We hope the police will now leave the Beatles alone."

82
DIALOGUE/ DIALOGUE/ DIALOGUE

A NY NEWS?"

"*Carolina in My Mind* is getting some extensive air play on the FM stations but as far as the major AM market goes it's only middle-of-the-road interest. Mary's follow-up single is called *Goodbye* and you remember the spoken-word series that we keep talking about? Our 'paperback record concept'? Well, we're launching Zapple very shortly."

"Zapple?"

"That's what it's going to be called. Paul has designed a cover for the series with a big apple-shaped cutout on the front and a picture printed on the inner sleeve. George has an album he's done with the Moog synthesizer called "Electronic Sound" and John and Yoko have another one called "Unfinished Music Number 2 Life with the Lions" and I understand that Miles has been doing a lot of recording with all those literary heavies like Charles Bukowski, Ken Weaver, Charles Olson, Kenneth Patchen, Richard Brautigan, Michael McClure and Lawrence Ferlinghetti—"

"Yeah—"

"The Iveys' record looks as though it's gone as far as it's going. Air play, chart positions and sales are rapidly dropping but Paul's working on getting them to do the music for Ringo's film so that's something but I'm afraid we've got a spot of bad news for Tony Meehan and White Trash—"

"From the tone of your voice it sounds like a massive bringdown—"

"Near enough and it's really a fucking pity after the way it's been going for them. We really thought we had a monster with *Road to Nowhere*, what with all the major top-forty air play in Buffalo and Minneapolis and that was only the beginning! The record's potential started to show when it jumped into the number-two slot on WJET in Erie, Pennsylvania—"

"Erie, Pennsylvania!"

"Now don't laugh, that's the number-one top-forty station in that very crucial secondary market. Then a week later we got that ecstatic cable from Capitol quoting a sales figure over a three-week period of fifty-five thousand records—"

"Well?"

"Well, their computer fucked up! It was only twenty-three thousand against the original quote so that's it for their IAP. Capitol says there's no point in going ahead with the promotional film they did and they've decided to scrap the poster. They said it doesn't look like the American public is ready for White Trash yet so you better call Tony Meehan and oh! I almost forgot! Guess who got married in Gibraltar this morning?"

"It couldn't be John and Yoko, could it?"

"It sure could and it certainly was!"

83

THE AMSTERDAM BED-IN

BEGIN—"

"Beatle John Lennon and Japanese artist Yoko Ono were turned away at the Thoresen passenger terminal in Southampton fifteen minutes before the departure of the ferry *Dragon* to France, owing to inconsistencies in their passports—"

"Stop—"

"The couple took an early-morning flight to Paris where they spent four days, passing virtually unnoticed in the French capital—"

"Break—"

". . . before departing in a privately chartered Hawker Siddeley jet piloted by Captain Trevor Coppleston. With them was The Beatles' social coordinator and personal assistant Peter Brown and photographer David Nutter—"

"Go on—"

"They landed in Gibraltar March 20, 1969, at 8:30 A.M. and arrived at the registrar's office shortly after 9 A.M. Yoko Ono was wearing a white minidress, white wide-brimmed hat and white knee socks. John Lennon wore a white pullover, white jacket and unmatched white trousers. Both were wearing white tennis shoes—"

"All right—"

"Mr. Cecil Joseph Wheeler performed the three-minute ceremony pursuant to the marriage ordinance of the City and Garrison of Gibraltar. The license by special issue cost four pounds fourteen shillings—"

"And—"

"John Lennon repeated the marriage vows with a cigarette in one hand and Yoko Ono wore dark glasses throughout the brief ceremony—"

"Leave that bit out—"

"Apple spokesman Derek Taylor said the cost of the wedding, which included the chartered jet from Luton to Gibraltar, hotel accommodations for the Lennons and their two witnesses and clothing, was about eight thousand pounds—"

"Finish it—"

John and Yoko at the Amsterdam Bed-In. Posters facing them include such slogans as "Stay In-Bed," "Grow Your Hair," "Bagism," and "I Love Yoko: I Love John" which is on a picture of themselves in the very same bed.

"Beatle John Lennon said, 'We chose Gibraltar because it is quiet, British and friendly.' Returning to Paris, Mrs. Lennon announced from their luxury suite at the Plaza Athenée Hotel near the Champs Elysées after Thursday's civil ceremony that the couple were planning a big happening within the next seven days—"

"Fine—"

"What's the big happening they're planning in the next seven days?"

"It's already started in room 902 of the Amsterdam Hilton. They're having a Bed-In."

"A Bed-In? I don't follow you—"

"They're spending seven days of their honeymoon in bed as a humorous protest against all forms of violence. They've invited the world press up to see them and to discuss their campaign to bring about world peace. It's John's latest project. The other day they had over forty journalists, photographers, disk jockeys and television people in the room at once. They're talking ten hours a day nonstop—"

"Is Derek PR-ing the thing?"

"No, they've got some people from Dutch EMI to handle it. Peter Brown stayed for a day but he's flying back tonight and every paper in town is flying one of their boys over for it. Richard's going over the day after tomorrow—"

"Richard? What the hell's he going for?"

"White Trash are doing their record for Dutch television and Ron Kass thought it would be nice if he went along. Don't forget he is the Client Liaison Officer—"

"Yeah but—"

"It's a real scene at the Hilton, I understand. They were pelted with tulips when they arrived as a symbol of love and appreciation on the first day and the Dutch vice squad are keeping an eye out because someone told them that they were going to fuck for the cameras—"

"Are they?"

"No, and all the kids keep rushing the door in packs trying to get through the lobby and the hotel management is going nuts but they love the business."

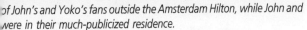
of John's and Yoko's fans outside the Amsterdam Hilton, while John and were in their much-publicized residence.

The Amsterdam Hilton, scene of the historic Bed-In.

"And they're just having fun—"

"And it is for world peace – And have Richard write us a memo about Amsterdam when he gets back—"

WHITE TRASH IN AMSTERDAM – A TRUE STORY

From the Client Liaison Officer to Ron Kass, Neil Aspinall, Derek Taylor, Peter Asher and Tony Meehan . . .

White Trash left London on March 27 at 8:45 and arrived at Schiphol Airport at 9:35 A.M. We were met by Olaf Stein of Bovema, Dutch EMI, who drove us directly to Haalversum where the *Doebiedoe Show* is filmed. We were given a dressing room, a pot of coffee and an hour to kill. The first program run-through was completed by midday, at which time Ronald Leahy, White Trash organist, Olaf and myself went to Radio Veronica to do an interview. When that was finished we went to another radio station and did a second interview concerning White Trash and Apple. It came off well.

We had lunch courtesy of Bovema. White Trash then went through a second rehearsal followed by a photo session with *Hit Week* magazine. The final run-through was completed by six that evening.

White Trash had been booked to fly back to London the same day but I asked Olaf if there was a possibility of their playing at the Paradiso in Amsterdam, one of the major underground ballrooms. He thought it a good idea and called the Paradiso who also thought it a good idea and arranged to

171

The Amsterdam Bed-In.

have the needed equipment as the group had only an electric bass and guitar with them.

Bovema paid White Trash 200 gulden and told me that another 1200 was being sent to Apple on Monday. They booked the group into the American Hotel where a single room for me had been reserved by Apple.

Thursday at the Paradiso was an off night and there had been no previous announcement of White Trash appearing in concert but despite the short notice there were five hundred in attendance. They did two 45-minute sets and were very well received. Payment for the two sets to White Trash was 18 glasses of beer, six posters and one ounce of hashish.

At the American Hotel we asked that five beds for the group be charged to Bovema as they had booked the rooms. The management called Bovema and were informed by Olaf that in fact Bovema would not pay for the rooms as the contract stipulated, that they were to return that night and no other arrangements had been agreed upon. Not wanting to complicate matters we said OK and left it at that. White Trash used the 200 gulden to pay for their bed and breakfast.

The result of their playing at the Paradiso that night was an offer by Jan Paul of the Lijn 3 Club for White Trash to play there the following night, Friday, for a percentage of the house take. I agreed and so did the group. Also in attendance that night was a promoter named John Seine who, after hearing the group, expressed a desire to arrange a two-week tour of the Netherlands for White Trash once working papers had been contracted.

Friday, March 28, White Trash checked out of The American Hotel as all their earnings had been used up to pay their hotel expenses. The early afternoon was devoted to photographs and at three o'clock we went to the Amsterdam Hilton to see John and Yoko.

We spent a very pleasant hour with John and Yoko, during which time I spoke to Mr. Hiller who was chief of protocol for the Bed-In that afternoon and explained the situation of the hotel rooms and lack of funds.

He expressed some dismay at Bovema refusing to pay for

the group's hotel expenses, as their performance the previous night at the Paradiso was an excellent promotional concert. He told me that *Road to Nowhere* was at number 15 in the Dutch charts and still climbing. He told me to come back later that afternoon and talk to his superior, Hans Boskamp.

I went back to the Hilton that evening and explained the situation to Mr. Boskamp. He was genuinely concerned about us and arranged for me to collect 300 gulden from him at eight o'clock that evening. I told him that Ron Kass had said if there was anything else the group needed to let him know and he would look after us.

Friday evening White Trash appeared as special guests at the Lijn 3 Club. The owner was pleased with their performance and said the group had played the longest set in the history of the club.

We were then told by him that he could not pay us until Saturday night at eight. At this point rampant paranoia set in as we had rebooked White Trash back into the American Hotel. It looked as if we had been taken for a ride. Such was not the case, such was our paranoia.

Saturday afternoon I decided to go see Boskamp again and ask him for another 300 gulden to get us by. He was a bit taken back by this request and asked why. I explained the situation to him and he said he would ask John for the money, as it was Saturday and the banks were closed.

John had Boskamp call Peter Brown, who said "Forget it" because the group was supposed to return to London on Thursday evening. I told him not to worry, that somehow we would manage; perhaps we would cash in our plane tickets and hitchhike back.

Our financial fears were quelled that evening when we phoned Jan Paul asking for our money. He came across and paid the band 250 gulden. He said he wanted to work a deal whereby White Trash would perform in Amsterdam with a normal contract with substantial money for a concert at the Paradiso, the Fantasio, his club, and two other venues as yet unspecified.

It appears that White Trash will be able to receive double

the money after the *Doebiedoe Show* is aired on April 4. Being an unknown quantity, this comes as good news.

There are a lot of dykes in Holland and Amsterdam has six hundred canals and over 500,000 bicycles. Amsterdam was a stoned groove. Thank you for letting me go along and if there is a possibility of me going to Japan in September with Mary Hopkin I wouldn't say no. White Trash's guitarist, Fraser Watson, would like to go too.

FINANCIAL STATEMENT FOR WHITE TRASH

INCOME
   Received from *Doebiedoe*: 200 gulden
   Received from Lijn 3 for performance: 250 gulden and 25 glasses of beer
   Received from Paradiso: 18 glasses of beer, six posters and one ounce of hashish
   Plus an additional 1200 gulden payable to Apple Corps, Ltd.

OUTLAY FOR WHITE TRASH
   Hotel with breakfast: 485.72 gulden
   Spending money: 120 gulden
   Meals exclusive of hotel breakfast: 15 gulden
   Airport tax and group transport: 106 gulden
   Received from Hans Boskamp for Hotel bill and charged to Apple: 300 gulden

"Well, I read your report but what was it really like?"

"We didn't get laid for starters but other than that it was Top City. Everything was just right, the weather, the vibes, the beer, the hash. We had a beautiful time with J and Y at the Hilton and we were just out of our heads with the excitement of it all and Yoko was looking fantastic and John let us scrounge through the baskets of fruit and he laid packs of cigarettes on us and rice and vegetables and he said, 'Go on, go on take anything you want.'"

"So you had a good time—"

"It's already a solid-gold memory—"

"They get nicer as the years roll by."

84

DIALOGUE/
DIALOGUE/
DIALOGUE

WHAT'S THAT BARREL doing in the Black Room?"

"That's the one we had at Mary's reception."

"I know that but what's it *doing* there?"

"I just never got around to returning it but we'll find a use for it someday."

"Well the press in this country is certainly going out of their way to make John and Yoko look like two deranged gorillas and do you ever read those cuttings you're always filing away?"

"Fuck you! Of course I do."

"They've just blasted them with ridicule. Donald Zec slashed them to ribbons in print and I didn't *believe* the way they were treated on the *Eamonn Andrews Show!* It was disgusting and the hostility isn't going to stop either because this is just the first Bed-In, which reminds me. Take this down. It's the caption for the Ono pics for Camera Press. Dateline today. John Lennon and Yoko Ono have codirected a startling and revolutionary TV film subtitled *Rape*, which is expected to run into censorship trouble. Lennon and Miss Ono in collaboration with Austrian TV producer Hans Preiner have carried out 'rape by camera' of a Hungarian girl known as Eva, an unsuspecting member of the public. Says Yoko, who names the work *Film Number 6* and subtitles it *Rape*, 'It is an ambitious film, the unveiling of more of human nature than we normally see. It is going deeper than skin deep, much deeper.' Eva is followed over a three-day period by a relentlessly probing, searching movie camera. A camera which will not let her be. The results, a one-hour thirteen-minute film, premiered on Austrian National Network Television on March 31 because, says John Lennon, 'TV is where it's at!' in color and it will later be shown at the Montreux television festival in Switzerland in late April. It is then aimed at major cinema circuits. Read it back."

"John Lennon and Yoko Ono have codirected . . ."

"All right. And you know about Vienna?"

"No—"

176

"Well, they conducted a press conference from inside a white bag in Vienna's most exclusive hotel, Sacher's, an hour before the premier of *Rape* and the hotel was in complete pandemonium. The management was totally freaked out of their brains and didn't know how to handle it and anyway John has finally verbalized what they've been doing with that bag routine of theirs. He calls it Bagism and we've got to get our hands on one hundred acorns because John wants them sent to all the world leaders, kings, presidents, prime ministers, the lot—"

"Acorns?"

"Yes, acorns. To be planted for World Peace in the spring of 1969."

W E'VE ALREADY TOLD them that Ringo's filming and he's not giving any interviews. It's not that he isn't willing to, it's just that he *doesn't* have the time."

"They said they called the studio and spoke to the film's PR man and he said they should call here."

"Well now that they've called that's the answer and what's the story on the Iveys?"

"Paul's definitely got them the gig doing the music for the film and he's written a song called *Come and Get It* which is going to be used in the film and released as their next single and they're also thinking of changing their name."

What's the matter with the one they've got?"

"They're sick of it, that's all. Paul thinks they're a fantastic group but that they need a lot of working on and he's been trying to give their musical ideas some direction *and* he's succeeded but he's told them that they're on their own after this one."

"Does anyone have any idea what Ken Kesey's record

85

THERE'S A HOT-DOG STAND ON THE CORNER OF THE UNITED STATES OF AMERICA AND IT'S CALLING ME BACK HOME

sounds like? He's been running around London with that tape recorder for weeks now."

"We'd have some idea if we just sat down and listened to it. Every time he comes in here I think he gets a little confused by all the motion and he's picking up on the indifference we're generating."

"Indifference?"

"Well, it's not fair to tell someone, 'Here's a tape recorder, here's a typewriter, here's our blessing now go out and make a record,' and then three weeks later begin a withdrawal of good will and start giving off paranoid vibrations. You can't pin Peter Asher down to an answer and Ron Kass isn't sure and the Press Office is all for the idea but you can't pin them down to an answer, either, because they've been told some-one's gotten uptight that the go-ahead was given in the first place."

"And whatever happened to the Hell's Angels and the rest of that crew? They were in here all the time and suddenly, pfft! they've disappeared."

"They got fed up with Apple and London. They probably thought it was going to be just like California but better only they found out it wasn't like California and in fact worse, and it's not that it's worse it's just that they didn't know what they were in for in the first place. No one wanted to be converted and no one gave a fuck. They were left alone and no one bothered them and what bugged them to death in the end was the absolute lack of aggravation. They had no idea what Apple was going to be like and once they were faced with it the whole thing confused them even more because they landed right in the middle of all the confusion and their presence just generated more confusion and they started going nuts. So to distract themselves from it all they thought, 'Ahh ha! We'll go out and get drunk and stoned and laid.' Well the pubs were charming and they liked the beer as a novelty but when they were full of it they asked someone where was a good place to go get some 'diversion' and some asshole told them 'Go to the Revolution!' and when they went there they saw all these fabulous, beautiful, delectable creatures running around but what no one had warned them about was the London dolly-bird mentality. They figured 'Shit! Look at all these beautiful, hip-looking broads!' but when they hit on those 'beautiful, hip-looking broads' they found that behind those lovely front porches there was *nothing* going on that even faintly resembled what they called soul. And the sun never shines in London."

"And Emily's Family?"

"They shoved off too. Disappointed in the failure of their fantasy of John and Yoko. Selfish suppositions. They felt their acid vision gave them the right to demand and expect their demands to be met. And the sun never shines in London."

"But it shines in the Fiji Islands—"

"Kesey's still here and Spider's still around and Frankie Hart, a California girl if ever there was one, has stayed and done the building a lot of good but someone's bound to get uptight with her because she's so *un*-uptight and start asking, 'What's she doing here?'"

"But not for a while because if you haven't heard, George has hired her as his personal assistant and she's also getting to work on the Jackie Lomax campaign which is designed to make Jackie a star and George knows good *karma* when he sees it. Twiggy thinks Jackie is better looking than the best of all of El Greco's paintings and Justin is going to be his manager and Paul is helping him out with another single—"

"And his album?"

"We're having a fucking hard time moving that one. It's another inexplicable fluke just like *Sour Milk Sea* was. It's sitting there in the record shops, quality going to waste."

"And Mary?"

"Mary is not doing badly for a young girl who's just starting in show business even though she'll tell you she was playing workingmen's clubs in Wales long before she was discovered by Apple, correction, by Twiggy and *launched* by Apple. There was *Those Were the Days* which we all know about and she's had *Lontano Dagli Occhi* released in Italy and *Prince en Avignon* released in France and both doing very well and

Goodbye, which was released only last month, is crashing its way up the US charts even if it's only drifting here."

"And Peter Asher has brought in those three American kids who are an acoustic group calling themselves Mortimer and he's already started working on giving them some form. He's doing everything himself, the photographs, the dialogue, the lot. He's talked Paul into giving them a song off the last Beatle album and they're downstairs at this very moment knocking it together in the rehearsal room—"

"Capitol called Jack Oliver this morning—"

"And?"

"They said they've received the lacquer masters and the master tapes for the album and they've gone ahead and made a large number of special dubs for the field promotion staff. They'd like to start air play in the States on Monday and of course they lay all their usual dialogue on us like, 'Once more it looks like The Beatles are grabbing the reins and carrying the industry aeons ahead and will be setting musical trends for months to come.' They're always going on like that and I wish someone would turn them off. Don't they know that The Fabs are tired of that stuff and know it *anyway?* And then the corker to the whole thing is that four days away from air-play target on The Beatles' album a bootleg version of the entire LP starts getting played day and night on the radio. Havoc! Litigation City! Of course no one knows where the fuck it was heisted from and then the *Get Back* single was played on London Radio last Sunday afternoon in case you weren't listening and again no one will cough up and answer where *that* came from so the album is being put back a while because they've decided it sounds all wrong but no one can get it together to decide what it's supposed to sound like to sound *right*—"

"And the film?"

"Still editing—"

"And the book?"

"Dalton and Cott are just about finished with it but then it has to go through EMI for censoring and then back to The Beatles for approval. Ethan Russell has got all his photographs and John Kosh has designed the book but, and it's always the big *but*, they can't find a printer to print it. They found one printer who halfheartedly said yes but then he said it had to be done in *just* black and white! And then another printer who couldn't meet the quote or our schedule. Already they've had half a dozen color separations done and all of them terrible and it looks like they're going to have to go out of the country to get the plates made once someone can come up with a workable separation! It says very little for the initiative of industry in this country. A nice juicy account like ours and they turn up their noses and say, 'We couldn't possibly manage it in the time you've asked but do come back in six years and maybe we can work *something* out.' "

"Peter Asher said that Richard Brautigan is all ready to go—"

"He's all ready to go as a special Zapple release but not until the contracts have been finalized. The pressings and the sleeves aren't getting the go-ahead until that happens and I've got a feeling that that one is going to be on ice now that the new regime has begun. It's probably going to die a slow death and Richard Brautigan will never walk through that white door downstairs. By the way, Bramwell says that the Zapple logo artwork and the position guides are being sent out on Friday and we won't be using Paul's original design and George has done his own cover and J and Y have one of their own already. The copy for the inner sleeves on those two has to go with it and Bramwell says from now on that's the accepted work pattern. Oh, and just for a bit of gossip, I hear that Ron Kass's movements are under close scrutiny from Klein. The pressure is starting. Oliver and Bramwell say that if Ron goes, whatever the circumstances, then they're going too."

"Do you think they'll stick to it?"

"It'll be interesting to see."

86

ALLEN KLEIN AND THE DEOPPILATION OF APPLE

I F KLEIN DIDN'T know it before he started he knows it now. He's walked into a financial cesspool."

"Do you think he can swim?"

"I'd venture to say that he's got a few bronze medals to prove it if anyone should ask."

"Do you think all that shit people say about him is true?"

"Like most rumors you hear, some of them are true and the rest, well, there's so much bad-mouthing and backbiting dialogue running around this building that emotion has all but made it impossible to tell the shit from the Shinola. My guess is that he's not really the bastard everyone says he is. It's just that he will not go out of his way to be charming to anyone."

"He should be admired for that, not *hated*."

"Yes but you know how much stock people put in the capacity to charm?"

"What do you think is going to happen to this place?"

"Massive, radical changes. You see, Klein's vision of what this place should be is diametrically opposed to everything it is now, to what it was supposed to be, to what everyone on the outside thinks it is and should be. Which will make his image an even more assailable target, but not for him, because he's invulnerable. Because he doesn't think of himself as having an image that needs tending. All he's thinking about is how to straighten the place out."

"Where do you start?"

"With the money-makers, with The Fabs. To hell with the Taylors, the Lomaxes, the White Trashes. Just sort out *them*, then it will be easy to think about the rest.

Klein doesn't seem particularly interested in making this the greatest record company on earth. He'd rather just get The Fabs what's coming to them. For him that's the challenge, that's his album cover, that's where he's going to be happiest."

"Get The Fabs what's coming to them?"

"Of course! I mean don't you know that for years now they've been cheated, robbed, ripped-off – there's no pleasant way of saying a nasty thing in a nice way without avoiding the truth *completely*. More people have been making more money off of their work than they have, and Klein aims to turn the tables on that situation. As far as Apple being the Mecca for deserving artists goes, Klein just sees that as a lot of Hippie shit and so do they, now that they've had a good hard second look."

"Well, if he's just interested in making The Fabs richer than they are now what's going to happen to the rest of the artists?"

"It's very simple. Sink or swim. If they don't make it they're out!"

"But what are the massive radical changes?"

"Say when a Republican president gets into office, he finds it very helpful to have a Republican Congress. If he doesn't, the job's a lot more difficult. He either has to wait until all his opponents croak or somehow, perhaps through brain surgery, alter their thought patterns. But this is the music business, man! You don't have to go through all that shit, all you have to do is fire everyone and bring in your own people."

"Do you think he's right for The Fabs?"

"On a deal like this you can't really tell for at least five to seven years. But one thing is for sure, The Fabs are better off now than they were before. Mr. Klein is coming on like the Rainmaker and heaven is opening up. He renegotiated song-writing contracts with Dick James and he's put the elbow into EMI and Capitol for a better deal and he's getting results."

"Are they all for him?"

"Well, they're all for a change."

W HAT DID SHE WANT?"

"Mick's home phone number and some acid."

"Mick's home phone number and some acid? Christ, what the fuck do they think this place is! Why do they always come *here?!?*"

"Because this is the most famous place in town. Because if you've just stepped off a plane from New York or LA or San

## 87

IT'S A GREAT PLACE TO GET STONED BUT I WOULDN'T WANT TO WORK THERE

Francisco, curiosity demands that you come here even if you invariably get the runaround."

"Sure, sure. Look we've got Dominic Behan coming in this afternoon to see if he can get Lennon for a television show he's been asked to do up north and if he gets Lennon they'll give him the show. The Fabs are all in for a board meeting this afternoon so we'll have to squeeze him in either before or after."

He was dawdling at the Rupert Street market, stretching his lunch hour out to an hour and a half, when The House Hippie heard someone hiss at him, "Get yer 'air cut!" Turning around he found Paul and Linda McCartney standing next to him, looking exquisite, arms around each other, out for an afternoon's bop and browse about London.

They talked for 20 minutes and The House Hippie left them, trying to list the number of requests from his employer before he immediately forgot them: photographs, press coverage on the wedding, say hi to Derek. He was hoping he would make it back to the office before The Press Officer had returned from his lunch because he had neglected to set the bar that morning and it looked to be a very frantic afternoon. He had just finished setting out the ice and glasses when The Press Officer sprinted into the room, whipping off his coat and lighting a cigarette in one single motion.

"Hey, Derek—" he called across the room.

"What—"

"I just ran into Paul and Linda on the street and they said to say hi and they want me to photograph them."

The Press Officer didn't reply to this information but instantly jotted the request onto his mental pad and ten minutes later phoned through to Peter Brown.

"Listen, Peter, our House Hippie just met Mr. and Mrs. McCartney on the street and they asked him to photograph them. So if you'll find out the time and place, this office will take care of the rest and I've got to tell you that finding one hundred acorns in London is taking more than I thought it would. We had this arsehole in yesterday who had a dozen to sell at a pound apiece and he was very politely turned around and pointed in the direction of the door and we're still waiting for the list of names and addresses of those world leaders that that fellow at the BBC told John he'd draw up for him and I'll ask Yoko later on today if she's designed the box they're to go in and don't forget we've got Dominic Behan in this afternoon and that's all for the moment," said The Press Officer, returning the phone to its resting place and calling for a scotch and Coke.

Thirty minutes later Peter Brown returned The Press Officer's call.

"Hmm, yes, all right, I see, OK, fine, thanks."

The Press Officer looked over at The House Hippie.

"Hey—"

"What's up, chief?"

"That was Peter Brown and he said he just spoke to Paul and he didn't ask you to photograph him and Linda, he just asked for any photographs of the *wedding* that might have come into the office and any of the outstanding cuttings."

"Ohh—"

"So look, the next time one of The Fabs asks for something, try and pay a little more attention to him, otherwise it looks like we're perpetually fumbling the ball, which we're not, but you must understand that they get very impatient because they've grown used to having everything they ask for as soon as they ask for it."

"OK."

"So get onto John Kelly right now and have him send over in a cab all of his photographs of the wedding and then go through that bag of cuttings I've seen hidden away behind the filing cabinet and sort out the best of the lot for them."

The Pineapple Archives had come a long way from those early summer days of 1968. Every month had brought the opening of a new file; the catalogue had become bloated with history. The recent Amsterdam Bed-In and the double-barreled weddings of John and Paul had produced such a massive volume of cuttings as to discourage even the most ambitious librarian, let alone this particular keeper of the clippings.

"Ahh, you mean I have to go through all that paper?"

Alas, The House Hippie had grown bored with the daily ritual of filing it all away and he could no longer conceal his disinterest. When The Press Officer heard his remark he exploded.

"What do you mean, 'Do I have to go through all that paper? 'That's your job, if you'll excuse me for reminding you, you lazy bastard! And when McCartney asks me for those cuttings do you expect *me* to say to *him*, 'Ahh what do you want with all that paper?'"

"The American cuttings *too?*"

"Yes, the American cuttings *too!*"

"All right, but how about telling me about the time you and John got stoned on acid and went to meet Brigitte Bardot—"

"Not now, man, *please!*"

The Press Office was moving along like a well-oiled nut-house. The Press Officer, in his immense white wicker chair with the scalloped back, was juggling the flow of journalists and friends from behind his desk when the receptionist announced that Dominic Behan, Brendan's brother, was in reception. "Send him up!"

Dominic Behan and The Press Officer greeted each other with the familiarity of two men who had survived the combined horrors of Belleau Wood, Chateau Thierry and the Argonne-Meuse together. No sooner had the gifted Irishman sat himself down than another gifted son of Eire walked in, Tony Meehan, the brains behind White Trash.

The Press Officer introduced Meehan to Behan, cementing the introduction with two double scotches, and excused himself for a brief five minutes. "I'll see if John's ready yet," he said and left the room.

Meehan and Behan glommed on to each other like only two Irish nationalists could. By their second double scotch they were reciting Irish poems and discussing passionately, tears filling their eyes, in *Gaelic*, everything from Molly Bloom's knickers to the fate of the snakes driven out of Ireland by St. Patrick. No doubt they had wound up in England.

When The Press Officer returned to his room he found the Office Zombie in a half lotus on the edge of the white leather

186

couch which was occupied by three lovely California girls looking for a recording contract and wondering if this was the place they'd find it. Stocky was contentedly drawing pictures of an incredible entanglement of genitalia.

The Press Officer told The House Hippie to get them all drinks. As he handed Dominic Behan his fourth double scotch, which due to a slip of the hand had turned into a heavy, triple scotch, he heard The Press Officer say, "I think John is ready to see you now, Dominic, but finish your drink first, there's no rush."

All of this was being photographed for an upcoming series by Tommy Hanley for the *TV Times* called "Inside the Crazy World of Apple." His word half, Mike Hennessey, was objectively making notes. The House Hippie asked the Office Zombie and the female trio from California if they'd care to retire to the Black Room for a quiet blast on a Benson and Hashish B-52 Bomber, away from the raucous and nerve-shattering commotion of the front room.

Just before he closed the door he saw The Press Officer giving Dominic Behan instructions on how to get down to Peter Brown's office where he would find John Lennon. It would have been more appropriate to have given him a seeing eye dog and a pair of crutches, he was smashed out of his skull. The door of the Black Room closed in a grateful puff of smoke.

Eight minutes later the intercom on The Press Officer's desk began rining furiously. Answering its call, The Press Officer was ordered down to Peter Brown's office *immediately* to escort the disastrously inebriated and violent Dominic Behan *out* of the building. John Lennon would *not* be taking part in the television show up north.

88

**FURTHER DETAILS
AVAILABLE FROM
APPLE/REGENT 8232**

PRESS OFFICE RELEASE to UPI, AP, Reuters, PA: Apple's world sales since August 1968 now total 16, 192, 126 records.

"Ron Kass is gone!!! Don't ask me the particulars because no one's saying anything, he's just gone and I wouldn't be surprised if Peter Asher hands in his resignation very soon and I've heard there's going to be a full-scale review of the staff and anyone who is not considered absolutely essential to the operation is going to be made redundant. The massive, radical changes have begun!"

"Well, I guess we all have to swing with the times—"

"Swing by the neck is more like it!"

"What about Bramwell and Oliver? Didn't they say if Ron goes they were going too?"

"They did but like you said we all have to swing with the times. Bramwell is staying right where he is and Jack Oliver has moved from back-room obscurity to the dazzling heights of the most prestigious record company in the world."

"'From back-room obscurity to the dazzling heights of the most prestigious record company in the world'? What's that mean?"

"They've just made Jack Oliver head of Apple Records!"

89

**TOREADOR, DON'T
SPIT ON THE FLOOR**

PRESS OFFICE RELEASE to UPI, AP, Reuters, PA: Beatle John Winston Lennon today changed his name to John Ono Lennon at a brief ceremony on the roof of the Beatles' Apple Company Headquarters at 3 Savile Row, London W1. The change of name was effected by Senor Bueno de Mesquita, Commissioner for Oaths (April 22, 1969).

Yoko Ono Lennon
John Ono Lennon

John says: "Yoko changed hers for me, I've changed mine for her. One for both, both for each other. She has a ring. I have a ring. It gives us nine 'O's between us, which is good luck. Ten would not be good luck. Three names is enough for anyone. Four would be greedy."

"There they go again—"

"I keep telling you it's just the beginning of John and Yoko. They've got themselves a personal assistant now. His name's Anthony Fawcett and John's just knighted him 'Superchicken.'"

"Superchicken?"

"Yes, he just pointed to him and said, 'You are Super-chicken!'"

"Where does he come from?"

"The London art scene. He's a bachelor of arts or one of those numbers. A bright kid but he'll probably go nuts working for them in a few months."

"Mary's sister Carol got married last week to an architect named Stan Sherrington."

"Good for her—"

"But there's more to it—"

"How much more?"

"Stan Sherrington is now Mary's manager."

"Well, well, well! The joint just keeps rocking and the punches just keep coming! Do you have his phone number?"

"Yes—"

"Well, call him up right now and ask him if Mary's going to be appearing, according to rumors that we, as her record company, can never get an answer to, at the Royal Box at the Americana Hotel in New York in June and find out if she's doing another album with Paul."

F OLLOWING THE Amsterdam Bed-In, 3 Savile Row underwent a psychic facelift. On the surface nothing much had altered. If you did a quick walk through the lobby and caught it all from the corner of your eye, the place still looked a bit like the waiting room of a VD clinic in Haight-Ashbury in 1967. And sometimes like the casting office for extras in a spaghetti

90
JOHN AND YOKO
FOREVER!

Western epic. And on some days just like the special canteen the Hollywood studios had to build for the cast of Tod Browning's film, *Freaks*. Above the ground-floor level sounded echoes of the more fashionable drawing rooms during the last days of the court of Louis XIV. It was still the most flamboyant record company in London.

The appointment of Allen Klein as Commander-in-Chief of Apple Corps, Ltd., was the backstage drama running parallel with the front and center John Lennon-Yoko Ono Road Show for Peace, with Derek Taylor as Ringmaster. John Lennon took his campaign up with all the foam and fury of any self-respecting fanatic burning with his vision.

The Lennons had instructed The Press Officer to fix the particulars; they would do the rest. The objective was media saturation. Cajole, convert, argue, bully but keep saying it over and over again: Peace! Peace! Peace! To the point of being bores, to the frayed edges of deadly overexposure, right into the belly of ridicule. It didn't matter much just as long as there was a soapbox to stand on and one pair of ears to hear it: Peace! Peace! Peace!

After the departure of Ron Kass, John and Yoko moved into the ground-floor office and redecorated it to exorcise the old spirits. They immediately created a rhythm in the building that until then had been frantically erratic and massively shapeless.

The Press Officer would have to stagger the interviews. There were an average of five a day in a five-day working week beginning at 11 A.M. and running through until 5:30 P.M., with a 15-minute interval between the arrival and departure of one team of writers and photographers and the next. The Press Office was filled with the overlapping flood of representatives of the world's press, each nervously awaiting his turn to be ushered in on cue to the office downstairs with the high white ceiling.

Besides the media members eager to discuss the Peace Campaign, there was the usual run of Lennonmaniacs with their propositions and deals that had to be sounded out and sifted through, juggled and processed. The work load at 3 Savile Row had quadrupled. The results were there to be seen in the burgeoning files of the Pineapple Archives; the press coverage returns were titanic. John and Yoko had become the King Kong of the Peace Movement.

91

I T SEEMS THAT every time George Harrison walks into this office, I'm eating a pizza, Carol is fixing her eyelashes and you're rolling a joint. I wonder what he thinks," said Mavis Smith looking at The House Hippie who was rolling a joint on top of the Amsterdam Bed-In presscutting file.

"Mavis," The House Hippie said, "our timing might be a little off but if I were George I wouldn't be worrying too much. Do you realize that between August and December of '68 *alone*, this place has grossed world sales of over one million four hundred thousand pounds and mostly on sales of Mary's record and George's 'Wonderwall' and that does not include *any* of The Beatles' records?"

"Yes, but still—"

"*Vogue* has been on three times now with that request for Linda to do a picture feature on Paul and for the third time we've passed it on to Peter Brown and still no reply! And what about those acorns?"

"Ahh, those friggin' acorns! The last batch were all bruised and moldy and you couldn't *possibly* send them to *anyone* let alone Ho Chi Minh and Haile Selassie."

"Keep trying—"

"If McCartney asked you to cut off your balls for Apple, would you do it?"

"Well, I'd have to think about it for a while—"

"There's a new Beatle single out at the end of May written by John called *The Ballad of John and Yoko* and they're also getting together a deluxe package called 'The Wedding Album,' which is going to include a book of the press coverage of the wedding and the Bed-In, postcards and posters and a whole slew of other goodies and David Dalton and Jonathan Cott have finished their book on The Beatles' album but as soon as EMI saw it they said, 'This will never do!' They've bowdlerized the whole thing. They've taken out all the 'shits' and 'fucks' and 'pisses,' all that stuff. Anything that vaguely suggests that they're anything but sugar-coated mop tops and when The Fabs saw the text all they said was, 'A little less Wordsworth and a little more *us*.' So if you're looking for artistic freedom I'm beginning to wonder if this is the place you'll find it. Remember this was the company where you weren't going to have to come in on your hands and knees but it looks like pretty soon the only way you're going to be allowed in is on your belly!"

"*Melody Maker* wants an interview with Paul, and *Rolling Stone* called and—"

"Every fucking journalist in the world wants an interview with McCartney but he's not doing any and Ringo's got his film and George likes being interviewed even *less* than he likes being photographed and *John*, well, he'll give any interview to *anybody!* So that's how it stands at the moment. No Beatles! Ringo is taking Derek to New York with him on the *QE2* when he goes to finish the final scenes on *The Magic Christian* and the Iveys have lost an Ivey and are looking for a replacement."

"So who's left?"

"Mike, Pete and Tom."

"Do you really think they're going to make it?"

"It's hard to say. George is going to be producing Billy—"

"And White Trash?"

"They're looking around for another single. I suggested they do that Frank Zappa-Reuben and the Jets number, *Jelly Roll Gumdrop*, but they can't take it seriously."

"And Ken Kesey?"

"Poor Kesey. He was finally asked to turn in his tape recorder and typewriter and he did. He brought them back and left the typewriter in reception and of course no one bothered to look after it and a few days later Jack the Ripper-

Offer struck again and the typewriter vanishes and then someone starts the rumor, 'Kesey did it!' What a fucking mess! He'll go back to California and they'll ask him, 'Hey did you meet The Beatles? What was Apple like?' and what can he say but 'Shitty!' and Sid Bernstein's offered The Beatles four million dollars to do a few concerts but they're not interested."

"How is Jack Oliver taking the transition of his sudden promotion?"

"Very well. He understands all that dialogue about coordinating record releases and cover artwork and advertising and the foreign-market affiliates and production marketing. I think he's just about finalized the completion of that enormous billboard on Shaftesbury Avenue that's going to carry the Apple catalogue. The first ad is for *The Ballad of John and Yoko* and he's booked the escalator sites on the tube and do you realize that something like six million people a day travel on the London Underground? We've also got this problem with EMI that's been a headache from the beginning and Jack's working on that one too.

"He's trying to get Apple extricated from the swamp of the monthly EMI mailings. You see, the record dealers, the people that place the orders from the actual record distributors, have lost sight of the fact that Apple is not just a subsidiary of EMI. And it's going to be the same story with Zapple if we're not careful. The foreign licensees have been brought up to date by him as well because they've been overlooked in the rush of the last six months."

"How is Peter Asher getting on with Mortimer?"

"They're all ready to go. They've finished their album, the tapes are done all except for the single, *On Our Way Home*, which just needs some strings knocked onto it and the album cover artwork is finished and at the platemakers and we've been promised proofs within a week."

"You know Ron Kass was negotiating to bring out a Lenny Bruce record before the ax fell and—"

"Well?"

"Whatever happened to it?"

"It got shelved because we couldn't decide on a release date or whether it should be on Apple or Zapple and I doubt if it ever will get out. It was some old Lenny Bruce and some new Lenny Bruce but nothing really extraordinary . . ."

92

TEN POUNDS A WEEK AND ALL YOU CAN STEAL

THE HOUSE HIPPIE had been thinking about it all morning. Ever since Frankie Hart had told him the unbelievable double salary she was receiving as George's personal assistant and as a part-time Press Office assistant he'd been thinking of the best way to approach it. He had to wait until the right moment to pop it to The Press Officer.

"Hey, Derek, I want a raise." It seemed like the right moment.

"We call it a rise in this country."

"Raise, rise, whatever you call it I still want more money."

"What's the matter with what you're getting?"

"What, ten pounds a week?"

"Well, when I was a lad—"

"Ohh, come on, man, don't give me any of that! I need more money because I just can't make it on what I'm getting—"

"Well what can I do about it? It's not my department—"

"Come on, you're The Press Officer here, you're a big wheel, and all you have to do is ask for anything and you get it and you know it too! When Frankie told me what she's earning just as a part-time Press Office girl Friday I almost went through the ceiling! And she's only been here a few months! It's not fair and you know it!"

"Well, I can't ask for any more for you. What do the other boys get? I'm sure they're getting the same as you—"

"I'm not a boy! I'm twenty-three fucking years old and this is London 1969 we're living in just in case you forgot! Do you

194

have any idea how much you have to spend on rent alone in this city?"

"Move to a cheaper neighborhood—"

"Cheaper than Ladbroke Grove! You're joking—"

"I'm not joking—"

"People laugh when I tell them what I make working here!"

"Well then, don't tell them—"

"Look, I thought this was supposed to be the new world! That's our whole scam, that we're fresh as apples and this is the new deal but as far as I can see it's as rotten and corrupt as the world we said we were turning our backs on! It's immoral to work for a place as rich and famous as this at these slave wages and you know it! You're perpetuating a decaying and antiquated system! Ten pounds is a really solid English wage. Give an Englishman ten pounds and four tea bags and maybe he can live on it for the next twelve years but I'm finding it a little difficult—"

"That's what happens when you come from affluent middle-class America—"

"Hey, fuck you! Do you realize that there is no scale of wages in this joint? There is nothing proportionate to what anyone does. Your salary, which is extraordinary by any standards, is comparable to nothing else and of course you deserve it but don't you think I should be getting more than I am now? Come on, man. It's really a joke! Just say something to George, he'll listen to you—"

"Why don't you?"

"You know why and it's unfair to put me on the spot like that and because I'm afraid of them like everyone else around here and so are you but you've just been around so long that you're a little more *comfortable* with them, that's all. Do you know how I subsidize that shitty income I pull in every week?"

"How?"

"I take imaginary cab rides, that's how! About four times every day I go upstairs to Accounts and say, 'Hey, Brian, hey, Allen, can I have fifteen shillings for that cab ride to the *Evening Standard*.'"

"Then what do you need a rise for?"

"Because I'm running out of newspapers to go to! Because I'm running out of lies! Because I'm sick of the performance! Because it is a scive and a low scive at that! Because I'm tired of this system that's sucked me into this life of crime and because I don't want to go on stealing from The Fabs! And mind you I'm only *one* of the low-life scavengers. You should see some of the scams some of the other characters in this building have going for them. I'm almost beginning to feel like I should be paying Apple for the privilege of working here—"

"Why don't you put your request on paper?"

"Because it'll take two years before it gets answered. Because I'll die of beriberi before anyone acts on it!"

"You should see what some of the other offices are like to work in—"

"Thanks! You're all living in another world that has nothing to do with the one going on outside here! You just *can't* go on living in this hermetically sealed dream! I'm telling you! Wake up! You can't go on being Marie Antoinette forever or you'll come to the same bad end as she did!"

"All right, all right, all right, I'll see what I can do. How about a drink?"

"The ice machine's broken—"

"Then without ice!"

One Week Later.

To Whom It May Concern:

I've been employed at Apple for a year and a half as Beatle librarian and personal assistant to Derek Taylor.

I've known Derek Taylor for five years. In the light of existing circumstances I think it only fair that a reconsideration be given to my salary.

I would like to make at least as much as the guy who sweeps up the factory in America. This is not asking for much. I would like the English equivalent of seventy dollars a week. This is not an outrageous amount when you consider that I've been here a year and a half and am employed as Derek Taylor's P.A. who happens to be the world's highest paid Press Officer to the four most famous people in the world at the most prestigious record company in the universe. Besides, I add a lot of class to this place.

Respectfully,
Richard DiLello

PRESS OFFICE RELEASE to UPI, AP, Reuters, PA: Apple Records announces that their next single release. *The King of Fuh*, turned down by EMI as unsuitable for distribution under the terms of their deal with Apple, is now to be released by Apple themselves on May 16. Apple plans to market the single, written, sung and produced in New York by Brute Force, a twenty-year-old discovery of George Harrison, through certain specially selected record stores in London and the provinces and review copies have already been sent to the BBC. Mr. Jack Oliver, head of Production, says, "We plan to use mail-order outlets to distribute *The King of Fuh*. We have a comprehensive system to ensure that we do not have to submit to yesterday's means to achieve today's ends."

"So bollocks to them!!! Get this out right now and what about Bonnie and Delaney? When are we releasing their album?"

"Well, the records have been pressed and the sleeves printed and the Press Office biographies and photographs done up and the tentative release date is for mid-May but now I've heard that the whole thing has been nixed because we can't come to a settlement."

"What kind of a settlement?"

"I don't know. That's all that's been said 'We can't come to a settlement.'"

"Deals! deals! deals! All these fucking deals that start out with a bang and then go pfft! Makes you want to puke! And are we going to do anything with those girls?"

93

A GALAXY OF STARS

"Michelle, Karen and Cynthia?"

"Yeah, those three. They're very good but they said they need a producer and who are we going to get to produce them? George? We should give them an answer instead of telling them to keep coming back every day even though it's nice having them around. And that other one, Maureen, she's good too. Someone should do something with her, too. We've got to find Mary Hopkin's antithesis. It's unhealthy having—"

"Well, Nicole is about as far away from Mary Hopkin as you're going to get and she's downstairs right now and she says she wants another audition with George and she's not going to leave until she gets it."

"Christ, not Nicole again! Did you hear what happened with her the other night?"

"No—"

"Well, she was up here with that same line, ramming it down our throat. She said as soon as she gets her teeth capped she's going to be the best-looking broad that you ever saw and *then* she'd really open her mouth and show us how to sing the blues and that if we only gave her half a chance she was going to be bigger than Janis Joplin and we listened and said, 'Sure, OK, whatever you say honey but please stop *screaming!*' Christ, once she starts you can't shut her up! And then horror of horrors, George walks in and she goes all weak at the knees and suddenly clams right up. George and Derek start talking and there are at least twenty people in the office all broken up into little groups, juicing and gabbing, and the Black Room is packed with smoke and another half-dozen bodies when suddenly she picks up this guitar and starts wailing! Jesus Christ! She *does* have a powerful voice. She almost knocked the goddamn pictures off the wall! It's just that she went about it in the wrong way that blew it for her. George told her to shut up, that he was trying to carry on a conversation. Well, that's all she had to hear. It completely wiped her out. She became hysterical and George just couldn't take the aggro anymore and left. Then she started in on Derek telling him how tough things were, how she didn't have anyplace to sleep, no warm clothes, how sick of it all she was. So Derek lays her on Richard and he takes her back to his place and puts her to bed very drunk because after George told her to shut up she had to drink half a bottle of scotch to blot out the horror of it all so about half an hour later she comes back downstairs where he's watching television and she starts crying and moaning and carrying on about how the whole fucking world is against her and so he tells her she's welcome to stay as long as she cools it with all that screaming so she shuts up and says, 'OK fuck you. I don't need your charity,' and walks out the door. Well, it's snowing and she doesn't know anyone in London and it's quite obvious that she needs *something* and charity, well, there are worse things than charity when there's a blizzard raging outside, so ten minutes later there's a knock on the door and she's back smiling and says, 'I've changed my mind.' He turns around and next minute she's gone completely berserk! She hits him in the head with a saltshaker and then picks up every bottle and plate in sight and starts whacking them all over the place, knocking big chunks out of the wall. She breaks a window, destroys the teakettle, almost shatters the television screen and then he and his friend jump on her and it takes the *two of them* to stop her from completely destroying the place. His friend says, 'Hey why don't you try one of these pills?' Well, that was the magic question. She stops dead and says, 'Oh yeah, wadda ya have? 'Oh just some sleeping pills.' Next morning she wakes up and asks him, 'Did I misbehave last night?' That was just the beginning. So she had a bad night, it happens to us all but then she's back here every day bugging the shit out of everyone. She walks right in on White Trash while they're rehearsing and starts singing some song that has nothIng to do with anything they're doing. Then she's cadging cigarettes and spare change oft of all the secretaries and office boys and just anyone who walks in. *Then* the other night she got drunk again in the Press Office, so drunk that we had to get Jimmy Clark to physically remove her from the building and she's kicking up a storm like you wouldn't believe and it's pouring down with rain and she falls in the gutter and by the time he gets her into a taxi she makes the Bride of Franken-stein look like a piece of ass so Jimmy figures that once she's in the cab she'll cool herself out but then guess what happens?"

"What?"

"She drops her knickers, squats down and *pisses* right there in the back of the taxi! Imagine a chick pissing in the back of your cab! Then she jumps out and runs away. Well, the drive comes back here and gives Jimmy a bollocking, 'If this is the kind of place Apple is then don't bother to call us again,' the whole routine and I can't say as I blame him because that kind of customer is certainly no recommendation."

"Well, I hope she doesn't start pissing in reception because they've just re-covered all the chairs down there and put in a new carpet."

"Well, as soon as Jimmy sees her she's going to get her ass thrown out of here again because George has banned her from the building as public nuisance number one and I've heard that she's also been banned from about every pub in the King's Road for unruly conduct and wouldn't you know it she's back asking, 'When can I have an audition?'"

94

A GOOD SPOT OF PR FOR JOHN AND YOKO

THE TELEPHONES *never* stopped ringing. The music might go off for a few minutes and reception might empty out for a long half-hour stretch but the telephones never stopped ring-ing. It was the constant reminder that to the outside world, every action of this empire was laced with significance. It was the single reassurance that everyone was still loved.

The telephone rang. The House Hippie answered it.

"Hello, yes, yes, I'm not sure, well I didn't ask him – what? – what? – *You Go Fuck Yourself, You Prick!!!*" Blam! The telephone went rocketing into its cradle and bounced back with the force of the impact; dangling by its cord, twisting back and forth – a dead line hanging from the edge of the desk.

"Now what was *that* all about!?" asked The Press Officer.

"Th-th-th-that-t d-d-demented f-f-fucker." The House Hippie sputtered like Porky Pig.

"Now wait a minute! Calm down and start from the beginning," The Press Officer soothed.

"I answered the phone and, and, there was this guy and he said he saw John and Yoko on that television program the other night talking about peace and then he asked me, 'Will you please tell me what he was doing wearing an army jacket with sergeant's stripes on it?' and I told him I didn't know and anyway then he says, 'Well, someone like him doesn't have any business wearing an army jacket,' and then I finally caught on and figured, 'Oh shit, another one, all right,' and then he went on and said the sight of John and Yoko on the television screen was disgusting enough but the fact that two monkeys like that were given air time to spout their inane views was an insult to the public and *then* he says, 'And besides what does Yoko Ono know about anything? I heard her say no one gets any pleasure from killing another person. You don't feel good when you're doing it—' and then he said, 'Well, I'll tell *you* something,' and then his breathing got heavier, 'When I was in the army during the war I killed people all the time and nothing, but *nothing*, gave me greater pleasure than killing Japs. I *loved* it and my biggest regret was that the war had to end and there were no more Japs to *kill!* So don't tell *me* that no one takes any pleasure in killing other people. Don't you *dare* to be so presumptuous!' You should have heard his voice. My skin started to *creep* up in folds."

The telephone rang.

"Derek, call on fourteen." The Press Officer reached for the line.

"Yes, yes, this is Taylor, yes that's right I understand you just had a conversation with my colleague and he told you to go fuck yourself and, now wait a minute, I don't expect anyone in my office to use language like that with the public but then I don't expect anyone to phone up and start telling us what pleasure he gets from killing people and using words like 'Japs' either. What's that? No, no one is going to offer you an apology. Now listen! I want you to understand this very clearly and it's of no concern to me whether you report this organization to the Press Council and I'm not worried if you are six foot three and weigh fifteen stone. I'm not going to have you threaten any of my staff with violence and I'm warning you right now that if you pursue this line of unbalanced reasoning I'm going to phone the West End Central Police Station which is one block from us and I'll have you dealt with immediately and I mean that. Don't you dare tell me you're going to smash in anyone's face and don't you ever call back here with a mouth full of evil words like that and a heart filled with hate. I might remind you that this is a record company and we're quite unprepared to deal with individuals in your state of mind. *That* is the end of this conversation!" The Press Officer hung up. "That," he continued, visibly shaken, "was a real dyed-in-the-wool psychotic. I see what you mean about his voice. He said he was six foot three and weighed fifteen stone and if we didn't apologize for the foul language we used with him he was going to come in here and 'punch that American's face in' – that's *you* kid."

"Uhh ohh! We better tell Debbie if anyone answering that description comes in here to tell him that the American working in the Press Office has gone home! Do you think this could mushroom into a tragedy? Do you think he could come in here and work J and Y over?"

"No, no I think that's the last we'll hear of him, it was all talk. He just wanted a bit of aggravation but keep an eye out all the same for the next few days because I don't want you getting your head broken for *anyone*. I think it's my duty to warn you that you wouldn't even receive a 'thank you' for your trouble and it's nothing personal, that's just the way it is."

PRESS OFFICE RELEASE to UPI, AP, Reuters, Pa: The Lennon/McCartney composition, *Hey Jude*, today received (May 22) the Ivor Novello Award for the highest certified British sales in 1968, though not released until August 1968.

"The Iveys have placed ads in all the trades advertising for a rhythm guitarist and singer. They've auditioned about thirty musicians already but no luck. Some of them look good and sound awful and others sound good and look awful. The rest have been adequate but there was no thread of communication so they're still looking. Derek's flying back from New York tomorrow afternoon. He called this morning and said the trip over with Ringo on the *QE2* was fine but he's got to get back because John is planning another Bed-In as soon as he gets his visa which is being withheld because of his drug bust. He was made an offer by the visa people. They said, 'We'll let you into the States if you allow yourself to be interviewed on radio and television by a handpicked team and publicly denounce your former flirtation with drugs as a foolish and dangerous escapade and tell the young people of the United States that it is in their best interests to bring an immediate halt to any further use of *all* drugs.' They're trying to break his back over that barrel but he won't go along with them. It's blackmail of the lowest order and they must be quite naive if they think they can make him cop out on that level. They're afraid that if they let him into the States for a repeat of the Amsterdam Bed-In he's going to fuck up their works but all he's saying and has been saying since *Revolution* is 'Stop all this bloodletting, *everybody*,' but they never bothered to listen to the words. You'd think that they actually want all that goddamn discord to continue. When *Revolution* came out it was expressing a very unpopular sentiment as a contribution from the youth faction in the wake of the May '68 riots in Paris and his passive stand at the moment is in direct opposition to what is going on in the universities in California and the rest of America. John wants to talk to Nixon on the phone with a radio link-up broadcast but of course there's no chance that that will happen."

"So how is he going to get into the States?"

"Well, The Beatles are too important an economic commodity to blackball indefinitely so it's going to take time and a lot of string-pulling but after a while they'll just drop it but they've got to maintain the pretense that there are grounds for refusal on a moral issue which they are bound to uphold."

"What else is in the wind?"

"Housecleaning—"

"Housecleaning?"

"Alistair Taylor was declared redundant after seven years as a devoted Beatle aide and the Publishing department was completely cleared out for the time being and Brian Lewis and Dennis O'Dell have resigned and Neil has been removed as the managing director of Apple Corps, Ltd."

"Neil!"

"Yeah, but he's not going anywhere, he's just going on paper. Don't forget he's practically *married* to The Fabs. There's a handful of secretaries and at first glance it looks like a full-scale slaughter but once the smoke clears it *might* not seem so bad. Peter Asher has also handed in his resignation. He said he finds the new regime and the prospect of having to account to Klein too much to take—"

"Well then, what's happening with James Taylor? It's a hand and hand deal it would seem—"

"Exactly. So James will piss off with Peter, which doesn't really come as a surprise to any of us because he's discouraged with his lack of any tangible success through us. Nothing's jelled the way any of us thought it would and I don't have any explanation why he's not a star yet or why Jackie Lomax isn't or why White Trash's record failed. There *are* a lot of excuses but damned few reasons. I'd venture to say, though, that any of those other rosebuds that bloomed, like Elektra and Atlantic and Motown, went through a few years of shit and disappointment before someone could sit up and say, 'Hey they're doing all right!' but then again this place is truly singular and comparable to nothing before it and if anything is to blame it's that all our energy has been so multidirectional that, like Derek says, 'Our records are hits but our misses are magnified,' and I hope like he also says that, 'Our future is magnificent.' But the hands our future has been placed in are the ones we said we were trying to get away from, so ideologically we're a failure on that score and we're back at peg one and starting all over again.''

T HE PRESS OFFICER bought himself a splendid white linen suit for the event. He called it his Bed-In suit and it was most appropriate for their destination – the Bahamas. John and Yoko Lennon had wanted to stage their next peace spectacular in the United States but since John's application for a visa was still on appeal and pending approval, they decided the next best place, owing to its geographical proximity to the USA, was Freeport in the Bahamas.

The Lennons' entourage included Derek Taylor, a two-man film crew, Yoko's daughter, Kyoko, and their personal assistant, Anthony Fawcett, plus 26 pieces of John and Yoko's personal luggage which cost $1200 in overweight every time they moved. They changed planes twice, at Bermuda and at Nassau, before arriving in Freeport.

When they arrived in Freeport it seemed that everything was against them. The weather was oppressively hot and the local residents turned out to be aggressively belligerent. They were shamelessly charged $2.50 for a glass of orange juice by the hotel management and the food appeared to be nastily cooked on purpose. All of that might have been ignored and the Bed-In could have gone on had it not been for one fatal flaw. The hotel rooms only had *twin beds* and they were *cemented* to the floor.

That night a strategy meeting was held and it was decided that Canada was the next to the next best place for a Bed-In for peace.

At Toronto Immigration the Lennons' party met with more aggravation. The authorities seized their passports and put a block on their leaving the airport lounge pending a special appeal for entry into North America. After four hours of bullying and bad treatment they were reluctantly granted a provisionary entry. They were, however, refused permission to hold a scheduled press conference.

A restless night at the King Edward Hotel was passed before flying out next morning to Montreal. In the midst of all this movement there had been a string of desperate telephone calls to Allen Klein who was working on securing John his visa to the USA, hoping it had come through or might do so at any minute. No such luck.

The Bed-In took place at the Queen Elizabeth Hotel in Montreal and in the space of ten days the Lennons dished out over 60 interviews to the world press. On Saturday between 8 P.M. and 3 A.M. the next morning, a song called *Give Peace a Chance* was rehearsed and with John Lennon conducting an assembled roomfull of friends and well-wishers that included Tommy Smothers, Rosemary and Tim Leary and the Canadian chapter of the Radha Krishna Temple, the Capitol Records mobile sound unit recorded the song that was soon to become the anthem of the world-push-for-peace movement.

The entire run-through and recording of the song was being documented on film by a triangle that included John's camera-man for Bag Films, Nick Knowland, the CBC, the BCBC, and Murray the K filming the entire John Lennon/Yoko Ono Peace Choir at work.

Sunday afternoon John and Yoko gave a string of interviews that included a Quebec Separatist and the most unpleasant experience of the voyage, Al Capp, who came on as Ace Professional Heckler sent to do battle with the Yellow Peril & Co. In the space of a few short minutes Capp's rage at the sight of John and Yoko became evident.

When he began hurling blatant racial jabs at Yoko, The Press Officer could no longer contain himself. He told him to get out. John Lennon at that point waded in and reminded The Press Officer that Al Capp was *their* guest and even if *he* could not keep a civil tongue, John expected his staff to show some restraint. He asked The Press Officer to apologize to Al Capp. It would have been easier to eat a bar of brown laundry soap than to apologize to Al Capp but in his great love for John Lennon The Press Officer swallowed hard and made his apologies for having interrupted Mr. Capp's tirade.

The Lennons' party, by now aware that the hoped-for visa would never come through, still with its 26 pieces of luggage, left Montreal by road heading for Ottawa where they boarded a train that took them to Toronto where they were told that there was no direct flight back to London. Their frustrating detour dropped them at Frankfurt on the anniversary of D-Day, where they had to crawl through the mud of more antagonistic bureaucratic abuse before making it home free all to England. It had been a very exhausting Bed-In.

97
HOW GREEN WAS OUR VALLEY

THEY'RE DRIVING ME nuts! Stan Sherrington was just up in the Press Office looking very dejected and vibrating utter neglect, moaning about the total lack of press coverage on Mary, which seems a little out of line under the circumstances since they're the ones that are so fucking apathetic about their own public relations *and* the press know it too! You'd get the impression that they're out to deliberately undermine our working policy of cultivating publicity. For instance, that interview with Anne Nightingale was just forgotten completely and the suggestion that Mary do a photo session with *Fabulous* was *ignored*. We had three scheduled interviews that were held up because Mary was late and when she finally arrived no apologies were offered to the journalists. That entire period following the release of *Postcard* and *Goodbye*, when we asked Stan about Mary's availability and willingness to do interviews, he said, 'Oh don't worry, she won't have to do too much, the record's going to take care of it for us.' *Then* on Mary's birthday when we tried to arrange a picture session with the *Daily Express* for Mary's first birthday as a star we couldn't, for the life of us, get in touch with either Mary or Stan. On her first tour, telegrams and messages were left all over the place to contact Stan without any success whatsoever. I mean he must have received *one* of those telegrams. Then Alan Smith of the *New Musical Express* tried to get in touch with Mary to do a story, he tried to get her in New York and Canada – failure! Complete communications breakdown. Every week we call her agent's office for a few newsworthy lines and if we're lucky they blurt out a few monosyllables. If one of the nationals is given a story they expect a quote and usually like to send around one of their own photographers to take a few pictures and more often than not Mary is unavailable or doesn't feel up to it. We give her to John Kelly to photograph and he turns out a beautiful session of her with bare shoulders and her father goes up the wall! Bare shoulders, that's *all!* So will you please tell me what the fuck are we supposed to do?!''

98
THE HOUSE OF THE OPEN DOOR

HE NEVER SAID VERY much but it was obvious that Stocky was an intelligence going to waste. His artistic talent was in evidence in the reams of poetry and the pen and ink drawings that were left scattered over the Press Office floors, stuck to the walls and crammed into desk drawers.

Stocky woke one morning and realized that if his soul were going to flourish and take flight it would have to be from a vantage point other than on top of the filing cabinets of the Pineapple Archives. As the existentialist fly on the wall he had become an unquestioned part of the office furniture. The news that he was going home to Massachusetts was met with a mixture of delight for his own salvation and ultimate regret at the loss of this amicable and gentle soul.

Before he left Stocky had discovered that the enormous barrel in the Black Room, that souvenir of Mary Hopkin's press reception, was a vehicle of pleasure in disguise. All you had to do was jump in the barrel, ignite one Benson and Hashish B-52 Bomber, squat down, swing an improvised lid over the top and *blast off!* Having finished the spliff in the tranquil belly of the barrel one would emerge throughly saturated and totally zonked.

One afternoon as The House Hippie oozed out from a super session in the barrel into the Press Office, the shriek of an internal telephone drew him to his desk. It was Tony Bramwell at the other end.

"There's some guy down here who says he used to play with the Quicksilver Messenger Service and he wants to see someone in the Press Office."

"About what?"

"I don't know."

"What's his name?"

"The Sundance Kid."

99
DIALOGUE/ DIALOGUE/ DIALOGUE

I T'S PRETTY QUIET at the moment. Paul and Linda are in the south of France, George and Patti are in Sardinia, Ringo's taking it easy for a while and *The Ballad of John and Yoko* is moving up the charts like electric vaseline. Chris O'Dell is now doing the studio bookings and is going to head Apple's album-promotion campaign. Captain Beefheart called Derek and asked him if there was a chance of his getting onto Apple but somehow I can't see that happening. The word from Klein's office is that there is going to be a drastic cutback in the liquor supply allowed for entertaining—"

"Oh my God!"

". . . and he's established a system of purchase orders so that no one working for the company can go out like they've been doing and charge anything they want to Apple. Now anytime that you've got to buy something you get an order form from the Accounts office which has the name of the supplier it's coming from, what it is, what it's for and how much it costs. Then it goes through Klein's office for clearance and approval. It's a deadly efficient system and Klein's moved his left-hand man, Peter Howard, into the empty office opposite Derek's room and he's going to be looking after the whole show when Klein's not here. *Get Back* chalked up another gold record by the last week in April and Jackie's single, *New Day*, is still hanging around doing nothing which is a motherfucker because we figured if the A side didn't make it, the B side, *Fall Inside Your Eyes*, was sure to act as the flip-side eleventh-hour rescue job. *That's The Way God Planned It* by Billy is out on the twenty-fifth of June and it looks like George just can't sit still. You know all those guys with the shaved heads and the saffron robes? Well, they're the devotees of that Indian god Krishna and their number is going around chanting this mantra—"

"A what?"

"It's like the Indian 'Hail Mary' and anyway this mantra zonks them out of their heads and sends them into a state of cosmic bliss and George is really far fucking into *it* and *them* and is going to be producing a single for them. J and Y have conceived of an extension for their musical collaborations. They're calling it the Plastic Ono Band. They're having a unit built which is representative of a quartet made of molded plastic. One figure is cylindrical, another square and two are rectangular. Inside one there's going to be a Sony tape recorder, in another a standard record turntable, a speaker cabinet in another and then a closed-circuit television set to play films through and to see your own reflection in to complete the show. Nice idea, huh? J and Y have also got their own breakaway splinter company called Bag Productions to handle all their stuff and John's told Derek he wants a big press launching for the Plastic Ono Band's first record, which is *Give Peace a Chance* from the Montreal Bed-In and it's set for an early July release. They're going to be cooling it a bit with all their interviews and Yoko says they're thinking of taking a motoring holiday in England and Scotland and they certainly could use the rest because they're dangerously overloading their circuits with all these projects but no one dares to even suggest that they lay off it for a while. Other than that there really isn't much going on right now."

FROM DEREK TAYLOR to Peter Howard: Dear Peter, Can I buy a £150 light show for the Press Office? It has no commercial merit but it looks nice. Even in our present hours of ease we get visits from people who would like that sort of thing and feel happier because it's there. Many of the presidents of large organizations who have, however, not yet lost their sensitivity and who still, even between the hours of nine and five, possess the capacity to respond joyfully when they see something beautiful are to be found among our guests; and certainly they are prolific tale bearers, and many of them, indeed, are drug addicts. However, if you think this is a misspending of apple's money then I could always order filing cabinets or something like it and kid you and our masters . . . Jesus, I wish I were still on holiday.

"A light show?"

"Well, you know what he's like. Go on, let him have his light show. Anyway it's impossible to say no to Derek and besides I wouldn't want to."

100
SAY PLEASE

MAVIS SAYS THE Chelsea Town Hall is the place for our *Give Peace a Chance* press reception. She's over there now checking it out," said The Press Officer. Five minutes later The House Hippie asked The Press Officer about the four articles on The Beatles he had been commissioned to write for one of the musical papers.

101
GIVE PEACE A CHANCE

"Glad you reminded me. Ringo is done, George is done, Paul is done, even though that wasn't really an article because I just submitted ten false starts which is indicative of—"

"And John?"

"Well, that's finished today but I can't decide about the title."

"What did you have in mind?"

"I thought of calling it – Lennon! The Greatest Man That Ever Lived! What do you think about that?"

"Well he'd probably agree with you but—"

"But what?"

"Don't you think it's a bit excessive?"

"Excessive!"

"Well, maybe you're right, maybe it is isn't, yeah, sure, why not, you could probably get away with it, yeah actually that sounds pretty good – Lennon! The Greatest Man That Ever Lived! do it—"

"Well, I'll think about it some more. Yoko's designed the acorn box—" which reminded The House Hippie, "Shit I almost forgot about that! The guy's coming in this afternoon who's going to wrap all those packages for us and all we have to do is give him the materials. I gave all the address labels to the printer but when he brought them back they looked *awful* and they're going to have to be done all over again. What do the acorn boxes look like?"

"Clear plastic and round, filled with white cotton wool padding. There's the two acorns and then a round white card with black letters reading 'Acorn Peace by John and Yoko – Spring 1969.' They're very good-looking in that minimal way she does her work but we've got to get a move on with them because they should have been out of here last week. It's getting to the point where the next time John asks me, 'Are they ready?' they fucking better be ready or we'll all lose our jobs."

"No, we won't."

"Of course we won't but it's a guaranted bollocking and what was the matter with the printing on the labels?"

"The usual English printer's fuck-up. If it's not one thing it's—"

"Sure, sure, but what was the matter?"

"They were all cockeyed and only half the impression on some of the letters registered and they looked like shit and I told the guy, 'That's the last time we're using you,' and then he promised to do an ace patch-up job to make up for it and at half price and—"

When Mavis Smith returned to 3 Savile Row, Chelsea Town Hall was decided on as the best place for the *Give Peace a Chance* press reception. It would easily hold as many people as the Press Office could think of inviting and it had an elevated stage on which the perspex robots of the Plastic Ono Band could be comfortably displayed with all its electrical parapher-nalia. At the same time an enormous black-and-white photo-graphic collage/backdrop for the Plastic Ono Band had been ordered and was by now nearing completion.

"And John and Yoko are going to launch the reception which will make it an actual event and we're having invitations printed which are postcards with a black and white photograph of the Plastic Ono Band and on the back it reads, 'Apple Peace/ Postcard/Communication/John and Yoko and Apple Records invite you to join them on Thursday this week, July 3, to meet the Plastic Ono Band in Chelsea Town Hall, Kings Road.'

"Says what has to be said and when are J and Y getting back from wherever it is they are?"

"John said they'd be back in plenty of time to liaise with us on the reception and as far as I know they've been up in Scotland just driving around looking at the hills and the heather and I'd say that's a fucking good light show we got for this office, wouldn't you?"

July 1, 1969

The vehicle careened into the ditch by the side of the road. The front of the car took the impact and was badly crushed. The chassis was also badly damaged. The main impact was taken by the front suspension and the engine. The car is not navigable. John received 17 stitches, Yoko 14 and Yoko's daughter, Kyoko, 4. They are resting comfortably in hospital.

"Christ, they must have fucking awful headaches but a total

213

of thirty-one stitches between them isn't that bad when you think they could have killed themselves as easily – and two days before the reception!"

"Should we cancel it?"

"Fuck no! I spoke to John this morning, you know he was driving when it happened and he isn't a driving man, hasn't driven for years, he must have forgotten what he was supposed to be doing and next minute it's screaming pandemonium in the ditch with fucking blood and broken glass everywhere."

"So anyway what did he say when you spoke to him?"

"To send up a film crew and we'll tape a greeting from the hospital bed and then play it back through the closed-circuit television in the Plastic Ono Band. So they'll be there on film and in spirit anyway. It's a bad omen for that to have happened right now."

July 2, three o'clock in the afternoon.

"The film crew called me an hour ago and said that when they arrived this morning John and Yoko were feeling so shitty that they wouldn't see them. So they're on their way back now without the film and we'll just have to go ahead without it and them. Try and be at the Town Hall no later than eleven o'clock on Thursday morning, there's going to be a lot to do before they all start arriving."

July 3

In the humid early-morning hours of July 3, Brain Jones choked to death on the anguish of his own life in a swimming pool in the English countryside. A pall clung to the day with a fierce tenacity that no one could shake.

By two o'clock that afternoon the electrical idiosyncrasies that had been harrassing the Plastic Ono Band had been ironed out to perfection and the stage-filling backdrop had been erected and the elaborate floral arrangements placed throughout the hall. The room leading off the main hall was fitted out with the caterer's banquet tables and though only 300 invitations had been sent out, food and drink for 500 had been ordered with a reserve supply on call. The white banners

214

with the black letters reading Love and Peace that had seemed so large in the Press Office were reduced to postage-stamp proportions in the enormous belly of this meeting hall, more suited for mass bar examinations and choral recitals than a press reception for a record by the Plastic Ono Band.

Everything was ready by 5:30 when the first guests arrived. The Press Officer gave an inspired speech explaining John and Yoko's absence and their hope for the message behind *Give Peace a Chance*. He encouraged everyone to eat and drink and above all to dance. The 300 people scattered across the plain of the hardwood floor under the cathedral-like ceiling seemed very, very small and isolated from each other. The volume of the PA system that was swinging somewhere below distortion and above comprehension yelped out Apple's fourteenth single release over and over again.

It took gargantuan amounts of alcohol before anyone could be coaxed into dancing. Finally, on someone's slurred suggestion, a line of bodies was formed back to front and an inebriated and demented snake chain began bunny-hopping to the only record that was heard that day. It coiled its way around the hall, back and forth, mindless and dazed by the rhythm of its own locomotion.

Mercifully the event called itself off by eight o'clock.

102

"LISTEN, IF YOU CAN GET THE PAPERS DRAWN UP REAL QUICK I'VE GOT SOMEONE WHO IS READY TO BUY THE BROOKLYN BRIDGE"

PRESS OFFICE RELEASE to UPI, AP, Reuters, PA: On behalf of Apple Corps and associated companies Apple spokesman Derek Taylor today said, "Allen Klein, who one month ago signed a business contract with The Beatles and their company Apple Corps, Ltd., is not, as was reported in *Variety*, July 2, in any way terminating his relationship with The Beatles or with their associated companies. It is not true as suggested in *Variety* that his representation of the Rolling Stones and Donovan has impaired his relationship with The Beatles. The New York firm of Eastman and Eastman, said by *Variety* to be taking a more active role in managing the Beatles' business affairs, in fact acts solely as representatives of Beatle Paul McCartney as an individual. Eastman and Eastman does not act as general counsel for The Beatles or any of their companies. Apple, Beatles, Eastman and Klein have over the past few months established a warm, workable relationship which is to their benefit.''

"A warm, workable relationship! If it goes on like it's going on right now and if the split gets any wider this show-business dynasty is going to look like the OK Corral and that garage in Chicago on St. Valentine's Day.''
"Well, what do they have against each other?''
"It's not so much that they've got anything against each other personally but that they're all going after the big fish, the ultimate prize—''
"And that is?''
"Control of The Beatle millions!''

103
THE SALVATORE GULIANO COMMANDO UNIT OF THE POPULAR FRONT FOR THE LIBERATION OF REGGIO CALABRIA AND THE SUNDANCE KID

THE SUNDANCE KID RODE into Apple on an imitation white Fender Stratocaster guitar. Delicately opening its case he looked up at The House Hippie and asked, "Hey, man, do you know where I can sell this ax?''
"Is it hot?''
"Nahh, I just need some bread to hold me over till I get back on my feet. By the way I'm the Sundance Kid.''
"So I heard.''
"But you can call me Sundance.''
"OK, Sundance. I heard that you play with the Quicksilver Messenger Service.''
"Yeah I gigged with them for awhile.''
"Did you play on that 'Happy Trails' album?''
"Yeah I did a little work on that.''
"Well, that's one of our favorite albums around here. We've

already worn out one copy of it and you know a really freaky thing about it is that there's a bass note in the middle of *Who Do You Love?* that has exactly the same frequency as the call buzzer on the Press Office intercom system."

"Oh yeah?"

"Yeah. So what can we do for you?"

"Well, I thought while I was in London I'd see if I could get together and gig with some musicians and I thought maybe you could put me in touch with some of them."

"Who'd you have in mind?"

"Oh, Mick Jagger, Steve Winwood, Eric Clapton, cats like that, cats that are *into* something."

A while later.

The Press Officer looked at The House Hippie, the strain and pressures of his job etched deep into his usually boyish face. He stood with his hands in his back pocket and with a backward toss of his head shook his hair from his forehead.

"What the hell does that guy who calls himself the Sundance Kid want from us?" he asked.

"Come on, Derek, you know what he wants! He just wants to hang around the office and get high and meet The Beatles, the usual routine. He's OK, man, he's really quite harmless."

"Yeah sure! Every time I turn around he's shoving those poems of his into my face, 'Hey, man, you wanna read some Sundance poems?' Well, I've read them and I'll tell you he's another one of those California acid-casualty mind-wreck jobs and you know it too! If anyone should recognize the symptoms I expect it to be *you!*"

"Yeah, I know, Derek, but what the fuck, he's kind of, well, *simpatico.*"

"*Simpatico!* He's scrawling those drawings of his all over the place! Look at the walls! George says, 'I don't want any smoking in the building, understand?' which doesn't mean we can't have the odd smoke in the bog, it just means be *discreet.* So what happens? George walks in the other day and there he is rolling joints on the press table with this big grin on his face and an enormous bag of grass just sitting there in front of him. George says, 'Who the fuck is that?' and as his highly respected and extremely well paid Press Officer all I can say is, 'That's the Sundance Kid.' He gave me a very *strange* look."

"Well, I tried, man. I said to him, "Hey, Sundance, why don't you go see Jo Bergman at the Stones office? They're just down the block and she can probably turn you onto some good people!"

"What did he say to that?"

" 'Oh that's cool, man, don't worry about it, I'll be all right. Besides I'm so stoned I couldn't even walk to the bathroom.' "

"We certainly get all the winners—"

"Has John got his visa yet?"

"No but Klein's working on it. He'll get it sooner or later."

"What did Paul say when you spoke to him?"

"Oh just that he doesn't want to give any more interviews for the next ten years and to pass the word around."

"Well, that makes the gig a lot easier."

"It's not a gig anymore, it's a scive."

At that moment the door opened. The familiar, dirty, wide-brimmed hat of the Sundance Kid walked in with its owner. His face was creased with its permanent grin, his eyes were the usual slits. He looked at The Press Officer and then at The House Hippie." Hey, you guys," he said, "you feel like smokin' some outta sight shit?"

104

PRESS OFFICE RELEASE

RESS OFFICE RELEASE to UPI, AP, Reuters, PA: To Linda (née Eastman) and Paul McCartney, a daughter (6 lb. 8 oz.) Mary, at 1:30 A.M. today, August 28, 1969, in St. John's Wood. London. All well.

THE PRESS OFFICER called for a drink and shook his head uttering a sardonic, under-the-breath chuckle. "I don't believe it!" he moaned.

"It's one of those things, chief," observed The House Hippie. "It only goes to show you that there are very few people you can trust."

Mavis Smith looked at him with genuine concern and asked, "But who is this guy, Derek? What actually happened?"

"The guy? He was just another one of those kids that keeps coming through this place. He came in one day and said, 'I've got a magazine,'' and he showed it to me. 'OK, fine, what can we do for you?' He told me, 'Nothing right now,' and then he sat down and started helping the girls stuff envelopes. Next time he came in to 'help out' he asked me if John and Yoko would contribute a record to his magazine, one of those paper jobs. He said he found someone to manufacture them for him and there wouldn't be any financial involvement from us. All he wanted was the record. I told him that I'd ask them, thinking they'd probably say no, but they said yes. I told him and then he asked me when could he expect it because he had to let his advertisers know. I asked them and they said you can have it by so-and-so and then I got back to him and gave him the promised date. Then he pulls this piece of paper out of his pocket and fills in the date and asks me to sign it. He said it was just a formality and that he needed a guarantee to show the advertisers that he'd gotten John and Yoko to donate a record which would be the vote of confidence they were looking for. So I signed it. Now I just thought he was some kid being efficient but what I didn't know was that his uncle was a lawyer and had been giving him advice as he was going along. To make it short, the day of the deadline comes up and of course there's no record. Next thing I got a letter saying, 'You're being sued!' A breach of contract. So I tell John and he says, 'Don't worry, we've got something you can give him.' So I call him back and tell him we've got the record and he says that if we can give him a second date of delivery he'll drop the whole thing. Well 'that something' turns out to be a

219

recording John made of the baby's heartbeat that Yoko miscarried last year. It was just five seconds but it was rerecorded and stretched out to four minutes. Some solid Lennon social commentary. Then he comes over with his uncle and we go downstairs and play the dead baby's heartbeat to them and they just couldn't believe it! They said, 'That's quite unacceptable and in the poorest taste,' and left. So now I'm getting sued and then after I've been sued I've got to sue John to even it up so that we break even but of course we haven't broken even at all."

106

**DIALOGUE/
DIALOGUE/
DIALOGUE**

FRANKIE HART HAS GONE back to California and now Terry Doran is George's personal assistant and The Beatles have begun another album over at EMI and we've got a press reception to launch the Hare Krishna Mantra at a marquee in Sydenham which George said he's going to attend and on top of Billy and the Krishnas he's found this chick named Doris Troy who's being signed to Apple and who he's going to produce as well. Billy's album is out and in the shops and Chris O'Dell is working to get some action to boost sales and what *can* we tell the press about Magic Alex and Apple Electronics? For all the thousands of pounds poured into it we've got nothing to show, no major break-through, no industry-shattering inventions, just a lot of dialogue, that's all. Our first birthday is on August 30 and there's going to be a party in Jack Oliver's office to celebrate the fact and someone just told me that Apple has been declared the most successful new record company of the year due largely to the efforts of Ron Kass."

SO LAUREN BACALL telephones this morning and says that she's in town for a while with her daughter Leslie Bogart and her son Sam Robards and would we mind if she brought them over to meet the Beatles and of course we wouldn't mind. We'll do anything to oblige anyone at any time but first I have to check it out and see if there are going to be any Beatles in the building to fill the request. Paul's at home with Linda and the kids so forget him and John and Yoko are out editing some film and George might be coming in and Ringo says sure. So we call her back and tell her to come over at one o'clock. By one o'clock they're in reception. Lauren Bacall! With all that silky hair and still as handsome a woman as any of those movies of hers that you've seen. Her daughter Leslie Bogart is one of those tall, scrubbed teenage American beauties with the dark hair parted in the middle and Sam Robards couldn't have been more than eleven and just a little chap who was in London and was about to meet The Beatles. Together the three of them were like some impossibly perfect picture postcard. They went upstairs and met Ringo who had arrived an hour before and God bless him! He was charming and chatty and amusing and so together that he created the illusion that they had met all four Beatles. It was the nicest kind of PR job done in the nicest way. Then it was time for them to go and we were standing in reception making our farewells and she was thanking us for being so nice and hoped we might be able to get together next time around when George walks in loaded down with tapes and records and looking very preoccupied. Well, little Sam sees him and freaks! There's George and it's two out of four and the excitement is too much for the kid. He rushes up to George and he's trying to make his way through the lobby on a quick, clean run. 'George!' he screams at him and George looks down at this kid who's just thrown his name at him full in the face and recoils in horror, shrinks back and makes it up the stairs two at a time. We're all standing there looking at each other and none of us knowing what to say because there's really nothing to say. Little Sam is totally bewildered by the whole thing and then Lauren says, 'That's all right. I always knew George was the mean one,' and then they left."

"But he's *not* mean!"

"Of course he's not! He's just a grown man who's been Beatled too many times now and won't play the game because it takes too fucking much out of you. It's a pain in the ass to always have people pounding on the roof of your car so that you'll look at them so that they can see what you look like when you look at them, to always have someone tugging on your arm to make you turn around so they can shoot their Instamatic off in your face and burn your retinas out, to hear that voice that says, 'Hey, George, give us a smile!' No, he just can't go along with it anymore, that's all."

108
CONSPECTUS

T HE LODESTAR OF THE Lennons' relentless peace campaign began tapering off with their car crash in Scotland and the beginning of the recording sessions in mid-July at EMI studios for The Beatles' thirteenth and final album. It was a run that had lasted four and a half months.

The previously recorded album with its accompanying film and documentary book had by now become a major migraine heartache. It had been decided that the film was no longer suited for a television audience and should be aimed at the major cinema circuit exclusively. The album itself was nothing more than dozens of tape cans of take after take of songs that had been laboriously and unenthusiastically ground out in January. It lay there, an almost forgotten effort that was more of a throwaway than a serious consideration for a Beatles album release.

The book of the filming of the album was not doing much better. EMI, in its insistence on censoring the script and the final sifting of approval from Apple, had reduced it from a potentially major work on The Beatles to a bowl of unpalatable pap. The writers, Jonathan Cott and David Dalton, were the first to admit it. When they received the final corrected proof they were horror-struck. Not only had any semblance of honesty and literacy been sucked out completely but massive chunks of dialogue that had come from Paul had somehow been credited to John and vice versa, cross and fire. Everyone was talking everyone else's lines.

The photographer and designer of the book, Ethan Russell and John Kosh, had to crawl through 14 different color separations to obtain a satisfactory set before they could think of having the photographic plates made. John Kosh, from the time the last transparencies had been delivered, up until the final printing of the book and its release with the album, had spent an accumulated four months in New York, courtesy of Allen Klein and Apple, in an attempt to get it looking as it had been visualized. It had become a major project that undeniably had been smacked by a plague of bad luck.

Allen Klein, in charge of placing the film in its most lucrative market, and Neil Aspinall, whose artistic child it had been from the beginning, became involved in a yoyo nightmare of deals and cross deals that shelved its debut for months to come. And all the while the press and the musical public kept asking, "When is it coming out?"

By August 1969, the Apple roster included The Beatles, Mary Hopkin, James Taylor in exile, Jackie Lomax, the Iveys, White Trash, Doris Troy, Billy Preston, the Radha Krishna Temple, the phantom Plastic Ono Band and the Modern Jazz Quartet.

The enormous rush of Mary Hopkin's first success was being tailed by a predictable and anticlimactic follow-up, financially and psychologically. She was cruising at a secure speed at a comfortable and unadventurous altitude. The opinion was voiced that she would celebrate her twenty-first birthday on the stage of the London Palladium hosting a gala night of the stars for some worthy charity.

James Taylor was the one that got away and no one seemed to have noticed. His departure was watched with a passive shrug of the shoulders and an attitude which said, "Well, that's less sweat for Father, now isn't it?" One seven-year cycle was about to end and no one except Peter Asher and James Taylor seemed to have any idea that he was the loaf in the oven that was *just* about to click into the new musical diet of the 1970s.

Billy Preston and Doris Troy were artists who had made it in a black market and were now in a position where their talents would receive wider and hopefully more lucrative recognition. That end, it was predicted, was going to be achieved with greater facility with George Harrison at the control knobs as their Svengali producer.

The Modern Jazz Quartet was the piece that had never quite fit the pattern of the jigsaw puzzle. They had been brought in by Ron Kass to give some class and diversification to a strictly pop stable. But there had never been a whisper about them. Not so much as a token biography or one press-handout photo had ever been sent the ravenous media. There was nothing which Apple could add to a success story that had been galloping on, unchecked, for the past ten years.

George Harrison's involvement with the Radha Krishna Temple and his running dialogue with the devotees of Krishna was the singular eccentric musical product from Apple that could have been nothing if not a labor of love for God. Their sexual appeal was instantly recognizable as being nonexistent. Spiritually it was known that they would find only a minority acceptance.

It was felt by now that Jackie Lomax was going to be one of those overnight successes that is usually years in the making. That he had everything that was needed to make it was never for one moment in doubt. But the question he asked was the same one being voiced by his record company – "When?"

White Trash had had to make violent personal adjustments when they moved from the wastelands of the Scottish ballroom circuit down to London. The cultural blitz that had met them at first stood in the way of their breaking from their tested and familiar repertoire of songs and attitudes. The belief in their abilities and the virtue of patience was the two-way split. They knew they were a good band with the potential to become a great one but somehow their record company had never bothered to have a listen.

224

The Plastic Ono Band was John Lennon's move from The Beatles into musical manhood and it came in a brilliant rush with the doped-up screaming agony of *Cold Turkey*. It was clearly visible that the steps would be taken in their logical sequence. There wasn't a chance in hell that he was about to jump straight into middle age. As a Lennon-driven and Ono-inspired musical unit, with Yoko's proclivity for science-fiction wipe-out vocals, nothing but success had been anticipated. The lingering cloud of self-doubt about that prediction was what gave the venture some excitement. Achievement is empty without a few butterflies in the stomach.

Like an iceberg with only one-tenth of its power showing above the surface, the Iveys' demo tape walked into Apple in that early summer of 1968 under Mal Evans' arm with only a fraction of the gleam of the light they were to become. It was their uncanny resemblance to the young Beatles that had made everyone sit up and listen but it was no conscious aping of their benefactors that had produced that similarity of sound. A year later they were still moving forward. It was too early in their career and too premature a phase in Apple's history for anyone to realize that they were about to become the best thing to walk through the fallout of the Longest Cocktail Party, looking like the Mediterranean on a beautiful day.

AN OUTSIDER COMING into Apple would say it's chaos, it's run by hippies and drug addicts, but it's not. It's run by people who know and it doesn't matter how long you take to do a thing. They set out to do it and they do it, they always do it." – Ian Clews, lead singer of White Trash in an interview with Tony Norman, *Top Pops* and *Music Now*.

The Press Officer, with some coaxing from The House Hippie, had grown quite fond of White Trash over the months. They had spent long afternoons draped over the Press Office

109
THE PULSE-POUNDING EXCITEMENT OF THE GOLDEN AGE OF SCOTTISH GORBALS ROCK CONTINUES

couches smoking, drinking and talking. That their career at the moment was at a dead standstill bothered him. That they were in need of encouragement from their record company was obvious. This was the most frequent complaint among the Apple artists: "Nothing is being done for us." It was usually only a half truth and came from frustration born out of desperation.

White Trash had been signed to Apple on a single-record contract with the option to be picked up by the record company, meaning that the relationship could be terminated on any number of lurking technicalities. They were therefore in a precarious position that did not allow for too many more chart misses.

The Press Officer addressed Mavis Smith and The House Hippie: "We've got to do something for that group and my suggestion is now that The Beatles have finished their album we let them have a listen to the tapes and pick out a song they think they can cover satifactorily and do it! I don't think any of The Fabs would mind and I'll ask John to make sure. What do you say to that?"

"Fine."

"The clouds have been gathering. The time has come."

The clouds had been gathering for some time. The House Hippie believed that with the proper direction they could very well turn into a successful group, justifying the Press Office's faith in them. Taking to heart Paul's letter which said, "In case you are ever worried about anything at Apple," he had done just that. The House Hippie told Peter Brown that he would like to have a few words with Paul next time he was in the building. Peter Brown had passed the message on. A few days later the call came through from Jack Oliver. "Paul's down in Neil's office and he'll see you now."

He had been thinking about what he was going to say to Paul and the best way of saying it for two days. It was very important to present the case for White Trash in an unhysterical, matter-of-fact fashion. No one except himself had actually heard them at work. They were a group that had recorded a powerful song that was intelligently and excitingly produced by their manager, a record that everyone had thought would be a hit and had been a flop.

The House Hippie realized that he could not barrel in ranting, "This is the greatest group in show business today!" No, you couldn't *possibly* say to Paul McCartney that this was the greatest group in show business today. A more realistic, understated approach had to be taken. Just before his hand touched the doorknob to Neil Aspinall's office. The House Hippie was struck by a momentary wave of uncertainty. "Wait a minute!" he thought, "Here I am going into ask Paul McCartney for help to relaunch White Trash and, well, maybe they're not *that* great after all. Maybe it's just that the more you smoke, the better they sound." But then his belief in the group returned, blotting all doubts from his mind. "No, they really are a great group and I know it so fuck it!"

Jack Oliver was there with Paul and Linda. The House Hippie told his employer that White Trash were a group that, with a bit of a push from Apple, could well turn into a money-spinning, chart-topping sensation. But at the moment what they needed was some studio time and an affirmative response from Paul so that they knew where they stood with their record company. They were in a very unhealthy state of mind to create music since they felt the ax might fall at any minute. Paul agreed.

He then asked Jack Oliver, chief of production for Apple Records, about the group and their musical abilities. Jack squirmed in his chair because in fact he knew very little about them or their music. Somehow he managed to summon up a "Yeah they're all right," response to his boss's question. At that moment Neil Aspinall walked in and said, "I've heard them rehearsing from John's office and they're no fucking good." The House Hippie remarked that it was grossly unfair to make that judgment after hearing them under such minimum conditions. Paul saw the logic behind that. "All right," he said, "tell them to go ahead and make some demos and then we'll listen to them and see if there's enough material for an album. And help them as much as you can, Jack."

So there it was. Paul McCartney had instructed the head of

Apple Records to do something for White Trash. The go-ahead had been given. They now had the single affirmative nod they needed to feel that their record company was behind them.

Throughout the late spring and into the summer, Apple and Track Records had amalgamated ranks by teaming White Trash with Track's Marsha Hunt, the luscious black beauty who had been the former hippie-chorus-girl star of the London company of *Hair*. They had become the Marsha Hunt with White Trash Road Show that had taken in the English university and club circuit with considerable crowd-pleasing success. Marsha Hunt and White Trash had been the perfect combination; like the werewolf and the vampire they were made for each other.

They went on with this double act until Marsha, pushed to the brink of collapse through overwork, ripped her vocal chords one night as she strained to be heard above the overamplification of White Trash's backing. A long rest was recommended for Marsha, and by mid-September White Trash found themselves rehearsing to perfection their version of *Golden Slumbers* from The Beatles' "Abbey Road" LP.

The Apple Press Office had its objective now: Get White Trash a hit record and maximum exposure. A harder, more decidedly wildcat publicity approach was being used in the regrooming of their image. They were to be billed as Apple's own "Home-baked blood-and-guts group." The House Hippie decided to capitalize on their cultural background. Taking vast liberties he rewrote the biography that was to go out in the blanket press mailing with their record.

"Let me hear that again," requested The Press Officer.

"White Trash come from Glasgow, the most violent and tempestuous city in the British Isles. A city in God's own country, inhabited by the devil's own people. A city that reeks of desperation under the cold, gray wash of the Scottish skies. They played their way through every club in the Gorbals, the Glasgow slum infamous for its rampaging gangs and razor kings, slashings, pummelings, stompings and copious pints of red blood in the gutter's sunset."

"Well, it's an improvement on 'They begin where the

Cream left off,' but that bit about playing their way through every club in the Gorbals, don't you think that's pushing it a bit?''

"Well, The Beatles didn't come from the 'slums' of Liverpool like everyone said but no one bothered to make the correction because it sounded pretty good as part of the whole and I mean what's a little bullshit? After all we're just trying to sell a few lousy records.''

"All right. And the pictures?''

"This afternoon.''

Every day The Press Officer would telephone Tony Meehan and ask him when the record would be finished. And always it was tomorrow. The panic was on because The Beatles album that included *Golden Slumbers* was scheduled for release on September 26 and if the White Trash single didn't follow almost immediately then the usual flood of cover versions would greatly reduce the chance of success their exclusive would give them.

The first recording session was a disaster. The mix was all wrong, a track in the studio wasn't working and the organ broke down in the middle of its solo. The Press Officer wanted to hear it anyway. "I must warn you, Derek,'' said Tony Meehan, "it sounds like shit right now.'' It did sound atrocious. "But we're going back into the studio for an all-night session until it's right and I'll have it back here by tomorrow afternoon.''

"Beautiful!'' said The Press Officer next afternoon. It was very difficult to tell the difference between The Beatle and White Trash versions on a first listening, so well had it been worked out. The lead vocal had a noticeably heavier delivery than the McCartney rendition and the organ solo on the middle break gave it the flourish that indentified it as pure White Trash. "Now all we've got to do is send it to Paul and have him OK it,'' he added.

With fingers crossed, everyone waited for Paul's verdict.

"Paul's furious!'' said Jack Oliver.

"What?''

"He said, 'I asked for a demo and I'm handed a finished

master of a full production with strings on it and the lot!' He wants to know who gave who permission to do it.''

''But I thought you—''

''That's funny because I thought you—''

''But didn't what's-his-name say that—''

''So what the fuck are we supposed to do now?''

''I don't know. He says he doesn't want it to come out at all.''

''And what the fuck are we supposed to tell those kids and their manager? They *need* this record right *now!* It's not like it's some piece of shit, they did a good job on it. What the fuck is going on here?!?''

''It's not my fault—''

''I know it's not your fault!''

''Well, that's it, I guess—''

''That's not it!'' screamed The Press Officer. ''Maybe you're afraid to say what you feel but I'm not. Give me that fucking record right now, I've had enough of this horseshit! I'm not letting that group down without a fight regardless what any of them say. I'm taking it to Lennon and if he says no then I'll reconsider but enough of this fucking around! It won't hurt any of us if this record goes out and you know it!''

The Press Officer grabbed the record and left the room at a gallop, headed for the ground-floor office. He explained the situation to John and then The Press Officer put the record on the turntable. When it was over John Lennon pointed to one of the speakers and declared, ''That's good imitation of us! *It's going out!!*''

110
WAIT TILL YOU HEAR THIS ONE!

PRESS OFFICE RELEASE to UPI, AP, Reuters, PA: Apple announced today, September 30, that John and Yoko are resting comfortably at Tittenhurst Park after their completion of mixing and recording with the Plastic Ono Band their single, *Cold Turkey.*

''So cancel that interview this afternoon,'' said The Press

230

Officer and then his eyes fell on the cardboard box half hidden under The House Hippie's desk. "And are those goddamn acorns still here?! What the hell are they doing under your desk!? Look, if those fucking things stay here any longer we're going to have an oak tree growing in the middle of this office! Do you realize that if John Lennon comes up here and sees those things sitting there after we've said, 'Oh, don't worry, John, they've already gone,' that you are in for the bollocking of your life?"

The House Hippie blinked at The Press Officer like a sleepy mole moving into the strong sunlight of a midsummer's day.

"Look, man," he said, "It's not *my* fault that the fucking printer is such a jerk-off artist. These things have been ready for weeks now but all they need is the labels and I called him again this morning and gave him a tongue-lashing and he's promised delivery this afternoon and besides, John hasn't been up here for years—"

"Never mind that! If they're not out of here in this evening's mail don't bother to come in tomorrow! Understand?"

"Yeah, sure, chief. Whatever you say."

The Iveys' manager walked in wreathed in his usual cloud of pipe smoke. "Christ, Bill, what the hell do you smoke in that thing? Your old acetates?" asked The House Hippie. Mavis Smith wrinkled the cute button of her nose in obvious distaste at the rancid-smelling tobacco. Bill smiled in a silent, benevolent reply.

"You know, Derek," he said, approaching The Press Officer, "the boys have been thinking of changing the group name now for some time."

"What for?"

"Well they feel that The Iveys is too *nice* a name. They want something with a little more of an edge to it."

"I thought we'd already been through this one before. The last time you mentioned it to me we drew up a list with a choice of sixteen names and you vetoed every one."

"Well, Neil's come up with a name that the boys and myself like and I think we're going to stick with this one."

"Well, come on, Bill! Spit it out! What is it?"

"Badfinger."

It was several minutes before anyone in the room could absorb what he'd just heard.

"Will you say that again please—"

"Badfinger."

"Badfinger? Are you sure that's what you want to be called?"

"Yes."

"Have you found your fourth man yet?"

"No, the boys are auditioning a lad from Liverpool this afternoon, but how do you feel about our new name?"

"Well, I suppose one can get used to anything after a while."

"So it's good-bye Iveys and hello Badfinger?"

"That's one way of putting it. Good-bye Iveys and hello Badfinger? Hmm. I think it's time for a drink."

111
WITH LOVE AND
ALL GOOD WISHES

Y OKO SAYS THE CRITICS won't touch it."

"Is it rude?"

"No, it's only a forty-five-minute color film of John Lennon's prick in various stages of erection, that's all. It's called *Self Portrait* and they'll be showing it along with the rest of their films in a three-hour spectacular at the Institute of Contemporary Arts."

"You've got to hand it to John."

"You sure do."

"It's not every managing director of a multimillion-pound organization that will stick his cock out like that for a laugh."

"That's the truth."

"Not only is he a brilliant songwriter but he's probably done more for the cause of male frontal nudity than any one single show-business personality."

"He sure has."

"The papers want to know when Yoko's having the baby and if they're going to call it Amsterdam like they said they would."

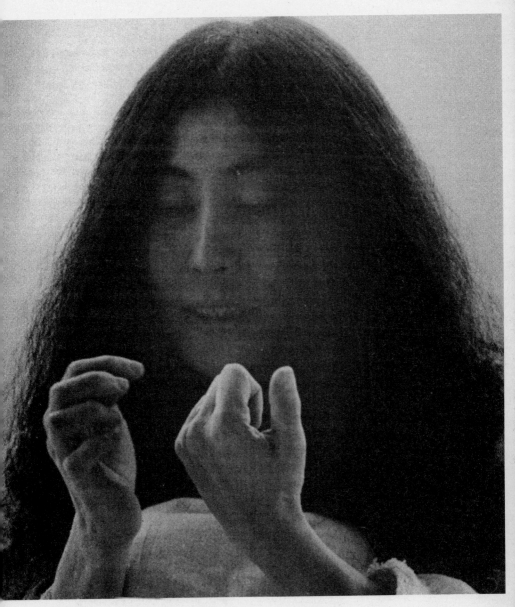

Yoko Ono at the Amsterdam Bed-In.

"No comment."

"What were they doing up in Canada last week?"

"They appeared at the Toronto Rock and Roll Revival Concert. It was a Plastic Ono Band special with Clapton, Klaus Voormann and Alan White. They've got an album out of it too."

"Haven't seen Paul around for a while, have you?"

"No, I haven't seen him for weeks now and somehow I don't think we're going to be seeing much more of him either. And at last the English press have got what they've been waiting for for so long. They've always begrudged The Beatles their success, their talent, their capacity to survive and now they're trying to write the whole thing off with feigned regret, only their regret reeks with glee. They keep going on about how they're all seeing less and less of each other and at last it looks like the end of a beautiful friendship and that it's Yoko's fault and Klein's fault but it's no one's fault. They've got the bitchiest public and it regards them as its private property and that public is *deranged*. They've just grown up and away from each other and pretty soon, as impossible as it seems, we're going to be living in a world where there are no Beatles. 'Good-bye' happens every day to every one of us so there really is nothing so extraordinary about it. If it can happen to you it can happen to them."

"But out there they think there has to be more to it than that. The public finds the obvious totally unacceptable."

"It's like that once-a-day, everyday question we get: 'What are they *really* like?' They don't want to believe that those beautiful songs, that gorgeous music coming out of those speakers has nothing to do with the flesh-and-bone reality of crawling through the day-to-day mud. That the gift of music has been planted in them and it simply *is*, just in much the same random way that some people have blue eyes and some have brown eyes but don't you dare answer that question with an 'Oh, they're just four guys' because you'll get laughed at. So how do you win? You don't. Like we said, the public is *deranged*."

WE'VE SIGNED A GROUP on a single-record deal who've done a *reggae* version of *Give Peace a Chance*. They brought it in and it was played for John and he said 'Put it out.' They didn't have a name when they came in so Mavis said, 'How about calling them The Hot Chocolate Band,' so they had one when they left. Billy Preston's single was a smash here and in the States but the album isn't moving. *Cold Turkey* is out on October 24 and the "Get Back" album is still shelved with the book and the movie. That group that Peter Asher brought in, Mortimer, are still hanging around asking us what's happening and are we going to release their album or not? No one knows what the hell to say except, 'Call back tomorrow.' It looks like White Trash could have a hit on their hands with *Golden Slumbers*. Derek has been working on it hard enough. He started a campaign that's going to run for two weeks. He's got all these freaks and dressed them up in black top hats, put false noses and mustaches on them, knocked a White Trash poster onto their sandwich boards and every morning sends them out into the streets to flap around. The record's already a Pick Hit and Power Play of the week and the musical reviews and all the provincials are ecstatic about it and if Bramwell can get them onto *Top of the Pops* that should do it for them. They're selling about nine hundred a day at the moment and any television appearances would easily knock it up to fifteen hundred, which would land them in the Top Ten. The only trouble is that EMI is pushing the Orange Bicycles' version of *Golden Slumbers* because that's one of their own groups and not moving Trash's version which is all part of the running story of our far from perfect relationship with the largest record company in the world. Badfinger auditioned this kid from Liverpool named Joey Molland the other day. He walked in with his guitar and plugged it in and they said, 'OK, play!' and he played along with them for a while and then they stopped and said, 'OK, sing!' and he sang. And that was it. They'd just found the fourth Badfinger."

113
BAD NEWS AND WILDCAT PUBLICITY

PRESS OFFICE RELEASE to UPI, AP, Reuters, PA: Yoko Ono Lennon lost the baby she was expecting today at King's College Hospital, Denmark Hill, London. Mrs. Lennon is resting comfortably.

"Sure enough, just like John said, there's bound to be some twat on Fleet Street who says, 'Oh, I suppose it's just another one of their publicity stunts.'"

"Bad news."

"Bad news indeed. Vicious tongues and humorless people. The Scottish dailies have raised one fuck of a stink over that biography we sent out with Trash's record. That one about them playing their way through every club in the Gorbals."

"What have they said?"

"Listen to this. Screaming headlines in the *Sunday Express*, 'Trash Pop Group Disowned by Lord Provost.' 'Glagow's image as a violent city took another knock last week – from Apple, the company the Beatles launched. In its publicity for a new record, Apple describes the people of Glasgow as "the devil's own children." It tells of pints of red blood in the gutters of the Gorbals. The pop group who made the record are called White Trash. They originally came from Glasgow and are now handled by Apple. Yesterday the publicity campaign was attacked by both Glasgow's chief constable and lord provost. Said Lord Provost Donald Liddle: "The members of the group may come from Glasgow but to my mind they are not Glasgow boys anymore – they are orphans. In my opinion this kind of publicity for publicity's sake is despicable. If this is the way you sell a record I can only hope it's a flop. But 'Trash' is very apt." And the Scottish *Sunday Mirror* headline reads, 'City Fumes Over Pop Disc Smear,' more of the same stuff."

"Dynamite!"

"We probably wouldn't have done as well if we'd tried. We'll have to do one of those numbers again. *Rolling Stone* says, 'Last word from an assistant chief constable of Glasgow, speaking in the absence of his boss, currently at an Interpol Laugh-In in Mexico, "I've never heard of this group and I'm very happy to be in that position of ignorance."

"That about says it all."

"Leave it to *Rolling Stone.*"

114

GIVE US OUR DAILY SPONGE

PRESS OFFICE RELEASE to UPI, AP, Reuters, PA: On behalf of The Beatles and their company, Apple Corps, their business manager Allen Klein of Abkco Industries after discussion with The Beatles announced in New York today that all negotiations between The Beatles, Associated Television and Northern Songs have been terminated by The Beatles. All of The Beatles and their companies intend to sell all their shares in Northern Songs to Associated Television at a price in accordance with the terms laid down by the takeover panel. John Lennon and Paul McCartney have no intention of involving themselves in any further relationship with Northern Songs or Associated Television beyond the fulfillment of their songwriting contract to February 1973. The Beatles intend to keep all their rights within their own company, Apple, which has divisions in records, music publishing, motion pictures and television. After discussions with The Beatles' solicitors and after taking advice of counsel, the writ served upon Northern Songs by The Beatles own Maclen Company will not be withdrawn and a statement of claim will be served within the next few days.

"Despite the immediate returns, even a man of Klein's abilities and reserves of energy is only able to scratch the surface of what's going on here. It's going to be years before this thing will make any sense to anyone. By then all of us will have just become the occasional brief mention tucked away in the corner of some newspaper and it will be difficult to imagine that it all had mattered so very much."

115

THIS GRISLY RUMOR RECEIVES "THE PRESS OFFICES OF THE WORLD AWARD" FOR BEING THE BIGGEST PAIN IN THE ASS OF 1969

ATTENTION PRESS OFFICE: Russ Gibbs, a Program Coordinator for WKNR Radio Detroit, Michigan, plans broadcast possibly this Sunday, suggesting that Paul is either dead or under death spell. He bases this on various symbols from The Beatles' albums including "Abbey Road." Paul is barefoot, which signifies a corpse in Eastern religion. Previous broadcasts by this station re this situation have resulted in mass hysteria and panic by Beatle fans, and certain radio stations and newspapers suggest you communicate with him to stop outrage. Urgent.

"Ahh, they're always trying to start one of those. It's happened before. The calls will stop coming in a few days."

But the calls didn't stop coming.

"What the hell is going on with all these goddamn calls?!"

"You were the one who said they'd stop in a few days."

"Well they have before—"

"But this looks like a different story. The substance of the rumor is developing. It's getting very intricate as it gets increasingly more ghoulish. They're picking up all the minutiae from the records and album covers and shaping it into something real. The American radio stations are feeding the rumor by complicity. The very weird thing about it is that there are quite a large number of people outside the lunatic fringe who have genuinely been taken in by it."

A few days later.

"Well, the calls are still coming in on an average of three an hour and most of them from America but the Continental ones are beginning to pick up and there was one from Japan this morning."

"Two radio stations, one in Colorado and the other in New York, have flown in their two top DJs to see if they can nail Peter Brown or Neil down to a statement of denial on the rumor. In the meantime they've been bugging anyone in the building they can lay their hands on. It's obviously a hot news item if they're sending those guys with their little cassette machines to London."

"Well, Paul's gone off to his farm in Scotland and says to deny it which is all we can do, and our official statement is that Paul McCartney is alive and well and unconcerned about rumors of his death because he figures that if he were dead he would in any case be the last to know. We'll use that one first and then if that doesn't satisfy them we can get a little flip and plagiarize Mark Twain who said that 'Rumors concerning my death have been greatly exaggerated.'"

"Is that what he said?"

"Close enough. We'll give them the quote and that's it! The mistake is to continue the dialogue. This fucking thing is taking up all our time."

"It's beginning to depress everyone—"

"It's put 'Magical Mystery Tour' and 'Sgt. Pepper' back into the charts—"

"It's still depressing."

A week later.

"Now they're saying that Paul's been dead for three and a half years and we've been using a lookalike stand-in. How about that?"

"A rumor invented by a jackass and perpetuated by an out-of-work grave digger."

"That disk jockey Russ Gibbs is the one who kicked this thing into national prominence, landing this whole bad trip onto our laps—"

"Russ Gibbs? He's downstairs in reception right now!"

A week later.

"It's still going on."

"But it *has* to drown itself sooner or later. I mean it just *can't* go on like this. I can't believe Russ Gibbs. He comes in here and makes a half-hearted apology for his part in this pop guignol and as soon as he sees how civil a reception he's receiving he drops the apologies and starts in with his requests for interviews with the other Beatles, the ones who are still alive and kicking around this building."

"There's so little else going on in the world at the moment, that *Life* magazine sent a team up to Paul's farm in Scotland and it's this week's cover story.''

''And that's the heart of the matter.''

''How—''

''He hasn't given any interviews for almost a year now and there was no way his public could get to him as he stepped further and further back and away from it all. They couldn't accept that. They didn't think it was right he was taking so much time out for self-reflection. So they said, 'All right, you're *dead!* You don't really exist anymore. You're just an amorphous memory now of someone who once played electric bass with The Beatles pop group from Liverpool. If we say you're dead then you're dead and if you're alive, *really alive*, then you'll come out and show us. You'll say, 'Here I am! Me! I *am* alive! I am not dead! I've just been sitting around with the old lady and the kids thinking about it all but I haven't really left you.' That's why this whole fucking thing has snowballed into this abominable yak. That demented public gets very ornery when it's denied its meat. *Life* magazine certainly had a surprise waiting for them when they got up there and Paul told them to fuck off and threw a bucket of water at them but then at the last minute he went down the road after them and said all right let's get this bollocks over with, take your goddamn pictures, write your frigging copy. They certainly weren't greeted by the Welcome Wagon. So as the calls keep coming, that leads us into our next and hopefully final statement: 'Paul McCartney is alive. He says so. His wife says so, his children show he is. The recent photos confirm it, the new songs make it concrete and the very fact that he is alive should be enough. If in doubt read *Life* magazine. If still in doubt then there is nothing we can do. The Paul McCartney who wrote *And I Love Her* still loves you and is still alive and has a lot to write. There are a thousand songs unwritten and much to do. Have faith and believe. He is alive and well and hopes to remain so as long as possible.'

''If that doesn't work then we'll start our own rumor that the public is dead from the neck up and they've been using a stand-in facsimile of a brain for the past three and a half years and then sit back and see who denies it.''

240

MILES WAS IN NEW YORK with instructions from us to record Allen Ginsberg for the spoken-word series and so they did a record and then what happens? Ginsberg gets a contract thrown in his face that all but allows him to breathe for the next five years and which in all good conscience he could not sign. So that scotches that!"

"Have you heard about the change from the West Coast to the East Coast?"

"No—"

"Well, since August of '68 Capitol has been dealing with all of Apple's products from the West Coast and then sending the finished product to New York for the final touches and media placement. Well, just before we released 'Abbey Road' the reverse happened and it was decided that for expediency it would be better if operations on all our products generated from New York under Abkco's wing because Klein has a greater interest in what happens to our stuff than Capitol does. He wants to let George have a crack at the singles market and says we're going to release *Something* as the next A-sided Beatles single. And Brute Force finally dropped in to see us to collect the master tapes for *The King of Fuh* which we never released and Derek's gotten a lot of bad feedback thrown at him over the White Trash press reception. He was told he spent too much money."

"After all the money that's been squandered on those other receptions?"

"Yes and it looks like their record has died at twenty-seven in the charts in spite of all the hopes pinned on it and all the effort exerted."

"Did you go to that staff meeting Klein called the other day?"

"Yeah."

"What was it about?"

"It was down in Peter Brown's office and everyone was very nervous, expecting to be told they'd just all been sacked but they needn't have. He first went over the procedure for the purchase orders and why he had initiated it and everyone knew anyway and just quietly nodded. Then he told us, and this was the meat of the whole thing, that his objective was to get The Fabs as financially secure as possible and what he expected from everyone in the building was the utmost respect for The Beatles. He said he wasn't going to tolerate any disrespect spect whatsoever and that whenever they came into the building they were to feel right at home."

"He should have saved his breath."

"Exactly. It was just a pep talk to lay down the law to us but it was wasted because it passed over everyone's head. No one had the nerve to ask, 'What do you mean by respect?' Bow down and kiss the carpet when they walk in? Is that respect? Because if it is then we don't have to be told because we practically do that anyway and always have done. Does respect mean not stealing from them when they're not looking?' And in the middle of all this Paul phones and wants to talk to him and his secretary announces it and he tells her to have him call back because he's very busy. Then she says he wants to speak with you right now, otherwise you should call him back on Monday. Everyone is sitting through this dialogue cringing and then he says, 'Call back on Monday!' Then he looks at us all and says, 'Are there any questions and have I made myself perfectly clear?' Everyone nodded, 'Yes, perfectly clear.' But even the most uncomprehending minds had understood the psychology of the meeting. He'd called us in to say that from here on in *he* was the boss and *he* was the one that demanded respect and whoever didn't like it could just fuck off out of here. You know, *just fuck off!*"

WHAT DOES HE want now?" asked The Press Officer.

"He says that he's got to get back to America only he doesn't have any money but if we can front him the air ticket as soon as he gets back he's going to sell his motorcycle and send us the money and there's nothing to worry about because he's not going to burn us."

"I'll believe anything at this point!"

"He'll be back this afternoon."

The Press Officer instructed his secretary to telephone the travel agents and have them deliver a one-way ticket to New York for the Sundance Kid.

"But what about Klein and the purchase orders? If you told him it was for the Sundance Kid he—"

"Fuck the purchase orders! I'll pay for it myself if I have to! I'll do anything to get rid of that guy!"

The Sundance Kid walked into the Apple Press Office later that afternoon: A Hollywood producer was calling from the States with an offer for Ringo to appear for $30,000 in a television spectacular that would only take two weeks out of his life if he could just pry himself away from his other commitments and the answer could be forwarded to the Waldorf-Astoria.

Badfinger were in for a huddle with Mavis Smith on the shape of their revised biography and press pictures.

Yoko's statement to the press was being double-checked by The Press Officer and Peter Brown. It read:

Every cent John earns goes into Apple at the moment. All that he means by saying that he would like to free his money is that he would like some pocket money, some spending money for some of our joint endeavors. It would be wrong to think that John is going to leave Apple because he, like the other Beatles, is a quarter of Apple but like everyone else he could do with some loose change which is entirely his own. He needs some freedom.

Apple's latest signee, Doris Troy, was being interviewed and talk of her collaboration with Jackie Lomax was being listened to with deep interest by one of the musical press who guzzled a scotch and Coke and checked the sound level of his tape machine every three minutes.

The Press Officer talked into a telephone, communicating the fact that John Lennon had written *Cold Turkey* in the morning, rehearsed it in the afternoon, called Phil Spector in and by that evening it had been produced and recorded to perfection. In John's estimate it was the best thing he had done except for what was to follow.

On another phone a journalist was hanging on for The Press Officer to ask if George and Patti would be attending Ravi Shankar's performance at the Royal Festival Hall. Someone noticed the phone off its hook and replaced it in its cradle.

Two-fifths of White Trash collided with Badfinger's manager and were asked how their record was doing. Neil Aspinall leaned over The Press Officer's shoulder and told him of the latest developments on the *Get Back* film, which was now going to be called *Let It Be*.

The designer, Gene Mahon, sat with his finished mechanical of the Plastic Ono Band "Live Peace in Toronto" album cover waiting for The Press Officer to show him the artwork for John and Yoko's album before delivering it downstairs.

Mavis Smith confirmed for the second time that day that Paul and Linda and Ringo and Maureen had attended the opening night of Mary Hopkin's debut at the Savoy Hotel and that Ringo had recently been to the States on a combination business and pleasure trip and upon his return intended to immediately begin work on his solo LP.

The journalist who had accidentally been hung up on had come back and wanted to know if George Harrison had any intention of joining the Bonnie and Delaney tour in Bristol as well as attending the Ravi Shankar concert.

When he looked up from his beleaguered desk The Press Officer saw the Sundance Kid looking down at him with an enormous, allknowing grin. "There you are," said The Press Officer. "Look, your ticket's right here and now all you have to do is climb on a bus which will take you to the airport and then climb on the airplane and you're halfway there."

The Sundance Kid tipped his hat and hitched his faded Levis, slowly nodding his head up and down. "That's really beautiful, man, I can't tell you how beautiful it is. Listen, man, I don't want you to think I'm going to burn you because as soon as I get to New York I'm going to sell my chopper and send you the bread for the ticket so you can cool yourself out on that score 'cause when it comes to a scene like that I'm straight as an arrow."

The Press Officer stood up and reached for the Sundance Kid's hand to give it a farewell shake. "I know you will and I'm not worried and I hope England was good to you and enjoy yourself and if you ever come back – well it was nice knowing you!" And abruptly he spun around and disappeared into the toilet. The Sundance Kid stood there looking at the empty space where The Press Officer had stood seconds before. His erratic departure had taken place in between blinks.

He turned around just as Badfinger's two ace roadies, Fergie and Nick, walked into the office. He crossed the room and told them he was leaving and they shook on it. He made the rounds saying good-bye, with everyone wishing him well. It was the loss of another lovable freak.

Walking up to The House Hippie he handed him an envelope. "Hey, man, that's for you and Derek. I was going to lay it on him but he looked like he was in a real rush to have himself a piss so just let him know when you see him."

"All right."

"Well, thanks, man, for everything. You've all been really beautiful and as soon as I get back—"

"Sure, Sundance, don't worry about it—"

"Well, adios, amigo!"

And then the Sundance Kid turned on the worn heels of his cowboy boots with the pointed toes and walked out of the Apple Press Office forever.

Ten minutes later The Press Officer emerged from the bog and looked uneasily into the cabaret of his office. "Is he gone?" he asked his secretary. "Yes." she replied.

245

Across the room The House Hippie carefully tore the edge from the large manila envelope. His eyes popped open two octaves. Inside was the biggest 2000-millimeter joint ever rolled by The Sundance Kid at The Longest Cocktail Party.

118
BOMBSHELL

J OHN'S GIVING ME THE statement within the hour," The Press Officer told his staff. "It's been coming for a long time." He covered his face with his hands and sighed into the darkness, turning silent thoughts in his head. He was looking very ill these days. The accumulation of the past two years was showing in his face. If he maintained his present pace it wouldn't be much longer before he came down with a severe case of the screaming heebie-jeebies.

The impressive thing about The Press Officer was that though he was in the employ of the biggest stars in show business, it was he who had become the star of this show – not by intent or devious design and certainly not by imposing his own ego on the ringmasters.

No, it had happened that way because he was the only one who had never forgotten the Declaration of Innocence that had been announced on the *Johnny Carson Show* in that long-past spring of 1968. He was the only one who still believed that Apple had half a chance, a greater hope of being better than all the corporations and holding companies that had preceded it. He still believed in the beauty and the power of The Beatles and right now he was finding it very hard to admit that The Beatles were no more.

They had all come to see Derek Taylor. Every freak and his brother, every straight and his sister. Peter Brown might be their social coordinator and Neil Aspinall and Mal Evans might have known them the longest but Derek Taylor was the one who had the articulate and immediate human touch. From the very beginning he was the one who had injected the energy into his employers' wishes to mold this nonstop schizophrenic dreamboat into reality. Almost singlehandedly he had created and sustained all the aspirations that the young Apple had announced so confidently. He had been its greatest fan.

He had held it all together; he had harnessed all the madness and kept the split worlds of the square and the straight satisfied, coping with their requests, their demands and their deals. But he was not so blinded by love or sentiment that he couldn't see what had once been a nice, stoned idea dreamed up on a warm, quiet afternoon had altered irrevocably. And right now, the only music he could hear was the sound of a burned-out record with the needle stuck in the last grooves, repeating itself over and over again.

"John says he's ready now, Derek," announced a voice.

The Press Officer looked up and sighed. In a single movement he raised himself from the white wicker throne and moved towards the door, leaving the room like a greased shadow.

He returned 20 minutes later.

"This is it!" He dictated:

"John Lennon has returned his MBE award in protest against Britain's involvement in the Nigerian and Vietnamese conflicts. In identical letters addressed to Her Majesty the Queen, the Prime Minister and the Secretary of the Central Chancery, John Lennon writes, 'I am returning this MBE in protest against Britain's involvement in the Nigeria-Biafra thing, against our support of America in Vietnam and against *Cold Turkey* slipping down the charts.' The letter is signed 'With love John Lennon' in his handwriting. Typed underneath is 'John Lennon of Bag.' The letters are written on notepaper headed 'Bag Productions, 3 Savile Row, London W1.' Bag is the company set up by Lennon and his wife Yoko Ono to handle their films, records and other merchandise. John Lennon and the other three Beatles were awarded the MBE in the Queen's Birthday Honors List in the summer of 1965."

Within the hour the calls would start coming in.

119
LOOK WHO'S TALKING NOW!

I HAVEN'T READ it yet, what does it say?"

"Oh the usual, that The Beatles are great but the people around them are a load of shits. It's very good on picayune details."

"What has she called it?"

"'Memories of an Apple Girl' by Francie Schwartz."

"Well, we knew it was coming. I'm just surprised that it took so long. Do you think she tried to turn it into a book?"

"Probably, but that's a lot of work and she wasn't around long enough."

"I've written *Rolling Stone* a letter about it."

"Read it to me."

"'Sirs: Everyone at Apple thinks "Memories of an Apple Girl" by Francie Schwartz is the funniest play of the season. Those of us in the Apple Press Office rise from our opium bunks to salute *Rolling Stone* for its fearless contribution to rock and roll journalism and the enlightenment of modern man in the second half of the twentieth century. Signed, The House Hippie, Apple Press Office, London.'"

"That's a nice bit of arch sarcasm."

"Well, what do you expect? After all, what kind of a person would sell his story?" said the House Hippie. "I'll be goddamned if I ever sell mine!"

120
DIALOGUE/ DIALOGUE/ DIALOGUE

K LEIN WANTS EVERYBODY to sign in their times of arrival and departure from now on."

"Just like real businesses, huh?"

"Yeah."

"I suppose it won't take much effort, just some getting used to but it is a bit regimented when you think what it's been like."

"Yeah."

"The trouble with this place has always been that it's a one-group record company."

"What do you mean? There's Badfinger and Jackie and—"

"Yeah, but they've always been secondary to *them*. The gig has been and always will be for *them*."

"It's understandable."

"Then it's understandable that people who do business with us get the feeling that they have to have a Beatle in their corner if they're going to get ahead, otherwise they've lucked out. I've heard it said more than once by people who don't work here that they get the distinct impression that you've got to kiss a Beatle's ass to make it and that we're all just The Beatles' slaves, rich men's lackeys—"

"Do you believe that?"

"I think that the circumstances don't allow for it to be any different but—"

"But what?"

"But the funny thing about it is that I really *enjoy* being a Beatle slave. In fact I *love* it!"

"You know something?"

"What's that?"

"So do I."

121
BUT WHO MURDERED BRITAIN?

PRESS OFFICE TO UPI, AP, Reuters, PA: John and Yoko Lennon today announced from their Apple Headquarters, 3 Savile Row, London W1, that they plan to make a film about James Hanratty, the convicted A6 murderer. After discussion with Hanratty's parents the Lennons, convinced that James Hanratty was innocent of the crime for which he was hung, said they are going to make a film that will insist that a new public inquiry be held and they themselves plan to reveal startling new facts about the case.

"I mean the Bed-Ins and the Bagism and giving back your MBE is fine but this is downright creepy! Do you realize that the guy who confessed to the actual rape and murder was in here yesterday with the rest of the Hanratty entourage? And poor Mr. and Mrs. Hanratty! They've been beating that drum a long time now with very little success. They spend most of their Sundays at Hyde Park Corner trying to whip up enough enthusiasm and signatures to get the case reopened and have their son's name vindicated and now this—"

"Will anything come of it?"

"I don't think the national conscience is that tormented anymore about what happened that night seven years ago on the A6 motorway. Time has erased the nagging notion that maybe, just maybe, it really committed a terrible mistake."

"John had posters made reading 'Britain Murdered Hanratty' and he and Yoko went to the premiere of *The Magic Christian* with them plastered all over the Rolls."

"I know."

122
ARRIVEDERCI 1969

WE'VE RELEASED fourteen singles and nine LPs this year. We've sold millions of records and raked in millions of dollars, undergone massive changes in our internal plumbing and ideology, been up and down and up again and we're still going. At the moment Apple Publishing is being handled by David Platz's Essex Music. He's been in the music publishing business for twenty years, copped fourteen Ivor Novello awards, has offices in every major country in the world, controls fifty other companies and has one of the most impressive catalogues in the business, so we're covered on that front. We've been spit upon and praised and there's nothing to indicate that public reaction and interpretation of our life style will be any different in the next twelve months. It's been a year jammed with so many events that most of them are lost forever. If you wanted, I suppose, there's quite a lot you could get sentimental about but tears distort the real picture and they taste salty besides. John and Yoko are kissing off the old year with a worldwide peace event with enormous billboards erected in twelve cities around the world reading 'War Is Over If You

Want It.' Ringo's in a TV special on Christmas Eve about George Martin called *With a Little Help from My Friends*, has made another film and almost finished his solo LP. George is producing three different artists and Paul is taking time off and there's a whisper that he's also making a solo LP. There's not much else to say except that it's been beautiful . . ."

PART THREE

1970

"WE DO NOT WISH TO ADD ANY MORE TO THE DIALOGUE ALREADY IN THE MEDIA"

George Harrison

JANUARY 1970

"The sales figures on Badfinger's single, Come and Get It, indicate that it's about to put them on the map of the record-buying public. The hard work seems to have paid off."

"But is it going to be a one-hit, nine-day wonder or are they capable of delivery on the follow-up?"

"Well, that album review in *Rolling Stone* was as close to ecstasy as we could have hoped for on a debut LP, and I think they're going to surprise the ass off us all."

"And White Trash?"

"Laying low and thinking about it."

"And Mortimer?"

"On ice."

"Things are a lot quieter these days."

"Yeah—"

"I wonder what it is?"

"Fucked if I know—"

"But things should pick up soon—"

"Maybe—"

"Hey, that chick as back in reception—"

"What chick?"

"That fucked-up and freaked-out one who says she's got a headache in her third eye and wants George to rub it and make it better."

"Can't you get rid of her?"

"She just won't leave. She stands there and cries quietly, never a sound, the tears just flow down her face and her eyes get all screwed up, not saying a word. No, she won't leave."

"Oh well—"

123

DIALOGUE/
DIALOGUE/
DIALOGUE

George Harrison, working out at Trident Studios.

124
ROLLER COASTER

EBRUARY 1970

"Yeah, sure I know John thinks we hate her and that we're all a bunch of two-faced fuckers running around behind his back sniveling and bad-mouthing her, sticking pins in our home-made Yoko Ono voodoo dolls but you know and I know what's happening and that's not happening at all! No one in this building *hates* her. *Hate*! That's a very strong accusation and an extreme assumption. I can't say as I blame him for thinking that sometimes, but the reason he feels that way is because we don't *love* her. That's the truth. I'd be a liar if I said we love her but we certainly don't hate her. If anything, we've just always wanted to get to know her better. It would be a welcome relief to walk into a room just *once* empty-handed, without an amplifier, without a cup of tea or a press cutting, without a list of people who want to interview them and a mouth full of questions. Just to walk in with yourself, that's all. But we're all so insecure and afraid of our status in their eyes that we need all those fucking props! It's a bad gig being a rich man's slave. We can't get to know *her* or *them* any better because we've passively accepted the roles that have been assigned to us and mindlessly act them out. Yoko's a Beatle now and that's that! She's achieved Beatle status around here and there's nothing more intimidating than that. I know it's not her choice but it's the reality just the same. When you hear the girls saying, 'Oh I can't stand her, she's so difficult to please, so impossible to get on with—' you know where that's at! It's the slave's backlash, it's chicks being catty, it's their safety valve for letting off steam, but there's no real malice behind the words, there's no real substance to any of it. It's just talk to relieve an oppressive situation and they're not easy people to work for. The pressure is mammoth and we've always moved at seven hundred miles an hour and everything is always wanted *right now!* So naturally everyone is very freaked and hypersensitive. I mean, how much more can we give of ourselves than we're giving now? What's expected of us that we're not doing? I'd like to know where all these so-called groovy people are that would do a better job than we're*

257

Three greats. Left to right: Pete Drake, Phil Spector and George Harrison.

doing. Where the fuck are they? The truth of it is we can't love them twenty-eight hours a day, always, every day, every week, every month of the year because we've got our own grubby little lives to attend to. OK, so we're not as blessed as they are but what do they have that we don't have besides beauty, immense wealth and talent and charisma? A little compassion is needed for the less exceptional specimens of this world, for all those not so fortunate people who didn't get a chance to walk down that one-way street called Success. The tragedy of this whole fucking thing is that we're all cut off from each other by the myth, by this cancerous charisma. It stands right in the way of everything and it's reduced us all to puppets in

258

Billy Preston, piano. Klaus Voormann with chair and Ringo Starr on drums, during the recording of George Harrison's album. "All Things Must Pass."

this asinine charade of bootlicking, and both sides know it. Well, we've got what we fucking deserve! We wanted to be in on this trip, to be here while it was going on and this is the price we're paying now. This is the creation. We've kept the afterbirth and thrown the child away. Fame? Look what it's done to us all. Fame? What a cruel, squalid joke!"

Badfinger, the musical heroes of The Longest Cocktail Party. Left to right: Joey Molland, Mike Gibbons. Pete Ham and Tom Evans.

125

THE FLAME FLICKERS

MARCH 1970

"Have you noticed how the place has gotten a lot quieter lately?"

"Yeah."

"We're just as busy in some ways as we've always been but somehow the place is changing."

"Yeah."

"We've got a lot of records coming out this month."

"Like what?"

"*All That I've Got* by Billy, *Temma Harbour* by Mary, *How the Web Was Woven* by Jackie, *Ain't That Cute* by Doris, *Instant Karma* by the Plastic Ono Band, *Let It Be* by The Beatles and *Govinda* by the Krishnas and Badfinger's LP. That's a couple of million more dollars here and there."

"Yeah."

TALK OF THE TOWN
SUNDAY, MARCH 15 FOR MONDAY MARCH 16, 1970

126
SENTIMENTAL JOURNEY

Press Office Release to UPI, AP, Reuters, PA: Beatle Ringo Starr spent the whole day filming for promotion of his forthcoming solo album, "Sentimental Journey." Dressed in a dark blue suit, a blue and pink striped shirt and a maxi-sized, shocking-pink bow tie, Ringo sang and danced through the title track in front of a specially invited audience of friends and friends of friends. The film, produced by Neil Aspinall and directed by John Gilbert, will be primarily for American promotion. The Talk of the Town Orchestra was under the direction of George Martin. The dancers, dressed in white, and the three backing singers were Apple's Doris Troy with Marsha Hunt and Madeleine Bell. A projected backdrop showed the album cover – a pub at the end of the street where Ringo lived in Liverpool.

THEY MUST HAVE CUT that dub with a broken nail . . . it's distorted . . . sibilant . . . out of phase . . ."
"Put the RIAA disk on . . . flat from forty to eighteen . . . let's hear the tape . . ."
"CCIR or NAB?"

127
DIALOGUE/ DIALOGUE/ DIALOGUE

"NAB."
"Dolby?"
"Yeah."
"Has it got tones on the front?"
"No "
"Where's the Ampex tape?"
"Line it up flat . . . no EQ . . . no filters . . . no EF . . . patch out the limiters . . ."
"Do it on tape mod . . ."
"It's nothing like the acetate . . ."
"Needs limiting . . ."
"It's too heavy in the low end . . ."

"Plug the Fairchilds in . . ."

"Eighty-cycle roll-off . . ."

"Still sounds rough . . ."

"Wind up the limiter . . ."

"Transients . . ."

"What's it like on the PPMs?"

"OK."

"VUs?"

"Not as high . . ."

"Sounds better but the phasing isn't good . . ."

"Azimuth?"

"Isn't very compatible . . . Ss are still nasty . . ."

"Pull three out at ten maybe and put an eleven K roll-off on it . . ."

"Right."

"The Dolbys are reading well past the DIN mark . . ."

"So what?"

"Let's do a test cut . . ."

"Minus three . . . five thou . . . a hundred and seventy-five pitch . . ."

"STLs aren't on, are they?"

"Yeah . . . minimum eighteen . . . are you on sapphires or rubies in the SX sixty-eight?"

"Rubies . . ."

"Look at those fucking Ortofons work!"

"Shit, it's tripped!"

"Pull six out at ten, othersie wind the Ortofons up to twenty . . . who forgot to put the helium on? . . . let's do another cut . . ."

"That looks better . . . the left Si Two is working like mad . . . it's that tambourine . . . fuck knows where the engineer was adding his top . . . OK play it back . . ."

"What does it look like?"

"Plenty of bass waves but the grooves don't touch . . . well only a bit . . ."

"Got a matrix number?"

"Yeah."

"Fuck it, let's cut the master . . ."

George Harrison and company during the recording of his brilliant album. "All Things Must Pass" at EMI Studios, London, 1970. Left to right, seated: George Harrison and Peter Drake, King of the Pedal Steel Guitar. Standing: Billy Preston, Klaus Voormann, Phil Spector, Ringo Starr.

128

WHEN SOPHIA LOREN WAS ASKED ABOUT THE SIMILARITY BETWEEN HER LOOKS AND THOSE OF GINA LOLLOBRIGIDA SHE REPLIED, "IT IS LIKE THE DIFFERENCE BETWEEN A FINE RACE HORSE AND A DONKEY BUT I'M NOT SAYING WHO IS WHAT"

THE PRESS OFFICER had just returned from a two-week vacation but the respite had not effected any noticeable improvement in his pallor, which still varied from yellow to green. He nervously skirted the room, looking very depressed, listlessly answering Beatle questions but more absorbed in the light show that splashed the walls with its erratic shower of color than in the voices blurting out requests from the other end.

Neil Aspinall came into the room and informed him that the *Let It Be* film was premiering in May in London and that the book that was scheduled for simultaneous release had been cancelled in the United States and was now being issued only in England and selected European countries. The Press Officer sighed with disgust, remarking what a pity it was because that book was the last and only visual documentation of The Beatles on such a grand scale ever assembled between two covers – but anyway.

A phone rang. It was Peter Brown.

"Yes . . . Apple band . . . maybe Klaus voormann and Alan White . . . flexible arrangement . . . hmm . . . yes . . . Beatles Today program maybe . . . George talking about The Beatles and himself as a musician and producer . . . yes . . . maybe Ringo talking with Pete Murray . . . yes Doris and the Krishnas on *Top of the Pops* . . . Mary for Eurovision . . . Mavis is going along with her . . . what? . . . *Knock Knock Who's There?* . . . I'll call *24 Hours* and cancel the profile on George . . . yes . . . all right."

He looked at his room, stood up, bolted for the lavatory, returned two minutes later, sat down, stood up, waltzed around the perimeter of the room like a skittish fox on stimulants and then blurted it out. "All right, you might as well know." Mavis Smith, the secretary and The House Hippie looked at him with varying degrees of interest.

"Know what?"

"John has fired this office," he said.

"What?"

"What do you mean?"

John and Yoko handing over their shorn locks to Michael X, to be auctioned at Sotheby's, proceeds to be donated to the Black Power movement of Great Britain, at the Black House, London, Spring 1970.

John and Yoko forever, Spring 1970.

"Why?"

"He called me this weekend and said he thought I had enough to do what with the other three and the rest of Apple and how tired I looked all the time and anyway he thought it might be better if he got someone who was a little more formal to clean up his and Yoko's image and so from now on all his requests for interviews etcetera go to Les Perrin because he's their new press officer."

"Les Perrin!"

"John told me not to take it personally, that he'd see me

265

John and Yoko at the Black House, London, Spring 1970.

around in the office as a human being rather than as a press officer and that was that. He wants to know what the taxi driver in the street thinks of him and her."

"I could have told him in one short sentence—"

"Well, you see, he thinks we're all freaked out of our brains up here and doped up to the eyeballs . . ."

"Well—"

". . . and can't get anything together and the only way he's going to establish a rapport with the straights is to get one and he knows that I don't dialogue with the press anymore and anyway I hate this place now. It's turned into a real shithole

266

and we've got fuck all to do and George says I should take off for six months and write a book."

"You mean you're leaving!?!"

"Well, I'll be coming in once a week to pick up the old pay packet and my mail and any messages but there isn't anything you and Mavis can't handle and besides George says he thinks you're all right and you've got good *karma*, he's always using those words with me."

"You haven't told him I've seen *A Hard Day's Night* thirteen times, have you?!?" panicked The House Hippie.

"No, and I'm not going to, so don't worry," reassured The Press Officer.

"I can't believe it's come to this."

"It's going to be very strange without you, Derek."

"And *you!* The greatest press officer that ever lived and now this!" wailed The House Hippie.

"Never mind all that shit," snapped The Press Officer, "just get me a drink and fix one for yourself while you're at it."

W HAT WE'LL DO IS lay that illustration across the center spread and it'll go two-thirds of the way and the fold won't make any difference and then we do a dot-for-dot four-color halftone and knock a black line around it and get rid of the sky and put in a Benday tint and that should match up perfectly because it's really coarse on the screen. Then we put black type on a white background on the right-hand side, range it left and right and that will leave room for the smaller illustrations to go in and that takes care of the center spread. Now we'll take that photograph and put it on the back and do an overall halftone that bleeds on all four sides and strip in a four-color apple on the bottom and range it with the type, overprint the type on the halftone and range it left and make it ragged right so it fits all around his head. For the front we'll

129

**DIALOGUE/
DIALOGUE/
DIALOGUE**

267

take that other illustration and do a cut-out halftone with the bottom vignetted so it just fades into the background and put straightforward type above and below the illustration, maybe a Goudy chiseled because of its three-dimensional qualities, it's black impressed and has a highlight down the left-hand side and it reads well and sets nice. We'll have that front-cover transparency retouched so it's already cut out on the transparency and we'll have that little bit retouched out and nobody will see it because we're the only ones who know it's there. For the mock-up we'll just whack those transparencies in the Lucy and get some quick black-and-white prints done from them and we're not going to have to bother with dyes or anything on this one. We'll work straight from the transparencies, trace them off and do the color rough, paste it all down and it'll look like it's going to look. It won't look *exactly* like the finished thing but it'll be close enough when we show them so they can see what's up. We're going to have to crop the back-cover photograph because the shape of the thirty-five-millimeter transparency doesn't fit the square of the cover so we'll just shift the image and then when he comes up in size there'll be just enough type to go down the left-hand side. We'll have the platemaker warm up the skin tones just a bit and punch the reds but they're going to have to be careful not to overdo it and, well, *that's our album cover!"*

130
FROM APPLE

WE IN THE PRESS OFFICE, as under-signed, are paying for this advertisement ourselves because we believe the record *Govinda* by the devotees of the Krishna Temple, produced by George, to be the best record ever made. You too?

"Where should I sign?"
"Right there's fine."
"But I don't have any bread to pay for it."

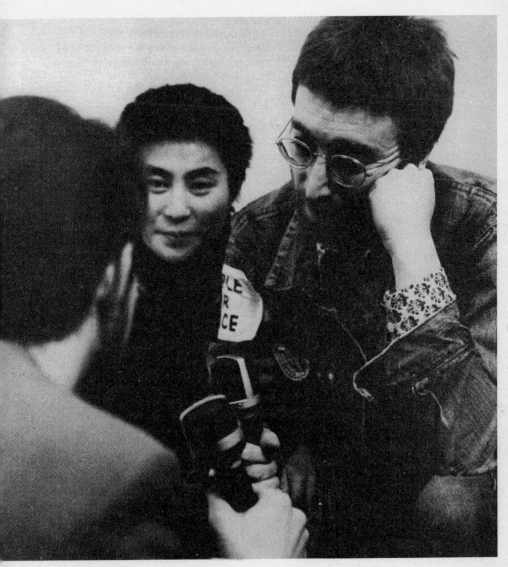

John and Yoko doing a spot of PR for world peace.

"Never mind, the Accounts department is taking care of it."

"But I thought that—"

"Never mind that, will you please just sign the fucking thing!"

"Yeah, sure."

131
JOHN AND PABLO

T*HE TIMES*. Thursday, April 2, 1970

LENNON AND PICASSO WORKS COMPARED
Christopher Warman

A Picasso lithograph and a catalogue of Picasso drawings were produced at Marlborough Street Magistrates' Court yesterday for comparison with a series of prints by John Lennon, seized by the police from an art gallery. The Picasso exhibits were shown by Mr. David Napley, defending Mr. Eugene Schuster and London Arts, Incorporated, of which Mr. Schuster is a director.

They pleaded Not Guilty on a summons alleging that between January 15 and 16 at the London Arts Gallery, New Bond Street, W1, they exhibited to public view eight indecent prints "to the annoyance of passengers" contrary to Section 54(12) of the Metropolitan Police Act, 1839, and the third schedule to the Criminal Justice Act, 1967.

The phrase "to the annoyance of passengers" was inserted after an application by Mr. Napley, who had submitted that, according to the authorities, this was an integral part of the offence.

He said that the warrant had originally been issued under the Obscene Publications Act, but it had been seen fit to proceed under an Act of 1839, which disposed of any defence of artistic merit or public interest and precluded the right of trial by jury.

Mr. Kenneth Horne, for the prosecution, said that on January 15 the gallery opened, free to the public, with an exhibition of prints by John Lennon. The 14 prints were for sale at £40 each, or £550 for the complete set.

As soon as the public were admitted complaints were received by Scotland Yard. Detective-inspector Patrick Luff, of the Central Office, New Scotland Yard, said that when he went to the gallery on January 15 about 40 people were viewing the prints.

Inspector Luff said: "I saw no display of annoyance from the younger age group, but one gentleman was clearly annoyed."

Mr. St. John Harmsworth, the magistrate, asked: "Did he stamp his foot?" Inspector Luff replied: "Anger was registered on his face."

Inspector Luff said that when he returned next day with a warrant, about 20 people were in the gallery. "I decided to take action when we went in," he said. They took possession of eight lithographs and told Mr. Schuster that the facts would be reported to the Director of Public Prosecutions.

Mr. Napley, handing over a set of the lithographs to the court, commented: "I hope the officer will not mark them, because no doubt by the end of this case they will be worth more than £550."

When Mr. Napley said that the prints appeared to depict the marriage and honeymoon of John Lennon and his wife, Inspector Luff replied: "Only if they were described and introduced in that way." He agreed that the gallery was highly reputable and that Mr. Schuster was a man of excellent character.

THE TIMES. Friday, April 10, 1970

McCARTNEY SPLIT WITH BEATLES DENIED

The Apple organization this morning denied reports that Paul McCartney had left the Beatles. Mrs. Mavis Smith, of the company's public relations department, said: "This is just not true."

132

**THE FLAME
FLICKERS SOME
MORE**

But she agreed that there were no plans at the moment for more recordings: "This is quite normal. Next month their new LP will be issued. It has already been recorded, so consequently as there is already material about there are no new plans."

She knew that Mr. McCartney intended issuing a statement today on the release of a new recording, but denied that any critical statements meant a real breakup of the group.

She said she hoped that the group would get together for another recording after the summer.

Although Mr. McCartney had not been to the Apple headquarters since before Christmas, "he communicates by telephone and, as he has got recording studios at his own home and all facilities, it is not necessary for him to come in."

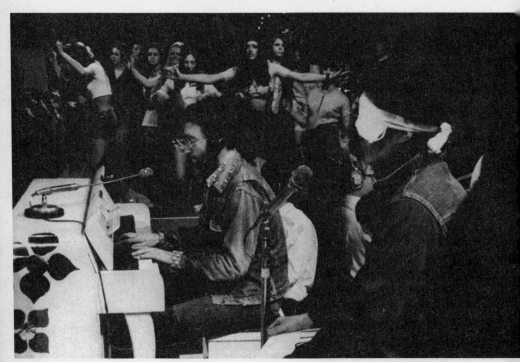

John gets 'em moving with his composition **Instant Karma** *at "Top of the Pops," BBC television program.*

"Well, how the fuck did Fleet Street find out what Paul said in that interview anyway? I didn't tell them and Radio Luxembourg announced it as a straight news story but I thought we were the only ones who knew what was in it."

"Well, we were."

"How did it come about in the first place?"

"Well, every journalist in town from Kenneth Tynan to the musical rags have kept up the barrage of requests for an interview with him but he keeps saying, 'No.' And then he says, 'All right, do this. Have Derek and Peter and Mavis draw up a list of questions like a straight interview and then I'll fill them in and we'll release it with the review albums, which by the way *no one* has heard, and that way for formality's sake we'll have obliged the media.' But someone must have told

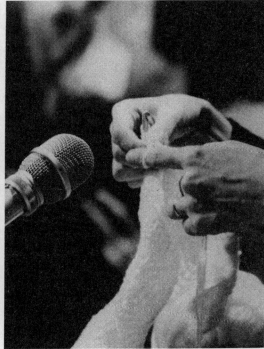

t "Top of the Pops."

Yoko knits up a storm during "Top of the Pops" filming of **Instant Karma**.

273

Don Short because he's the one who leaked the story. So there it is and anyway why deny it? It's the truth so don't get so fucking uptight with me.''

Paul McCartney Interview

Q: Why did you decide to make a solo album?

A: Because I got a Studer 4 track recording machine at home – practised on it (playing all instruments) – liked the results and decided to make it into an album.

Q: Were you influenced by John's adventures with the Plastic Ono Band, and Ringo's solo LP?

A: Sort of but not really.

Q: Are all the songs by Paul McCartney alone?

Klaus Voormann. artist, producer and Plastic Ono Band bassist during the filming of John's and Yoko's **Instant Karma**.

Alan White on drums at ''Top of the Pops''.

Mal Evans, on tambourine.

A: Yes sir.

Q: Will they be so credited: McCartney?

A: It's a bit daft for them to be Lennon-McCartney – credited, so "McCartney" it is.

Q: Did you enjoy working as a solo?

A: Very much. I only had me to ask for a decision, and I agreed with me. Remember Linda's on it too, so it's really a double act.

Q: What is Linda's contribution?

A: Strictly speaking she harmonises, but of course it's more than that because she is a shoulder to lean on, a second opinion, and a photographer of renown. More than all this, she believes in me – constantly.

Q: Where was the album recorded?

J and Y

A: At home, at EMI (no. 2 studio) and at Morgan Studios (Willesden!)

Q: What is your home equipment (in some detail)?

A: Studer 4 track machine. I only had, however, one mike, and, as Mr. Pender, Mr. Sweatenham and others only managed to take six months or so (slight delay) I worked without V.U. meters or a mixer, which meant that everything had to be listened to first (for distortion, etc . . .) then recorded. So the answer – Studer, I mike and nerve.

Q: Why did you choose to work in the studios you chose?

A: They were available. EMI is technically good, and Morgan is cosy.

Q: The album was not known about until it was nearly completed. Was this deliberate?

A: Yes, because normally an album is old before it comes out. (aside) Witness "Get Back."

Q: Why?

A: I've always wanted to buy a Beatles album like "people" do and be as surprised as they must be. So this was the next best thing. Linda and I are the only two who will be sick of it by the release date. We love it really.

Q: Are you able to describe the texture or the feel of the theme of the album in a few words?

A: Home, Family, Love.

Q: How long did it take to complete – from when to when?

A: From just before (I think) Xmas, until now. *The Lovely Linda* was the first thing I recorded at home, and was originally to test the equipment. That was around Xmas.

Q: Assuming all the songs are new to the public, how new are they to you? Are they recent?

A: One was 1959 (*Hot as Sun*) two from India, *Junk, Teddy Boy*, and the rest are pretty recent. *Valentine Day, Momma Miss America*, and *OO You*, were ad-libbed on the spot. T

Q: Which instruments have you played on the album?

A: Bass, drums, acoustic guitar, lead guitar, piano and organ-Mellotron, toy xylophone, bow and arrow.

Q: Have you played all these instruments on earlier recordings?

A: Yes – drums being the one that I wouldn't normally do.

Q: Why did you do all the instruments yourself?

A: I think I'm pretty good.

Q: Will Linda be heard on all future records?

A: Could be; we love singing together, and have plenty of opportunity for practice.

Q: Will Paul and Linda become a John and Yoko?

A: No, they will become Paul and Linda.

Q: Are you pleased with your work?

A: Yes.

Q: Will the other Beatles receive the first copies?

A: Wait and see.

Q: What has recording alone taught you?

A: That to make your own decisions about what you do is easy and playing with yourself is difficult but satisfying.

Q: Who has done the artwork?

A: Linda has taken all the photos, and she and I designed the package.

Q: Is it true that neither Allen Klein nor Abkco have been nor will be in any way involved with the production, manufacturing, distribution or promotion of this new album?

A: Not if I can help it.

Q: Did you miss the other Beatles and George Martin? Was there a moment, e.g., when you thought: "Wish Ringo was here for this break"?

A: No.

Q: Assuming this is a very big hit album, will you do another?

A: Even if it isn't, I will continue to do what I want – when I want to.

A: Are you planning a new album or single with The Beatles?

A: No.

Q: Is this album a rest away from The Beatles or the start of a solo career?

A: Time will tell. Being a solo album means it's "the start of a solo career" . . . and not being done with The Beatles means it's a rest. So it's both.

Q: Have you any plans for live appearances?

A: No.

Q: Is your break with The Beatles, temporary or permanent, due to personal differences or musical ones?

A: Personal differences, business differences, musical differences, but most of all because I have a better time with my family. Temporary or permanent? I don't know.

Q: Do you foresee a time when Lennon-McCartney becomes an active songwriting partnership again?

A: No.

Q: What do you feel about John's peace effort? The Plastic Ono Band? Giving back the MBE? Yoko's influence? Yoko?

A: I love John and respect what he does – it doesn't give *me* any pleasure.

Jackie Lomax at the Speakeasy, London, in repose and in action.

Q: Have you plans to produce any other artists?

A: No.

Q: Were any of the songs on the album originally written with The Beatles in mind?

A: The older ones were. *Junk* was intended for "Abbey Road," but something happened. *Teddy Boy* was for "Get Back" but something happened.

Q: Were you pleased with "Abbey Road"? Was it musically restricting?

A: It was a good album. (No. I for a long time.)

Q: What is your relationship with Klein?

A: It isn't. I am not in contact with him, and he does not represent me in *any* way.

Q: What is your relationship with Apple?

A: It is the office of a company which I part-own with the other three Beatles. I don't go there because I don't like offices or business, especially when I'm on holiday.

Q: Have you any plans to set up an independent production company?

A: McCartney Productions.

Q: What sort of music has influenced you on this album?

A: Light and loose.

Q: Are you writing more prolifically now? or less so?

A: About the same. I have a queue waiting to be recorded.

Q: What are your plans now? A holiday? A musical? A movie? Retirement?

A: My only plan is to grow up.

The following information accompanied Paul McCartney's solo LP, McCartney, Apple catalogue no. PCS7102. General release date, April 17, 1970.

1: THE LOVELY LINDA

When the Studer 4 track was installed at home, this was the first song I recorded, to test the machine. On the first track was vocal and guitar, second – another acoustic guitar – then overdubbed hand slaps on a book, and finally bass. Written in Scotland, the song is a trailer to the full song which will be recorded in the future.

2: THAT WOULD BE SOMETHING

This song was written in Scotland in 1969 and recorded at home in London – mixed later at EMI (No. 2). I only had one mike, as the mixer and V.U. meters hadn't arrived (still haven't).

First track

1 vocal, guitar.

2 tom-tom and cymbal

3 electric guitar

4 bass

3: VALENTINE DAY

Recorded at home. Made up as I went along – acoustic guitar first, then drums (maybe drums were first). Anyway –

electric guitar and bass were added and the track is all instrumental. Mixed at EMI. This one and *Momma Miss America* were ad-libbed, with more concern for testing the machine than anything else.

4: EVERY NIGHT (Blues)

This came from the first two lines, which I've had for a few years. They were added to in 1969 in Greece (Benitses) on holiday.

This was recorded at EMI with

1 vocal and
2 acoustic guitar.
3 drums.
4 bass.
5 lead guitar (acoustic).
6 harmony to the lead guitar.
7 double-tracked vocal in parts.
8 ? electric guitar (not used).
9 track.

5: HOT AS SUN

A song written in about 1958 or 9 or maybe earlier, when it was one of those songs that you play now and then. The middle was added in Morgan Studio, where the track was recorded recently.

1 acoustic guitar.
2 electric guitar.
3 drums.
4 rhythm guitar.
5 organ.
6 maracas.
7 bass.
8 bongos.

6: GLASSES

Wineglasses played at random and overdubbed on top of each other – the end is a section of a song called *Suicide* – not yet completed.

7: JUNK

Originally written in India, at Maharishi's camp, and completed bit by bit in London. Recorded vocal, two acoustic guitars, and bass at home, and later added to (bass drum, snare with brushes, and small xylophone and harmony) at Morgan.

8: MAN WE WAS LONELY

The chorus ("Man We Was Lonely") was written in bed at home, shortly before we finished recording the album. The middle ("I used to ride . . .") was done one lunchtime in a great hurry, as we were due to record the song that afternoon. Linda sings harmony on this song, which is our first duet together. The steel-guitar sound is my Telecaster played with a drum peg.

1 guitar.

2 voices (two tracks).

3 bass drum.

4 bass.

5 steel guitar.

9: OO YOU

The first three tracks were recorded at home as an instrumental that might someday become a song. This, like *Man We Was Lonely*, was given lyrics one day after lunch, just before we left for Morgan Studios, where it was finished that afternoon.

Vocals, electric guitar, tambourine, cow bell, and aerosol spray were added at Morgan, and it was mixed there.

On the mix, tape echo was used to move feedback from guitar from one side to another.

10: MOMMA MISS AMERICA

An instrumental recorded completely at home. Made up as I went along – first a sequence of chords, then a melody on top.

Piano, drums, acoustic guitar, electric guitar.

Originally it was two pieces, but they ran into each other by accident and became one.

11: TEDDY BOY

Another song started in India, and completed in Scotland, and London, gradually. This one was recorded for *Get Back* film, but later not used.

Rerecorded partly at home . . . (guitar, voices and bass) . . . and finished at Morgan.

Linda and I sing the backing harmonies on the chorus, and occasional oos.

12: SINGALONG JUNK

This was take 1, for the vocal version which was take 2, and a shorter version.

Guitars, and piano and bass, were put on at home, and the rest added at Morgan Studios.

The strings are Mellotron, and they were done at the same time as the electric guitar, bass drum, and sizzle cymbal.

13: MAYBE I'M AMAZED

Written in London, at the piano, with the second verse added slightly later, as if you cared.

Recorded at EMI, in No. 2 Studio. First

1 piano.
2 vocal.
3 drums.
4 bass.
5 and vocal backing.
6 and vocal backing.
7 solo guitar.
8 backing guitars.

Linda and I are the vocal backing group.

Mixed at EMI.

A movie was made, using Linda's slides and edited to this track.

14: KREEN-AKRORE

There was a film on TV about the Kreen-Akrore Indians living in the Brazilian jungle, their lives, and how the white man is trying to change their way of life to his, so the next day, after lunch, I did some drumming. The idea behind it was to get the feeling of their hunt. So later piano, guitar and organ were added to the first section.

The second had a few tracks of voices (Linda and I) and the end had overdubbed breathing, going into organ, and two lead guitars in harmony.

Done at Morgan. Engineer, Robin Black.

The end of the first section has Linda and I doing animal noises (speeded up) and an arrow sound (done live with bow and arrow – the bow broke), then animals stampeding across a guitar case.

There are two drum tracks.

We built a fire in the studio but didn't use it (but used the sound of the twigs breaking).

133

LET'S GO TO THE
MOVING PICTURES

AY 1970

The Directors of United Artists Corporation, Ltd., cordially invite you to attend the Gala Premiere

THE BEATLES
Apple
an Abkco-managed company
presents

LET IT BE

Produced by Neil Aspinall   Directed by Michael Lindsay-Hogg

On Wednesday May 20 at 8.00 P.M. for 8.45 P.M.
at the LONDON PAVILLION PICCADILLY CIRCUS W1
DRESS INFORMAL   R.S.V.P. MAY 13

"No, none of The Fabs is going but when the press ask just tell them you don't know. It doesn't look good if they don't look like they give two shits about their own movie. Yeah,

A conversation with Ringo Starr

that's right, United Artists is taking care of the tickets and all the seating arrangements. We certainly don't need that god-damned aggravation. Is anything else happening? I didn't think so."

134

THREE LITTLE INDIANS SITTING ON A FENCE

JUNE 1–10 1970

Mavis Smith smoked her tenth cigarette of the morning. Leafing through a magazine she heard her stomach growl from the nicotine abuse and contemplated having a pizza for lunch. Carol Paddon, The Press Officer's secretary, was playing with her Yorkshire terrier, Snatch, absorbed in that private and incomprehensible gibberish that people insist on using to converse with the lower species and babies. "And how is mommy wommy's wittle woodgikums today?" she asked the poor beast. Unable to articulate beyond a "woof, woof" Snatch rolled over on her back, spread her legs and waited for her soft stomach to be stroked. The House Hippie, catatonic as marble, stared blindly out the window, lost in some private alleyway of his mind with shuttling thought patterns, only half registering his dreams. *The telephones had undeniably stopped ringing.*

Upstairs on the third floor in the Accounts department, Ishmail Kassan, newly appointed office manager, attacked the morning's avalanche of invoices and aggravation. Young Nigel Oliver, office boy promoted to the Accounts department, looked at his desk with its equally intimidating mountain of red-tape garbage and paper work and wondered if maybe he wasn't better off as a carefree office boy.

Across from him, Allen Lewis and Brian Cappociama discussed the horses and the beaches of southern Europe, and never looking up from their moving pencils, plowed through the morning's allocation of monetary drudgery as methodically as they had been accustomed to for the past three years.

Ronald Tolson, accountant, 70-odd years, sitting catty-corner to Ishmail Kassan, maneuvered Beatle invoices from one side of his desk to the other, thinking of a time in life when there had been no Beatles and the world had been different from what it was now on this warm, June morning, glutted with so many bits and pieces of paper. Dee Meehan, with Apple from its embryonic beginnings, preened into a hand mirror, confirming her suspicions that she really was as beautiful as she thought she was.

Daniel Chavant, handsome dark-haired French office boy, launched into a tirade in French on the injustices of the overloaded house mailing system. Jimmy Clark, the Apple bouncer, exited from the kitchen with an enormously pregnant sandwich and his fifth glass of milk, saw Daniel talking to himself and gesticulating passionately to half a ton of mail, and almost cracked a joke about the French kittens, Un, Deux and Trois who cinq in the English Channel, but remembered his mouth was full.

In the kitchen, Margot, an Apple scruff who had graduated from the steps outside to second in command of the kitchen, talked with Penny about what Peter Brown and Peter Howard were having for lunch. Looking out into the back courtyard and then up at the blue sky she thought to herself what a nice day it was for a walk in the park just as the toast began burning.

On the fourth floor, Neil Aspinall had already begun work on his next film, a massively ambitious cinematic Beatle document that chronicled their rise from the Cavern to Savile Row. With his two assistants, Tony and Graham, he had amassed all existing footage of The Beatles' concerts, press conferences, hotel-room dialogues, airport arrivals and departures; in total, the entire gamut of Beatleological film history. Hundreds of hours of John Lennon, Paul McCartney, George Harrison and Ringo Starr that had to be pruned into 90 comprehensible minutes. Standing by the projector, watching the Shea Stadium concert for the seventy-fifth time, Neil relived the fantastic rush of his youth that was now committed to a flickering celluloid memory.

On the ground floor, cloistered in the shell of the switchboard unit, sat Judy and Laurie McCafferey, with The Beatles now for seven years, transferring calls to Jack Oliver, Tony Bramwell, the Accounts department and Peter Brown. From behind their glassed-off partition, manipulating the spider web of jack plugs, they looked for all the world as if the screaming had never stopped.

Breezing past the switchboard, heading for reception, Jack Oliver waved to his two secretaries, Sally and Shirley, sweating lightly and cursing heavily, under pressure from Allen Klein and four separate Beatle bosses to attend to a thousand separate details for the release of albums, singles, artwork, ad placement and all the attendant clutter that filled his life as the chief of Apple Records.

Tony Bramwell gazed at a larger-than-life-size color poster of his girl friend, Julie Ege, and half wondered who next he was going to be asked to get on *Top of the Pops*, what other records he was going to have to wave in the face of a BBC DJ, pleading for equal air time and currying favors.

Peter Brown, clipped, combed and immaculately dressed, sat behind his equally well-ordered desk giving crisp, precise instructions to his personal assistant, Bill Oakes, while his secretary, Barbara Bennett, passed him a stack of letter-perfect correspondence to sign on behalf of The Beatles and Apple Corps, Ltd.

In reception, Debbie Wellum, by now seasoned and toughened as a carpenter's callous to such scenes from the street freaks, listened unemotionally as a head of hair abused her, chagrined at being unable to gain an audience with John Lennon after having come all the way from California to get

288

into John's head, only to find that John had left for California where someone else was getting into his head.

Inside the ground-floor office, behind the one-way-mirrored door of John and Yoko's room, were the Lennons' two female personal assistants, Sally and Diane, gathering and wrapping an enormous package that they hoped contained everything that Yoko had requested in her telephone call on the previous day from California. Sally looked at Diane and asked, "Are you *sure* that's all she asked for?"

Mavis Smith, about to light her eleventh cigarette of the morning, caught herself in the act. She looked up at what had once been the highest-powered Press Office in London, England, and became instantly conscious of the fact that it now very much resembled a conservative mausoleum. "*I Can't Stand It Any More!*" she screamed to the walls, slamming shut a vacuous issue of *Vogue*. Snatch half-opened her eyes at this outburst and then closed them again, retreating into some delicious canine fantasy. The House Hippie and the secretary looked at her, only having half heard the pain in her statement. Their minds had become blunted by inactivity and the procession of days, stretching out as empty as the cloudless blue London summer sky.

"There's not a fucking thing to do in this Press Office anymore!" she continued. "Nothing! My mind is beginning to rot! Have you noticed how the phones only ring once every hour and a half and then when they do it's only some twat of a Brazilian journalist who's eight months behind the times and wants to know if he can have an interview with James Taylor. I feel terrible sitting here day in and day out with not one fucking thing to do, collecting a salary for just reading magazines!"

"I don't," said the secretary.

"Neither do I," added The House Hippie.

"Well, it's all right for you lazy twats but it's driving me *crazy!* I'd rather be at home puttering around, doing something for myself, than sitting in this graveyard! I mean we don't have any artists anymore, that's just it! White Trash are gone, their option wasn't picked up; Mary doesn't want to have anything to do with us; there aren't any more Beatles; John and Yoko are having their heads dry-cleaned in California and it was those two who gave us most of the work and excitement; Jackie's pissed off to another label; we never even saw the Modern Jazz Quartet—"

"But there's Badfinger!"

"Big deal! A record company with one group! Some catalogue after two years! No one comes in anymore and Derek is just biding his time because *he* knows it's all over and the phones don't ring anymore because *they* know out there that nothing is going on!"

"So what are you going to do about it?"

"I'm quitting!"

"But, Mavis—"

"You can't—"

"I have!" she said.

135

AND THEN THERE WERE TWO

R*ECORD RETAILER.* June 20, 1970

MAVIS SMITH LEAVES APPLE

Mavis Smith has resigned from the Apple Press Office, which she left last weekend. Assistant to Derek Taylor for the past 18 months, she previously worked with Leslie Perrin Associates.

In the absence of Derek Taylor, now writing a book, Mrs. Smith has been running the department together with Richard DiLello, who will now assume responsibility for press matters.

NOW THAT I'M The Press Officer," said The House Hippie to the secretary, "there are a couple of important things that want doing around here and I'll need your full cooperation."

"Like what!" she snapped at this cardboard cutout of a Press Officer.

"Like moving those fucking desks around. They don't look so hot they way they are now."

The new Press Officer, by virtue of the absence of the real one, and the retirement of the second in charge, knew full well what an empty victory his ascension was. He knew only too well that *this* was the ultimate irony, the final hilarious mockery of the system of office politics. He also knew time was running out, very fast and very thin.

"Oh yeah, there's something else that I want," he remembered.

"What?"

"I want to get a sign made for that door."

"That says what?"

"Press Office!"

HIS SABBATICAL WAS doing him good. The real Press Officer was looking healthier and more boyish than ever. But now, when he came in every Thursday, it was too painful to say that things would never be the same

again. His diminished staff had no news to report. The conversation that had once coursed so thickly through the room was now reduced to an anemic trickle of half-grunted monosyllables. The Press Officer would read his thinning mail, dictate a few replies and go out for a three-hour lunch so as not to have to face the empty horror of a Press Office where the telephones no longer rang.

"I'll see you next week," he would say over his shoulder and next week would come with nothing to distinguish it from the week before.

The days passed. By now the secretary and The House Hippie had become bloated lounge lizards. She was spending more and more time rolling on the floor with Snatch, absorbed in doggie conversations. He had become imprisoned in the magazines he could not stop reading.

"If George Harrison walks in here and finds you like that with that dog it's going to be all over for you. Besides it's a bad reflection on me as The Press Officer to have you carrying on in such a state," The House Hippie admonished.

"Oh piss off, you! You're not a real Press Officer and besides I'm getting married in August and I don't give a wank if I do lose this job because I'll get another one so—"

"Who the hell are you getting married to?" he interrupted, "that fucking dog? That'll change your name to Carol Snatch!"

"Fuck off, you arsehole! I can't marry Snatch because she's a girl! I'm marrying Gary so that makes me Carol Hudson."

"Well, congratulations, you old slag!"

"Don't mention it, shitface."

At that moment the internal telephone on the secretary's desk rang and interrupted the exchange of pleasantries. Anne Nightingale of the *Daily Sketch* and Radio One's only female DJ was in reception. "Oh Anne, yes certainly, send her up."

It was Friday, July 10, 1970.

138

OOPS!

M

ONDAY, JULY 13, 1970
When Peter Brown walked into the Press Office that Monday morning The House Hippie knew something was wrong.

"Have you seen the *Sketch* this morning?" he asked. It was a loaded question.

"No I haven't, Peter, why?"

"Well then, I suggest you do and when you're finished Derek wants you to call him at home." Peter Brown turned and left the room.

The House Hippie made it to the press table in three strides where the morning papers were scattered in sloppy disarray. The secretary's eyes followed him. He picked up the *Daily Sketch* and there it was, on page 17, smacking him right between the eyes. "Holy shit, Carol! Look at this!" Looking over his shoulder she saw it. "Cor!" she squeaked in her best cockney. They both went very white in the face and weak at the knees. "Get Derek on the phone right away!"

The Press Officer picked it up on the fourth ring.

"Hello, Derek?"

"Hi there, kid. Peter told me about it but I haven't seen it yet. What does it say?"

"It's Bad News City, chief. I don't know why the hell she did it, I mean we were just talking, you know casual conversation, and it wasn't like we were giving her an interview or anything she—"

"That's all right, just read it to me."

"Well, the headline screams 'Apple Coming Apart at the Core . . .'"

"Shit, not that one again," he gasped in disgust at the worked-to-death pun.

"'Apple, the pop utopia which The Beatles built themselves, seems to have become a crumbling dream. Its brain center, the gracious white house in Savile Row, is an empty, expensive monolith these days and the staff are resigning out of sheer boredom.'"

"Shit!"

"'"There's just nothing to do anymore," they say sadly. Yet two years ago Apple was the Mecca of World Pop. "We were the most prestigious name in the business," said Richard DiLello, Apple's resident hippie.'"

"Ouch! Go on—"

"'True enough. Clusters of girls camped out on Apple's front doorstep hoping to see a real Beatle emerging. And they often did. But now John, Paul, George and Ringo are not around at Apple anymore. Paul hasn't been there since last Christmas, John and Yoko, finally allowed a visa to America, have gone there for extensive psychotherapy and no one knows when they are coming back. George, always the most active musician of the four, is working on a solo album and Ringo has gone to Nashville, Tennessee, to make his next record. Meanwhile, the basement studio at Apple stays silent.' "

"What else?"

" 'The Beatles' promise that Apple would find, launch and finance new talent never properly materialized. Mary Hopkin, their one established star, still releases her records through Apple, but she has little else to do with the company.' "

"Ungrateful bi—"

" 'Not so long ago Apple's offices would be crammed every day with disk jockeys, TV interviewers, poets, Hell's Angels, Hollywood film stars, painters and children. It was a busy, happy place and Apple held a party every day.' "

"We sure as fucking hell did!"

" 'Not surprisingly its drinks bill rose to hundreds of pounds a month.' "

"We certainly did burn it up—"

" 'But even after John Lennon's freeze, when he announced "We're broke," Apple was still an active pop center with a successful if chaotic image.' "

"They all seem to think that the fun ended overnight but it didn't—"

"It sure didn't—"

"And?"

" 'Now its four bosses, having lost interest in each other, appear to have abandoned Apple too. Only a nucleus of staff remains headed by Allen Klein, The Beatles' business manager. "It looks as though we are going to end up as just an Accounts department," said secretary Carol Paddon unhappily, "collecting the Beatles' royalties." ' "

"Christ Almighty, talk about coffin nails!"

"It's not our fault, Derek, believe me," pressed The House Hippie.

294

"Come on now, man, you know I'm not uptight with you. I don't give a shit about it but how did it happen?"

"Like I told you, she just came in here like always and we were sitting around dialoguing and she wasn't even taking notes! It was Anne Nightingale the Beatlemaniac, our friend, not William Randolph Nightingale the journalist. She didn't say she was writing a story about Apple, nothing!"

"Well, that's not according to Hoyle."

"So, what happens now?"

"Well, now it's done so don't worry. I'll call you back this afternoon but in the meantime don't say anything to anyone."

"All right, chief."

Later that afternoon.

A few of the Apple Scruffs, the greatest Beatle fans in the world, as immortalized in words and song. November 1970

"All right, kid," said The Press Officer from his Sunning-dale home, "I've talked to Peter Brown and Klein has been on to him and he's furious about that story and from now on he wants Peter to handle all the press enquiries so what I suggest is you and Carol write out your resignations right now and have them ready when the time comes—"

"Resignation!" That word was the end of The House Hippie's world. "Resignation!" he screamed again, thunderstruck.

"Well, you don't want to get sacked, do you?" asked The Press Officer.

"You mean *it's over?! Curtains?!*"

"I'm afraid it's just a question of time, kid. We've had a good run."

"But—"

"I'll talk to you at the end of the week," said The Press Officer and signed off.

The House Hippie returned the phone to its cradle, dazed.

"Carol," he began, "Derek says we're not to talk to the press anymore, that Peter is going to be taking care of all that shit and we should write out our resignations now so when the time comes—"

"Fuckin' 'ell I'm not resigning from here," she broke in, "they can bloody well sack me. That way you get more money and besides there's no disgrace in getting the bullet from this place because everyone in the business knows what a joke it is," she added confidently, adjusting her eyelashes and running a comb through her heavy blonde hair, very much looking forward to a social evening out on the town.

T

HREE WEEKS LATER.
Since that Monday morning in July the Apple Press Office had not stirred. The death watch had been slowly drawing itself out to its ultimate, predictable demise.

A telephone rang.

The House Hippie answered it.

"Well, kid, I've just had the word." It was Derek Taylor, The Beatles' Press Officer.

"Oh yeah—"

"Peter Brown called me an hour ago. He just got the call from Klein."

"And?"

"He says that *Sketch* story has gotten a lot of coverage in the States and then he said, 'Have they left yet?'"

"Uhh oh!"

"Do you have your resignation ready?"

"Funny you should ask because I gave it to Peter Brown yesterday but then I found out that you get three times as much bread if they sack you so I went back to Peter this morning and asked him for it back and told him to fire me instead."

"Did he give it to you?"

"Sure he did."

"Well, kid, I know it's hard to believe but this looks like the end but you've got your photography now and we'll farm out some work to you so don't worry."

"I'm not worried but—"

"I know it's a bit of a shock after three years but it's not the end of anything except the finish of this so there you are and it was a good scene even when it was shitty, wasn't it?"

"It sure was, chief."

"So listen now, I want you to stay in touch and remember this is just a beginning, another stepping stone and well, I'll be seeing you around."

"OK, chief."

For The House Hippie and the secretary, the Longest Cocktail Party ever held had just dried up.

140

NEWS ITEM

THE EVENING STANDARD. August 4, 1970

Earlier this week the Apple Press Office was closed down and the two remaining employees dismissed. Since the breakup of The Beatles their Apple empire has diminished to little more than a center for collecting their royalties and dealing with their private affairs.

PART FOUR

1971

SILENCE IN THE COURT TILL THE JUDGE BLOWS HIS NOSE

Paul McCartney

The Times. Friday, January 1, 1971*

PAUL McCARTNEY TAKES COURT ACTION TO LEAVE BEA-
TLES
By Geoffrey Wansell

Paul McCartney, one of The Beatles who, with John Lennon, wrote the songs that established and maintained their
international reputation, yesterday started a High Court action
to dissolve all his remaining connexions with his three fellow
Beatles and their company.

The most impressive feature in the life of young people in
the past decade seems finally on the brink of dissolution.

There have been splits and arguments within the Beatles
over the past three years, but there have been hopes and
rumours of reconciliation. The rumours have been killed, and
the end formally proclaimed of the group known affectio-
nately to their devotees in the past as "the fabulous four."

The writ issued by Paul McCartney in the Chancery Division
of the High Court yesterday sought: "A declaration that the
partnership business carried on by the plaintiff and the defendants under the name of 'The Beatles and Co.' and
constituted by a deed of partnership dated 19 April 1967,
and made between the parties hereto ought to be dissolved
and that accordingly the same be dissolved."

The partnership was launched just before their LP record
"Sergeant Pepper's Lonely Hearts Club Band" was released in
Britain. This record was described by the music critic of *The
Times* soon after it appeared as "a sort of pop music master
class examining trends and correcting or tidying up inconsistencies and undisciplined work." It may well stand as their
most enduring piece of work.

Mr. McCartney also asks in the writ that the affairs of the
partnership should be wound up; that accounts and inquiries
should be taken, in particular of dealings between the

* All articles in Part Four are reproduced from *The Times* [London] by
permission.

partners; and that a receiver be appointed to collect debts accruing to the partnership.

The defendants in the action are John Lennon, who is sued as "John Ono Lennon," of Ascot, Berkshire; George Harrison of Henley-on-Thames, Berkshire; Ringo Starr who is sued under his real name of Richard Starkey, of Highgate, London; and The Beatles' company, Apple Corps, of Savile Row, London.

Mr. McCartney, whose address is given as St. John's Wood, London, also asks for costs in his writ before the High Court. The hearing is expected some time early in the next law term and it is thought that all four Beatles will attend.

This move formally to end The Beatles is not entirely unexpected. Some 15 months ago John Lennon announced his intention not to work with the members of the group again, as his recordings with his wife Yoko Ono and other interests were taking all his time.

In a newspaper interview last April immediately after he released his first solo record Paul McCartney explained that The Beatles had ceased to exist as a group. He said then that he was concerned that the individual members' earnings were tied closely in Apple.

The Apple company, which is run by Mr. Allen Klein, was formed early in 1968. One of its purposes was stated to be "to encourage unknown literary, graphic and performing artists."

Mr. McCartney is known not always to have seen eye to eye with Mr. Klein and there have been public disagreements over individual records. He is reported to want Mr. Lee Eastman, his father-in-law, to manage his business affairs and for each Beatle to look after his own interests.

The Beatles' press and public relations consultants said yesterday that they had no comment to make on behalf of any of the defendents of the case. Both Mr. Harrison and Mr. Starr declined to comment and Mr. Lennon, who is in New York, made no public comment on the action.

San Francisco, December 31.
John Lennon, in an interview in the pop music journal

Rolling Stone, says that Mr. McCartney's attempts to dominate the group led to its breakup.

Mr. Lennon said all the Beatles got "fed up being side men for Paul."

Mr. Lennon listed his experiences with drugs and said he stopped LSD because he just could not stand the bad trips. He started taking it in 1964 and made about 1,000 trips. He was on pills when he made his first film *Hard Day's Night* and had turned to marijuana when he made the second film *Help!*

He said: *"A Hard Day's Night* I was on pills, that's drugs, that's bigger drugs than pot, I started on pills when I was 15, no since I was 17, since I became a musician. The only way to survive in Hamburg, to play eight hours a night, was to take pills. I've always needed a drug to survive." Reuters.

The Times. Wednesday, January 20, 1971

Q C FEARS BEATLE CASH MAY NOT MEET TAX

The financial affairs of the Beatles partnership, whose estimated annual earnings are between £4m and £5m, are in a grave state, counsel said in the High Court yesterday.

"The latest accounts suggest that there is probably not enough in the kitty to meet even the individual Beatles' income and surtax liability," Mr. David Hirst, Q.C., declared. He added that "on a conservative estimate" the four's surtax liability must be £500,000.

Mr. Hirst was making a plea on behalf of Paul McCartney for a temporary appointment of a receiver of the partnership business, and for an order that Mr. McCartney be given information about the partnership finances.

The matter was adjourned on undertakings by Apple Corps, Ltd., to procure payment of money due to The Beatles into a solicitor's joint account, pending a full hearing in about a month's time, when evidence has been completed. The full hearing is expected to last about five days.

After a two-hour hearing yesterday lawyers talked outside

court for an hour and a half and then announced terms on which yesterday's application was adjourned.

Yesterday's hearing arose from a writ issued by Mr. McCartney on December 31 in which he seeks dissolution of "The Beatles and Co.," formed in 1967, in which he, John Lennon, George Harrison, Ringo Starr and Apple Corps, Ltd., are partners.

Each Beatle has a 5 percent interest in the partnership. Apple Corps holds the remaining 80 percent.

Mr. Hirst told Mr. Justice Stamp that the group's manager, Mr. Allen Klein, had instructed accountants not to give Mr. McCartney information about the group's financial affairs.

He said of Mr. Klein: "He is a man of bad commercial reputation. Mr. McCartney has never either accepted him as manager or trusted him. And on the evidence his attitude has been fully justified."

Mr. Hirst described the bookkeeping of the Beatles partnership as lamentable and said draft accounts delivered to the home of Mr. McCartney's solicitor last night disclosed a grave state of affairs.

Counsel gave three main reasons for the claim for dissolution:

(1) The Beatles had long since ceased to perform together as a group, so the whole purpose of the partnership had gone.

(2) In 1969 Mr. McCartney's partners, in the teeth of his opposition and in breach of the partnership deed, had appointed Mr. Klein's company, Abkco Industries, Ltd., as the partnership's exclusive business managers.

(3) Mr. McCartney had never been given audited accounts in the four years since the partnership was formed.

"Until 8:15 P.M. yesterday the only accounts we had received of the partnership were draft accounts for the 16 months up to March 31, 1968," counsel said.

Mr. Hirst said a receiver should be appointed because the partnership assets and income should be safeguarded to meet the potential tax liability.

Counsel said the partnership agreement was entered into in April 1967, before the death in August that year of The Beatles' manager, Mr. Brian Epstein.

The next year, and early in 1969, disagreements began to occur. Artistic differences arose, particularly between Paul McCartney and John Lennon, who had written most of the songs. In January, 1969, Mr. Klein was introduced by John Lennon, who proposed that he be appointed manager. George Harrison and Ringo Starr also became keen.

Mr. McCartney did not trust Mr. Klein and wanted a New York law firm, Eastman and Eastman, partners in which were his father-in-law and brother-in-law.

In May 1969, the other three insisted on appointing Mr. Klein, or rather Abkco Industries, Inc., as exclusive director. Mr. McCartney opposed and protested strongly. But Abkco were appointed managers "at a fee of no less than 20 percent of the gross income."

Mr. Hirst continued: "McCartney has never accepted, and does not accept, Mr. Klein as manager."

Up to 1965 Mr. Epstein had run their business affairs, selected their professional advisers, and been completely trusted by The Beatles. In 1965 the four decided to abandon touring and make records instead. That increased their financial success because of the enormous worldwide market.

On tour they had a close personal relationship. Once they switched to recording they began to drift apart.

After The Beatles' partnership deed was signed in 1967, the group activities began to decline. They made their last record in the summer of 1969, and that September John Lennon announced that he was leaving the group. Since then each Beatle had increasingly gone his own way.

Last spring, Paul McCartney decided that he, too, should leave the group.

Mr. McCartney's first solo record was released last April in spite of efforts by Mr. Klein, Mr. Harrison and Mr. Starr to postpone its release.

In June 1968, Mr. McCartney's accountant was told by the partnership accountants that the combined net profits of the partnership for the year to March 31, 1968, and for Apple Corps, for the year to December 31, 1967, were about £1.5m.

In December 1969, other figures were given: Beatle royalties to December 1968, £3.5m; due from Capitol Records, Inc., for three months United States record sales, $2.5m; Apple Corps' net income for 1969, about £2m; Beatles' share of United States record royalties from September 1969, to June 1970, $7,815,628.

Counsel said the rate of partnership income in the middle of last year was between £4m and £5m. By last September Paul McCartney's royalties from his solo record last year amounted to £487,000.

Mr. Hirst said that a quick reading of the draft balance sheet up to December 31, 1970, showed the total credit of the four individual Beatles, excluding the company, as £738,000.

On the figures produced by the partnership accountants, £678,000 was owing in income tax. The four Beatles must be liable for at least £500,000 surtax, Mr. Hirst continued. There was thus a tax deficiency of about £450,000.

Mr. Hirst said the net current assets of the partnership as a whole were shown at £1.56m, of which £1.55m was said to be owed by Apple Corps, Ltd.

The partnership's solvency would appear to depend on the ability of Apple Corps to pay, counsel said. It was manifest that Apple Corps must owe very large sums in corporation tax.

Mr. Klein's counsel, Mr. A.J. Balcombe, Q.C., said a letter from a bank showed that on January 15, 1971, Apple Corps had something over £2m on deposit.

After discussions between counsel, Mr. Hirst said undertakings acceptable to Mr. McCartney had been offered, to last until the full hearing of the motion.

Mr. Harrison, Mr. Starr and Apple Corps (but not Mr. Lennon, who was "on the high seas") would undertake that Apple Corps would procure payment into a solicitor's joint account of money due to The Beatles.

That would include $3m from associated companies; about £100,000 owed by associated companies to the partnership; 25 percent of all the group's gross receipts; and £487,000 McCartney royalties held by EMI.

No payment would be made out of the joint account without instructions from both sides' solicitors.

The evidence was to be completed within a month, and a date for the full hearing to be fixed as soon as possible after that.

The judge said it was obviously an urgent matter.

The Times. Thursday, January 21, 1971

BEATLES SOLVENT, MR. KLEIN SAYS

Mr. Allen Klein, American manager of The Beatles, has issued a statement in New York denying that their finances are in "an appalling state."

The statement released by a spokesman says:

"I wish to make it clear that the partnership is solvent and has more than sufficient net current assets to meet all income tax and surtax liabilities."

The Times, Wednesday, January 27, 1971

UNDERTAKING ON MONEY OWED TO THE BEATLES

More trouble has arisen over The Beatles' money, and the matter was again before a High Court judge yesterday. The new difficulties were over implementing the undertakings on which last week's case was adjourned.

Revised undertakings given yesterday will mean that money can be paid into a joint account in New York instead of London. Both sides were represented in a 10-minute hearing before Mr. Justice Stamp.

Mr. David Hirst, Q. C., for Paul McCartney, who wants to break up the group, told the judge that alternative undertakings had been agreed.

The revised undertakings concerned the opening of a second solicitor's joint account in New York, and the payment into of certain money owed to The Beatles.

The undertakings were given by Apple Corps, Ltd., who with John Lennon, George Harrison and Ringo Starr are defendants to Mr. McCartney's action, when it was agreed last Tuesday to adjourn Mr. McCartney's claim for appointment of a temporary receiver of the assets of "The Beatles and Co."

The judge said yesterday that he would hear the case again on February 19.

The Times. Saturday, February 20, 1971

TAX OFFENCES BY MANAGER OF BEATLES

Mr. Paul McCartney, of The Beatles, heard his counsel say in the High Court yesterday that Mr. Allen Klein, the group's American manager, had been convicted of tax offences in New York.

News of these convictions, Mr. David Hirst, Q. C., told Mr. Justice Stamp, had only recently come to light and it had not enhanced Mr. McCartney's confidence in Mr. Klein.

Counsel added: "On January 29 last year he was convicted of 10 tax offences by a jury in a New York federal district court even though, as he says, they are effectively under appeal. These were not mere technical offences. They consisted of unlawfully, willfully and knowingly failing to make and file returns of federal income tax which Mr. Klein was under a duty to make and file."

It seemed, Mr. Hirst went on, that Mr. Klein had demonstrated towards the United States federal tax authorities "a willful failure to account, comparable to that demonstrated towards the partners in The Beatles and Co."

Mr. Hirst was opening Mr. McCartney's application for the appointment of a receiver for the group's assets pending a full trial of his action to have the partnership dissolved.

He said that one ground for the application was that Mr. Klein had paid himself commission out of funds to which he was not entitled and was asserting entitlement to even more.

The seriousness of the position could be appreciated when one saw that the group's income ran into millions a year. Draft accounts for 1970 showed an income of about £4m, with a potentially huge income-tax liability. Each of The Beatles

308

would be liable for a share of that, apart from their individual surtax liabilities.

Defendants to the claim are the other three Beatles, Mr. John Lennon, Mr. George Harrison, and Mr. Ringo Starr, and the management company, Apple Corps, Ltd., Each of the Beatles has a 5 percent interest in the partnership and Apple Corps the remaining 80 percent.

Undertakings were given a month ago to pay certain money due to the group into solicitor's joint accounts in London and New York.

In his writ issued on December 31, Mr. McCartney claims a declaration that the partnership, formed in April 1967, should be dissolved. He also asks that the partnership affairs should be wound up; that accounts be taken and inquiries made – including in particular an account of all partnership dealings and transactions between the partners – and that a receiver be appointed of the partnership's assets.

The hearing is expected to last six days.

The Times. Tuesday, February 23, 1971

BEATLES SAVED FROM BANKRUPTCY

Mr. Morris Finer, Q. C., counsel for three of The Beatles, said in the High Court yesterday that Mr. Allen Klein, American manager of The Beatles, had saved them "from almost total bankruptcy."

Counsel added: "He inherited a situation and rightly or wrongly – and we say rightly – took the view that the vital thing from his point of view, having regard to the total mess, almost total bankruptcy, of their affairs, was to generate income "

Mr. Klein very largely left accountants to sort out the mess, Mr. Finer went on. He considered his main job was to try to get money to rescue the group from the dreadful situation in which he found them. And in that he was very successful.

Mr. Finer was appearing for John Lennon, George Harrison, Ringo Starr and Apple Corps, Ltd., on the second day of Paul

McCartney's application for the appointment of a receiver of the group's business affairs. The appointment is sought pending full trial of Mr. McCartney's action to dissolve the partnership.

Mr. Klein is not a party to the present application but is represented by Mr. A.J. Balcombe, Q. C., holding a watching brief.

Mr. Finer objected when Mr. David Hirst, Q. C., for Mr. McCartney, read from a newspaper cutting about The Beatles. Newspaper reports were hearsay evidence and not admissible, he declared,"

"I imagine the last thing any of us want is trial by newspaper," Mr. Finer added. He said none of the cuttings included in the evidence was backed by evidence from the reporter.

Smiling at the press bench, Mr. Justice Stamp remarked: "I am never very impressed, with all respect, with what I read in a newspaper."

In a later intervention Mr. Finer said The Beatles, other than Mr. McCartney, had always counted their individual earnings as a group assets.

This arrangement would not necessarily be disadvantageous to Mr. McCartney, who claims that the royalties from his solo record "McCartney" belong to him alone.

Counsel went on: "Mr. Harrison's royalties on his individual record this year are going to be nearly twice as much as Mr. McCartney's – nearly £1m." Mr. Harrison's record had been at the top of the charts for five weeks and was going to earn an enormous sum.

The hearing was adjourned until today.

The Times. Wednesday, February 24, 1971

BEATLES "COULD YET WORK THINGS OUT SATISFACTORILY"

Ringo Starr, drummer of The Beatles, suggested in the High Court yesterday that The Beatles' might yet stay together as group.

The inside story of The Beatles' troubles was told to Mr.

Justice Stamp in affidavits by John Lennon, George Harrison and Mr. Starr, who ended his by saying: "My own view is that all four of us together could even yet work out everything satisfactorily."

John Lennon, in written evidence, said that after the death of Brian Epstein (their first manager) The Beatles' company Apple was full of "hustlers" or "spongers." "The staff came and went as they pleased and were lavish with money and hospitality. We have since discovered that at around that time two of Apple's cars had completely disappeared and that we owned a house which no one can remember buying," he continued.

But a few weeks after their manager, Mr. Allen Klein, an American, had been authorized by him (Mr. Lennon) to make changes in the organization of Apple, the effects were felt.

Early in 1969 Mr. Klein dismissed incompetent or unnecessary staff; the "hustling" and lavish hospitality ended; discipline and order appeared in the Apple offices.

Mr. Lennon said the four Beatles started to receive monthly accounts of their personal spending, copies of bills and, where necessary, explanations. They also got regular bank statements and statements of their income and investments.

Mr. Lennon's evidence was read by Mr. Morris Finer, Q. C., yesterday, the third day of Paul McCartney's application for the appointment of a receiver of the group's business affairs.

Mr. McCartney's claim is being opposed by Mr. Lennon and the other Beatles, and Apple Corps, Ltd., against whom Mr. McCartney has started an action claiming dissolution of the group's partnership.

It was true, Mr. Lennon's affidavit continued, that when the group were touring, their work and social relationships were close, but there had been a lot of arguing, mainly about musical and artistic matters.

"I suppose Paul and George [Harrison] were the main offenders in this respect but from time to time we all gave displays of temperament and threatened to 'walk out.' Of necessity, we developed a pattern for sorting out our differences, by doing what any three of us decided. It sometimes took a long time and sometimes there was deadlock and nothing was done, but generally that was the rule we followed, and, until recent events, it worked quite well."

Even when they stopped touring they frequently visited each other's houses in or near London and personally were on terms as close as they had ever been. "If anything, Paul was the most sociable of all of us," Mr. Lennon said.

"From our earliest day in Liverpool, George and I on the one hand and Paul on the other had different musical tastes. Paul preferred 'pop type' music and we preferred what is now called 'underground.' This may have led to arguments, particularly between Paul and George, but the contrast in our tastes, I am sure, did more good than harm, musically speaking, and contributed to our success. If Paul is trying to break us up because of anything that happened before the Klein-Eastman power struggle, his reasoning does not make sense to me," Mr. Lennon went on.

After Mr. Epstein's death, he stated, he and Mr. McCartney in particular tried to be businesslike over Apple's affairs, but were handicapped by their ignorance of accounting and business practice and preoccupied with musical activities.

"Above all, although royalties were coming in, none of us had any idea at all about the state of our finances or our liabilities."

They decided that they must find a new manager and interviewed several people, but none seemed to have any idea of what was needed. He said he arranged to see Mr. Klein, whom he had heard about from Mr. Epstein. He was tough but the knew the entertainment business. He introduced Mr. Klein to the other Beatles.

"If Paul is suggesting that I was trying to rush him and the others into engaging Klein, or pushing him down their throats, that is a wrong impression," Mr. Lennon added. At all times Mr. Klein had shown himself on top of the job.

The only other major contenders for the manager's job were the Eastmans – father of Mr. McCartney's wife, Linda, and her brother. Mr. Lennon said he had opposed the idea of having as manager anyone in such a close relationship with any particular Beatle.

Mr. Lennon said Mr. McCartney's criticisms of Mr. Klein were not fair. "Klein is certainly forceful to an extreme but he does get results . . . So far as I know he has not taken any commission to which he was not entitled."

An affidavit by Mr. Harrison was then read. It said: "The only serious row was between Paul and me. In 1968 I went to the United States and had a very easy cooperation with many leading musicians. This contrasted with the superior attitude which for years past Paul had shown towards me musically."

He said they were making a film in a studio in Twickenham, "which was dismal and cold, and we were all getting a bit fed up with our surroundings. In front of the cameras, as we were actually being filmed, Paul started to 'get at' me about the way I was playing. I decided I had enough and told the others I was leaving. This was because I was musically dissatisfied."

Mr. Harrison's statement continued: "After a few days the others asked me to return and since I did not wish to leave them in the lurch in the middle of filming and recording, and since Paul agreed that he would not try to interfere or teach me how to play, I went back. Since the row Paul has treated me more as a musical equal; I think this whole episode shows how a disagreement could be worked out so that we all benefited."

He added: "I just could not believe it when just before Christmas I received a letter from Paul's lawyers. I still cannot understand why Paul acted as he did."

Ringo Starr, whose real name is Richard Starkey, stated: "Paul is the greatest bass player in the world. He is also very determined. He goes on and on to see if he can get his own way. While that may be a virtue, it did mean that musical disagreements inevitably arose from time to time. But such disagreements contributed to really great products."

Mr. Starr said he was shocked and dismayed after Mr. McCartney's promises about a meeting of all four Beatles in London in January that a writ should have been issued on

December 31. "I trust Paul and I know he would not lightly disregard his promise. Something serious, about which I have no knowledge, must have happened between Paul's meeting with George in New York, and the end of December."

Mr. Finer read evidence by accountants who estimated that Apple Corps' liability for corporation tax for the period April 1967, to December 31, 1970, was £1,935,000. The total surtax liability of the four individual members of the partnership was estimated at £630,000. The hearing was adjourned until today.

The Times. Thursday, February 25, 1971

BEATLES' ASSETS "NOT NOW IN JEOPARDY"

In an affidavit read in the High Court yesterday Mr. Allen Klein, American manager of The Beatles, stated that the group's partnership assets "are not in any sense now in jeopardy."

Earlier it was stated that Mr. Klein had more than doubled The Beatles' income in the first nine months after he took over as manager in May 1969. Last year he had increased it fivefold.

As a result of Mr. Klein's efforts, it was stated, The Beatles' partnership income increased from £850,667 for the year ended March 31, 1969, to £1,708,651 in the nine months and ended December 31, 1969. In the year to December 31, 1970, the income was £4,383,509.

The figures were given in an affidavit by Mr. John Darby, an accountant, who said Mr. Klein had been very successful.

Mr. Darby's affidavit was read by Mr. Morris Finer, Q. C., who is appearing for John Lennon, George Harrison, Ringo Starr and Apple Corps, Ltd. They oppose an application by Paul McCartney for appointment of a receiver of the group's business affairs pending trial of his action to have the partnership legally broken up. Mr. McCartney has criticized the management of the group's affairs by Mr. Klein.

Mr. Finer said yesterday that Apple Corps was solvent after

all tax liabilities, current and payable over the next two years, had been met.

The income-tax position of the partnership was manifestly capable of being covered from assets in hand and the tax certificates could be brought forward.

Mr. Finer then read an affidavit by Mr. Klein. In it he denied that The Beatles had been prejudiced by having him as their manager. He added: "On the contrary, they have greatly benefited."

Mr. Klein said Mr. McCartney had made attacks on his commercial integrity in general, and in his [Mr. Klein's] dealings with The Beatles in particular. Mr. McCartney had also declared that the assets of The Beatles' partnership were in jeopardy. Mr. Klein went on: "I am concerned to answer these attacks and to rebut this allegation."

Mr. Klein, who is 40, said he was a graduate in accountancy. In 1967 he acquired a controlling interest in Cameo-Parkway Records, Inc. In 1968 over-the-counter trading in Cameo-Parkway stock was suspended, its assets not meeting requirements for certain transactions.

"Since it has been suggested that the suspension and delisting of the stock is an indication of lack of commercial integrity on my part, I stress that there is no allegation by the American Stock Exchange of any dishonesty or improper conduct on my part," Mr. Klein continued.

Referring to tax offences of which he had been found guilty in a New York court, Mr. Klein stated that no allegation had been made of failure to pay any tax. The 10 offences had related to alleged failure to file tax returns, he said. The duty of filing these returns had been delegated by him to a member of his staff. No sentence had been imposed because the matter was under appeal.

Mr. Finer interrupted the reading of his affadavit and commented that before Mr. Klein represented The Beatles his recording company Abkco was used by such stars as the Rolling Stones, Herman's Hermits, the Kinks, the Animals, the Dave Clark Five and Marianne Faithfull.

Mr. Justice Stamp asked what was the relevance of some of

the evidence in Mr. Klein's statement. Mr. Finer replied: "The whole of the conduct of Mr. Klein, as an individual, as a manager and as a person, has been made the basis of an out-and-out attack. This naughty animal is defending himself to show that from the start he was acting properly and in The Beatles' interests."

A specific point made against Mr. Klein was that he had neglected the accounting position. The evidence showed that was not so.

The ultimate relevance of the evidence was that it had been suggested that his clients had employed a dishonest manager. They said they had done nothing of the kind and that there was no case for appointing a receiver.

Mr. Klein's affidavit said he appreciated before he became The Beatles' manager that he was taking over "a very perilous situation" which, according to the auditors, involved insolvency.

He made this position clear to The Beatles at many meetings, and his first task was to help them to generate enough income to alleviate this situation. The largest potential source of income was from royalties on records and he wanted to negotiate a new arrangement with EMI.

Discussions were held with The Beatles and with John Eastman as to how EMI should be approached and who should go to the meeting with them.

He went on: "It was decided by all four Beatles that I alone should go with them and have authority to negotiate. McCartney was anxious that Mr. Eastman should attend, but McCartney went along with the collective decision."

A meeting was held on May 7, 1969, attended by Mr. McCartney, Mr. Lennon, Mr. Harrison, Yoko Ono, himself and three representatives of EMI. Ringo Starr was not there as he was making a film.

No conclusion was reached at that meeting but EMI made it clear that they were not prepared to negotiate any new arrangements so long as the NEMS claim was outstanding.

Mr. Klein said that he had arranged for his company, Abkco, to take over from NEMS at considerable profit to The Beatles.

He added, "Notwithstanding, on July 8, 1969, Mr. John Eastman saw fit to write to each of The Beatles criticizing the settlement and alleging I had cost them £1.5m."

Referring to The Beatles' film *Let It Be*, Mr. Finer said: "It was suggested that Mr. Klein did something wrong in the arrangement of the film deal with United Artists. But it made an absolute fortune for all four Beatles."

The film's profits would be absolutely enormous, counsel added, but Mr. McCartney, his advisers or Mr. Eastman would not concede that Mr. Klein had done something that was entirely proper.

The hearing was adjourned until today.

The Times. Friday, February 26, 1971

INCOME OF THE BEATLES FOR 19 MONTHS UNDER KLEIN MANAGEMENT SAID TO BE OVER £9M

Mr. Allen Klein, American manager of The Beatles, said in an affidavit read in the High Court yesterday that he agreed that Paul McCartney, one of The Beatles, "never accepted me as his manager, but the partnership did, and I have continued as manager of the partnership."

He added: "McCartney has accepted the benefits which I have negotiated in that capacity. As regards my ability to make deals I am content to be judged on my record."

Mr. Klein's affidavit was read by Mr. Morris Finer, Q. C., who appears for the three other Beatles – John Lennon, George Harrison, Ringo Starr – and Apple Corps, Ltd. Mr. McCartney is claiming the appointment of a receiver of the group's business affairs.

He is asking to have the group's legal partnership ended. His application is opposed by the other three Beatles and Apple Corps.

Mr. Finer produced a schedule which he said showed the total income received by The Beatles from June 1962, until December 1969, but not including income from songwriting, which had never been part of the joint activities. In that six and a half years the total income of The Beatles from tours, films, record royalties and other sources was £7,864,126.

For the 19 months between May 1969, when the Klein management agreement was made, and December 1970, the total income was £9,142,533. More than £8m of it was from record royalties.

Mr. Klein denied ever having been untruthful, that he was unscrupulous, or that he had ever held himself out as Mr. McCartney's personal manager.

It was not true, he said, that any of The Beatles told him that the Capitol agreement was a "tricky one." "This is the big agreement which has been so responsible for the increase in income," Mr. Finer said.

The affidavit went on: "Still less did I advise The Beatles to enter into an agreement on a false basis. The agreement makes specific provision for records which might be made by The Beatles individually and expressly provides for the contingency that they might not perform as a group at all."

In spite of Mr. McCartney's reluctance, it was a fact that he signed it, Mr. Klein went on.

Mr. Finer commented: "Your Lordship may think it is pretty unlikely that EMI, which has been for years in such close association with the group, were under any kind of misapprehension at any time as to what the facts were regarding these young men and their relationship with each other. EMI has acted as father and mother to these young men for years. Everybody knew it."

The judge: Well, I did not.

Mr. Finer: That is why I am trying to bring these matters home to your Lordship.

Mr. Finer said it seemed obvious that Mr. Klein had been advising John Lennon and Apple in relation to Maclen (Music), Ltd., the music company in which Mr. McCartney and Mr. Lennon each held 40 percent holdings and Apple Corps 20 percent. Maclen consisted of valuable rights and potentials, and had to be managed.

He went on: "Mr. Klein gets, I think it is clear from the evidence, no management fee from Maclen, but Maclen pay a management service fee to Apple Corps and Mr. Klein gets a proportion of the fee through Apple.

"Under the ultimate agreement, Mr. Klein gave up his claim to commission that arose under the original management agreement, and said that if he did not get his permission under that agreement then Apple would manage the affairs of Maclen which had to be managed and obtain remuneration for doing so. The effect was that Apple got a gross commission of 20 percent which came back to McCartney and the other Beatles."

Mr. Finer said royalties from Mr. McCartney's solo record "McCartney" was "Beatle money." The same applied to Mr. Harrison and the record he made three months ago which was making double the money. He added: "No one is getting at Mr. McCartney on this."

Mr. Finer said that in 1969 and 1970, £760,000 had been paid in tax by Apple Corps, Maclen and Subafilms, Ltd. In addition £400,000 of tax certificates were being held, making a total paid or set aside for tax in those two years of Mr. Klein's management of £1,160,225.

The judge remarked that part of the Apple Corps tax paid in 1969 was for a very much earlier period. Mr. Finer agreed, but said that the amounts showed that Apple Corps was "perfectly solvent today."

Mr. Klein said neither Abkco nor he had received directly or indirectly any other benefit from their association with The Beatles than set out in schedules in evidence. At December 1968, the totality of the securities held by The Beatles, Apple Corps, and their other companies was £1,091,207.

At February 9, 1971, the total held in England by the companies, the partnership and Maclen was £4,097,948, and in the United States, including security at the Westminster Bank as a result of undertakings to the court, of £2,451,000.

The combined total of cash and securities for the whole Beatles outfit at that date was £6,549,668. This compared with £1,091,207 at December 31, 1968.

The hearing was adjourned until today.

The Times. Saturday, February 27, 1971

GROUP "NO LONGER THOUGHT OF AS THE BEATLES"

Since The Beatles stopped making group recordings they had stopped thinking of themselves as Beatles, Mr. Paul McCartney stated in the High Court yesterday.

He was answering evidence filed by Mr. John Lennon, Mr. George Harrison and Mr. Ringo Starr, the other three Beatles, in opposition to his claim for the appointment of a receiver of the group's assets pending trial of his action to have the group legally broken up.

Mr. Lennon had stated in his evidence: "We always thought of ourselves as Beatles, whether we recorded singly or in twos or threes." Mr. McCartney denied this.

He said: "One has only to look at recent recordings by John or George to see that neither thinks of himself as a Beatle." On his recent album John Lennon has listed things he did not believe in. One was "I don't believe in The Beatles."

Mr. McCartney stated that when the four entered into their partnership agreement in 1967 they did not consider the exact wording or give any thought to the agreement's legal implications. They had thought that if one of them had wanted to leave the group he would only have to say so. On the way in which the four had sorted out their differences in the past, he denied that it had been on a three-to-one basis. If one disagreed, they had discussed the problem until they reached agreement or let the matter drop. "I know of no decision taken on a three-to-one basis," he added.

Mr. McCartney denied that he and the Eastmans, the father of Mr. McCartney's wife and her brother, had obstructed Mr. Allen Klein in the preparation of accounts. Nor, he said, had the Eastmans been contenders for the job of manager of the group. He said he wanted them as managers, but when the rest of the group disagreed he had not pressed the matter.

Mr. Lennon had challenged his statement that Mr. Klein had sowed discord within the group. Mr. McCartney recalled a telephone conversation in which he said Mr. Klein had told him: "You know why John is angry with you? It is because you came off better than he did on *Let It Be*."

He added that Mr. Klein also said to him: "The real trouble is Yoko. She is the one with ambition." Mr. McCartney added: "I often wonder what John would have said if he had heard the remark."

When the four had talked about breaking up the group Mr. McCartney said Mr. Harrison had said: "If I could have my bit in an envelope, I'd love it."

Mr. McCartney also recalled the negotiations to acquire one of the NEMS companies for Apple. Mr. Klein, he said, had told The Beatles at the outset: "I'll get it for nothing."

That, Mr. McCartney went on, was a typical example of the exaggerated way Mr. Klein expressed himself to them. He added: "I became more and more determined that Klein was not the right man to be appointed manager."

Mr. McCartney ended his evidence by stating that none of the other three Beatles seemed to understand why he had acted in the way he had.

The short answer was that the group had broken up, each now had his own musical career, there were still no audited accounts and they still did not know what their tax positions were. None of these points, he added, had been denied by the other Beatles.

The hearing was adjourned until Monday, when counsel will make their final submissions.

The Times. Tuesday, March 2, 1971

FINAL SPEECHES IN BEATLES CASE

Mr. David Hirst, Q. C., said in the High Court yesterday that it was quite plain that The Beatles had irretrievably broken up. He was beginning his final submissions on the seventh day of the claim by Paul McCartney for the appointment of a receiver of the group's business affairs.

Counsel's summing-up and their arguments on the legal position are expected to occupy the next two days.

The Times. Wednesday, March 3, 1971

BEATLES CASE Q. C. SPEAKS OF RULE OF DEMOCRACY

Mr. Morris Finer, Q. C., appearing in the High Court for John Lennon, George Harrison and Ringo Starr of The Beatles, said yesterday: "There is a rule of democracy in partnership, as in other aspects of life, and the law enshrines it—the will of the majority should prevail."

It was the eighth day of the case in which Paul McCartney, the fourth member of The Beatles, asks for the appointment of a receiver of The Beatles' business affairs pending trial of his action for the legal dissolution of the group's partnership.

The three other Beatles and Apple Corps, Ltd., are opposing the application.

Mr. Finer in his final speech said it was incontrovertible that the appointment of a receiver would terminate the continued exploitation of all of the assets of the partnership and individual recordings.

"It is a trade which manifestly requires management," he went on. "This partnership has got a manager—Apple Corps, Ltd. But it has proved itself in the past, both as an organization and a company, as being incapable of properly managing the affairs of the partnership. One thing which is manifest is that if the interests of the partnership are properly to be looked after between now and the trial of this action it is vital that any order your Lordship makes—I shall ask you to make no order—must provide for management. The effect otherwise would give rise to loss and, indeed, chaos."

Mr. Justice Stamp said: "I am inclined to agree with you on that point."

Mr. Finer continued: "Mr. McCartney, through his counsel, seems to live in a world where everyone is either a seraphim or angel, or ape or viper . . . where there is precious little room for the intermediate atmosphere in which most people live."

Earlier Mr. David Hirst, Q. C., for Paul McCartney said that when Mr. Klein came on the scene The Beatles were on the crest of a wave. He could claim no credit for the wave, let alone the ocean across which it moved. The group had broken up and there was no prospect of its reconstitution. Whichever version of the disputed facts one accepted, it was manifest there was disharmony.

Mr. Hirst said four aspects had been clearly shown in support of Paul McCartney's case: jeopardy of the assets, exclusion of a partner, lack of good faith towards a partner by other partners, and the likelihood of eventual dissolution.

The hearing was adjourned until today.

The Times. Thursday, March 4, 1971

RECEIVER FOR BEATLES WOULD BE DISASTER, Q. C. SAYS

Mr. Morris Finer, Q. C., counsel for three of The Beatles, said in the High Court yesterday that in practice appointing a receiver of the group's business affairs would be an absolute disaster.

He was continuing his final argument in opposition to Paul McCartney's claim for the appointment of a temporary receiver.

It was the ninth day of the hearing, in which Mr. Finer is appearing for John Lennon, George Harrison, Ringo Starr, and Apple Corps, Ltd. Mr. McCartney seeks the appointment pending trial of his action to have the group's legal partnership disolved.

Mr. Finer said the case had been presented as making out that Mr. McCartney had been cheated. The truth was that it was a question of whether the commission payable to Mr. Klein (manager of the Beatles) was "of right."

Mr. Finer said: "There are a whole host of companies throughout the world, many in America, who simply could not take the risk of paying the partnership, if a receiver were appointed, in circumstances where there might be competing claims."

The appointment of a receiver would give the impression that the business had stopped and the reputation of The Beatles would be damaged.

Mr. Justice Stamp: Can you say that The Beatles' reputation is such a delicate blossom?

Mr. Finer said: "The reputation of Apple Corps, which is an active business, includes a lot more business than dealing with Beatles' records." The company's reputation was likely to be seriously affected if a receiver was appointed.

The case against the defendants had been pitched impossibly high. There might be all sorts of grounds for arguments but that was a different story from saying: "You must appoint a receiver because of this wicked man."

Counsel continued: "The whole object of this operation is to poison the court against Mr. Klein and say that he is dangerous and it is for the benefit of everybody to get him out." That was wrong when that was seen against what Mr. Klein had produced over the past 18 months. The hearing was adjourned until today.

The Times. Friday, March 5, 1971

THE BEATLES HAD £10,000 A MONTH, COUNSEL SAYS

Before Mr. Allen Klein, an American, took over the management of The Beatles the four partners had been overdrawing from a partnership account at the rate of £6,000 a month, counsel said in the High Court yesterday.

Mr. William Forbes told Mr. Justice Stamp that in the 28 months before the Klein era The Beatles had drawn a total of £272,000 from the account, although the combined net profit available to them was only £122,000.

He added: "In the pre-Klein era the four of them were drawing an average of £10,000 a month, an overdrawing of £6,000 a month." The result, according to Mr. Micawber, was misery.

Mr. Forbes was continuing final submissions begun on Wednesday by Mr. Morris Finer, Q. C., in opposition to Paul McCartney's claim for the appointment of a temporary receiver of The Beatles' business affairs.

It was the eleventh day of the hearing in which Mr. Finer

and Mr. Forbes appear for John Lennon, George Harrison, Ringo Starr and Apple Corps, Ltd. Mr. McCartney seeks the appointment pending trial for his action to have the group's legal partnership dissolved.

Mr. Forbes said that after Mr. Klein took over their management The Beatles' drawings continued at £11,000 a month but the amount available to them increased to £40,000 a month.

For the year ended December 31, 1970, the net profit available for them was £840,000, out of which they drew £184,965.

Mr. David Hirst, Q. C., for Mr. McCartney rejected the proposed undertakings offered by Mr. Finer on behalf of the other three Beatles and Apple Corps.

The basic objection was that the proposals would still leave Mr. Klein as manager. He went on: "Having regard to his record and his performance since he became manager, and what we now know of what has happened in America, and having regard to his evidence, we say he is not a suitable person to bear these responsibilities."

The hearing was adjourned until today.

The Times. Saturday, March 6, 1971

JUDGMENT TO BE GIVEN LATER IN BEATLES CASE

Judgement was reserved in the High Court yesterday on the claim by Mr. Paul McCartney for the appointment of a temporary receiver of The Beatles' business affairs.

It was the eleventh day of the hearing of the claim which had been opposed by Mr. McCartney's partners, Mr. John Lennon, Mr. George Harrison, and Mr. Ringo Starr and Apple Corps, Ltd.

Mr. Justice Stamp reserved judgement after failing to get agreement from the defendants' lawyers of his compromise suggestion that he should appoint a receiver and manager who would be told to appoint sub-managers including Mr. Allen Klein, present manager of The Beatles, to look after the individual records of Mr. McCartney on the one hand and the other three Beatles on the other.

Another judge in the High Court, Mr. Justice Plowman, granted an application by Northern Songs, Ltd., for temporary orders banning Maclen Music, Ltd. (the company of John Lennon and Paul McCartney) from publishing or causing to be published compositions by Mr. Lennon and Mr. McCartney and from asserting on sheet music or record labels any right to the copyright.

The Times. Thursday, March 11, 1971

BEATLES: RULING TOMORROW

Judgement will be given in the High Court concerning The Beatles tomorrow. Mr. Justice Stamp reserved judgement last Friday after hearing for 11 days Paul McCartney's claim for the appointment of a temporary receiver of the group's business affairs.

The appointment, sought until full trial of Mr. McCartney's action for the legal dissolution of the group, was opposed by John Lennon, George Harrison, Ringo Starr and The Beatles' company, Apple Corps, Ltd.

The Times. Saturday, March 13, 1971

RECEIVER APPOINTED FOR THE BEATLES By Geoffrey Wansell

Paul McCartney, of The Beatles, yesterday won the first stage of his legal battle to dissolve their partnership.

None of the four members of the group was in the High Court to hear Mr. Justice Stamp say that he was reasonably sure that in the circumstances a dissolution of the partnership would be ordered at the trial of Mr. McCartney's action for the legal breakup of the group.

Mr. Allen Klein, the group's American business manager, was also absent when the judge appointed Mr. James Douglas Spooner, a partner in a city firm of chartered accountants, as receiver and manager of the group's business interests, pending trial of the main action.

Mr. Spooner's appointment, however, was postponed for seven days pending a possible appeal against the judgement by the three other members of The Beatles, Mr. John Lennon, Mr. George Harrison and Mr. Ringo Starr.

The judge said: "The Beatles have long since ceased to perform as a group" and added that the case centered on the personality and activities of Mr. Klein.

Of the group's accounts, Mr. Justice Stamp said that their "condition is quite intolerable." He thought it would be many months, if not years, before an orderly position could be secured.

He accepted that Mr. McCartney could not be expected to go on dealing with Mr. Klein, about whom there had been such lengthy arguments during the hearing. But he did not think the appointment of a receiver would discourage the purchase of Beatles' records from which the group's income derived.

He added: "However successful Mr. Klein may have been in generating income, I am satisfied that the financial situations is confused, uncertain and inconclusive."

The judge said there was no evidence that Mr. Klein had or would put partnership money into his pocket.

Mr. Andrew Leggatt, for Mr. McCartney, told the court that his client's worst fears about the financial position of the partnership had been proved right.

The Times. Tuesday, April 27, 1971

THREE BEATLES ABANDON THEIR APPEAL

Three members of The Beatles pop group yesterday abandoned their appeal against a High Court order putting the affairs of their company, Apple, in the hands of a receiver. John Lennon, George Harrison and Ringo Starr now face a bill for legal costs estimated at £100,000.

The order had been made by Mr. Justice Stamp on March

12 on an application by Paul McCartney, pending trial of his action to dissolve the partnership.

Mr. Morris Finer, Q.C., for the three Beatles and Apple, said in the Court of Appeal yesterday that his clients considered it to be in the common interest to explore means whereby Mr. McCartney could disengage himself from the partnership by agreement. They felt that continuance of the appeal would be inimical to such negotiations.

The order appointing Mr. James Douglas Spooner as receiver and manager of the group's business pending trial of the action will take effect immediately.

Lord Justice Russell said: "I can only express the court's hope that the parties will come to some amicable and sensible arrangement."

WHEN I SPOKE TO George Harrison in his suite at the Park Lane Hotel two days before the August 1, 1971, concert for Bangladesh at Madison Square Garden, he asked me what I was doing these days.

"Well, I've just finished writing a history book about Apple." Silence. George blinked once, looked me right in the eye and said, "Well, it's only just beginning."

Richard DiLello
New York City
1972

APPENDIX 1

THE BEATLES FROM 1962

1962

January 1	First recording-company audition in London.
January, April, May	Back in Germany at Hamburg's Star Club.
June 9	"Welcome Home" night at Liverpool's Cavern Club.
August	Ringo quit Rory Storme's Hurricanes, shaved off his beard and joined The Beatles in place of Pete Best on drums.
August 23	John Lennon's wedding at Mount Pleasant Register Office, Liverpool, to Cynthia Powell.
September 4–11	First recording sessions at EMI Studios, St. John's Wood, London, with George Martin as producer.
October 5	First Parlophone single released: Love Me Do.
November	First television appearance: *People and Places*. (Granada TV) in Manchester.
November 26	Recorded second single: Please, Please Me.
December	Fifth and final trip to Hamburg.

1963

January 1	Commenced tour of Scotland.
January 12	Single: Please, Please Me.
February	First nationwide concert tour of U.K. in the Helen Shapiro Show. First national television appearance: *Thank Your Lucky Stars* (ABC TV).
February 16	First No. 1 record hit: Please, Please Me.
March 9–31	U.K. concert tour with Tommy and Chris Montez.

April 1	*New Musical Express* Poll Winner's Concert at the Empire Pool, Wembley.
April 8	Julian Lennon born at Sefton General Hospital, Liverpool.
April 11	Single: From Me to You.
	LP *Please, Please Me* No. 1 on LP charts for 6 months.
May 18–June 9	Tour with Gerry and the Pacemakers and Roy Orbison.
June 18	Paul's 21st birthday.
August 3	Final appearance at Liverpool's Cavern Club.
August 23	Single: She Loves You.
October 13	*Sunday Night at the London Palladium* (ATV).
October 24–29	Sweden: Concerts and television.
November 4	Royal Variety Performance at Prince of Wales Theater, London.
December 13	The Beatles Show tour with Peter Jay and the Jaywalkers and the Brook Brothers.
November 22	LP *With the Beatles*.
November 29	Single: I Want to Hold Your Hand.
December 7	*Juke Box Jury* (BBC TV). All four Beatles acted as the panel on this disk program. Also shown the same evening on BBC TV was a film of the Northern Area Convention of the Official Beatles Fan Club from the Liverpool Empire.
December 21	Bradford Gaumont
	The Beatles Christmas Show.
December 22	Liverpool Empire
	Also on the bill: Rolf Harris, the Barron-Knights,
December 24–January 11	Finsbury Park Astoria
	the Fourmost, Billy J. Kramer and the Dakotas, Tommy Quickly and Cilla Black.

1964

January	Paris, Olympia (3 weeks) with Trini Lopez and Sylvie Vartan.
February 7–21	First American visit. The Beatles appeared twice on *The Ed Sullivan Show* (CBS TV), Concerts at

	Coliseum, Washington, D.C. (Feb. 11), Carnegie Hall, New York (Feb. 12), Holiday in Miami.
February 25	George's 21st birthday.
March	Commenced work on first film, *A Hard Day's Night*.
March 20	Single: Can't Buy Me Love.
March 23	John Lennon's first book, *In His Own Write*, published.
May 6	*Around The Beatles* television film, repeated June 8.
June 4–6	Denmark: Concerts.
June 8	Commenced tour of Hong Kong, Australia and New Zealand. Ringo caught tonsillitis and missed concerts in Denmark and Hong Kong.
July 6	Royal premier of *A Hard Day's Night* at London Pavilion.
July 10	Single: A Hard Day's Night. LP: *A Hard Day's Night*.
July 25	George on BBC TV program *Juke Box Jury*. Ringo appeared on the panel the following Saturday.
August 19–September 20	5-week tour of U.S.A. and Canada.
October	Taped insert for America's *Shindig* (ABC TV) at Granville Theater, Fulham, London.
October 9–November 10	British tour with Mary Wells.
November 27	Single: I Feel Fine. LP: *Beatles for Sale*.
December	Ringo has operation for the removal of his tonsils at University College Hospital, London.
December 24–January 16	Another Beatles Christmas Show at Hammersmith, London, with Freddie and the Dreamers, the Yardbirds, Elkie Brooks, Jimmy Savile, Mike Haslam and the Mike Cotton Sound.

1965

February 11	Ringo Starr's wedding at Caxton Hall, London, to Maureen Cox.
February–March	Recording songs for next film, *Help!* Filming in Bahamas (February 22–March 12).

March 13	Commenced filming in Austria.
April 9	Single: Ticket to Ride.
April 11	*New Musical Express* Poll Winner's Concert at Empire Pool, Wembley. Televised by ABC TV (April 18). Appeared as panel on *The Eamonn Andrews Show* (ABC TV).
April–May	Continued filming at Twickenham Studios.
June 12	Announcement that The Beatles had been awarded the M.B.E. (Member of the Order of the British Empire).
June 20–July 4	European tour with concerts in France, Italy and Spain.
June 24	John Lennon's second book, *A Spaniard in the Works*, published.
July 23	Single: Help!
July 29	Royal Premiere of *Help!* at London Pavilion.
August 1	*Blackpool Night Out* (ABC TV).
August	LP: *Help!*
August 13–September 1	American tour. Taped *Ed Sullivan Show* for broadcast on September 9, 1965. Opening concert at Shea Stadium, New York, on August 15, 1965.
September 13	Zak Starkey born 8 A.M. at Queen Charlotte's Hospital, Hammersmith.
October 26	Investiture at Buckingham Palace. Presented with the M.B.E. medals by Her Majesty the Queen.
December 3	Single: Day Tripper/We Can Work It Out. LP: *Rubber Soul*.
December 3–12	British Tour with the Moody Blues, the Koobas and Beryl Marsden.
December 17	*The Music of Lennon and McCartney* (Granada TV, shown in the London area only on December 16).

1966

| January 21 | George Harrison's wedding at Epsom Register Office, Surrey, to Patricia Anne Boyd. |
| March 1 | First showing of *The Beatles at Shea Stadium* (BBC TV). |

April–June	Lengthy series of recording sessions.
May 1	*New Musical Express* Poll Winner's Concert, Empire Pool, Wembley.
June 10	Single: Paperback Writer/Rain.
June 24	German tour: Munich, Essen, Hamburg.
June 27	Hamburg–Tokyo flight.
June 30–July 2	Japan concerts: Budo Kan, Tokyo.
July 4	Manila concerts: National Football Stadium.
August 5	LP: *Revolver*.
August 8	Single: Eleanor Rigby/Yellow Submarine.
August 12–August 29	American tour beginning in Chicago and ending in San Francisco.
September–October	John Lennon's solo movie debut in *How I Won the War*, shooting on location in Germany and Spain.
October	George on holiday in India and Ringo on holiday in Spain.
November	Paul composed the sound-track music for the Boulting Brothers' film *The Family Way* and went on holiday, motoring through France and Spain and then flying to Nairobi, Kenya.
December	The Beatles reassembled in London for a new series of recording sessions.

1967

February 17	Single: Penny Lane/Strawberry Fields Forever.
April	Paul flew to America for Jane Asher's 21st birthday party in Denver, Colorado.
June 1	LP: *Sgt. Pepper's Lonely Hearts Club Band*.
June 25	*Our World*, a worldwide live television program, showed The Beatles recording All You Need Is Love in the EMI London studios.
July 7	Single: All You Need Is Love/Baby You're a Rich Man.
August	George and Patti fly to Hollywood to see the Ravi Shankar concert at the Hollywood Bowl and George wrote *Blue Jay Way*, naming it after the house he rented.

August 19	Jason Starkey born at Queen Charlotte's Hospital, Hammersmith, at 3:25 P.M.
September–November	Scripted, cast, directed, filmed and edited the color television film, *Magical Mystery Tour*.
October 18	World premiere of *How I Won the War* at the London Pavilion.
November 24	Single: Hello, Goodbye/I Am the Walrus.
December	*Magical Mystery Tour* record and book package. Ringo in Rome to film *Candy*.
December 7	Opening of The Beatles' Apple Boutique at 94 Baker Street, London.
December 25	Paul and Jane Asher engaged.
December 26	World premiere of *Magical Mystery Tour* on BBC-1.
December 29	John Lennon goes to Morocco for brief New Year holiday.

1968

January 5	*Magical Mystery Tour* shown in color on BBC-2.
January	George spent 10 days in Bombay composing, arranging and recording his own musical score for the sound track of the film *Wonderwall*.
February 6	Ringo's solo guest appearance on BBC-1 in *Cilla*, Cilla Black's TV series.
February–April	The Beatles to Rishikesh in India for Transcendental Meditation course at the Maharishi's academy. Ringo came home after a fortnight and Paul stayed a little longer. John and George returned towards the end of the three-month course.
March 15	Single: Lady Madonna/The Inner Light.

And God Created Apple

APPENDIX II
BEATLES' TOUR INFORMATION

1963
HELEN SHAPIRO TOUR with DANNY WILLIAMS, KENNY LYNCH, BEATLES, KESTRELS, RED PRICE ORCHESTRA

February 2	Bradford, Gaumont
February 3	Doncaster, Gaumont
February 4	Bedford, Granada
February 7	Wakefield, Odeon
February 8	Carlisle, ABC
February 9	Sunderland, Odeon
February 10	Peterborough, Embassy
February 23	Mansfield, Granada
February 24	Coventry Theater
February 26	Taunton, Odeon
February 27	York, Rialto
February 28	Shrewsbury, Granada
March 1	Southport, Odeon
March 2	Sheffield, City Hall
March 3	Hanley, Gaumont

1963
THE BEATLES GERRY AND THE PACEMAKERS ROY ORBISON

May 18	Slough, Granada
May 19	Hanley, Gaumont
May 20	Southampton, Gaumont

May 22	Ipswich, Gaumont
May 23	Nottingham, Odeon
May 24	Walthamstow, Granada
May 25	Sheffield, City Hall
May 26	Liverpool, Empire
May 27	Cardiff, Capitol
May 28	Worcester, Gaumont
May 29	York, Rialto
May 30	Manchester, Odeon
May 31	Southend, Odeon
June 1	Tooting, Granada
June 2	Brighton, Hippodrome
June 3	Woolwich, Granada
June 4	Birmingham, Town Hall
June 5	Leeds, Odeon
June 7	Glasgow, Odeon
June 8	Newcastle, City Hall
June 9	Blackburn, King George Hall

1963
BEATLES' SHORT TOUR OF SWEDEN
October 24–October 29

1963
*THE BEATLES' AUTUMN TOUR with PETER JAY and
THE JAYWALKERS BROOK BROTHERS*

November 1	Cheltenham, Gaumont
November 2	Sheffield, City Hall
November 3	Leeds, Odeon
November 5	Slough, Adelphi
November 6	Northampton, ABC
November 7	Dublin, Ritz
November 8	Belfast, Adelphi
November 9	East Ham, Granada
November 10	Birmingham, Hippodrome
November 12	Portsmouth, Guild Hall
November 13	Plymouth, ABC

November 14	Exeter, ABC
November 15	Bristol, Colston Hall
November 16	Bournemouth, Winter Gardens
November 17	Coventry, Coventry Theater
November 19	Wolverhampton, Gaumont
November 20	Manchester, Ardwick, Apollo
November 21	Carlisle, ABC
November 22	Stockton, Globe
November 23	Newcastle, City Hall
November 24	Hull, ABC
November 26	Cambridge, ABC
November 27	York, Rialto
November 28	Lincoln, ABC
November 29	Huddersfield, ABC
November 30	Sunderland, Empire
December 1	Leicester, De Montfort Hall
December 8	Lewisham, Odeon
December 9	Southend, Odeon
December 10	Doncaster, Gaumont
December 11	Scarborough, Futurist
December 12	Nottingham, Odeon
December 13	Southampton, Gaumont

1964
THE BEATLES AT THE PARIS OLYMPIA *Three weeks' engagement in January with TRINI LOPEZ and SYLVIE VARTAN*

First American visit – 1964
February 7–21
The Beatles appeared twice on *The Ed Sullivan Show*, with concerts at the Washington Coliseum, Washington, D.C. (February 11), and Carnegie Hall, New York (February 12).

1964 Denmark

June 4	Copenhagen
June 5	TV show in Amsterdam
June 6	Blokker Exhibition Hall

1964 Hong Kong, Australia, New Zealand Tour

June 9	Hong Kong
June 12	Adelaide
June 15	Melbourne
June 18	Sydney
June 22	Wellington, New Zealand
June 23	Wellington, New Zealand
June 24	Auckland, New Zealand
June 25	Auckland, New Zealand
June 26	Christchurch, New Zealand
June 27	Christchurch, New Zealand
June 29	Brisbane

1964 Five-week tour of the United States and Canada

August 19	San Francisco, Cow Palace
August 20	Las Vegas, Convention Hall
August 21	Seattle, Municipal Stadium
August 22	Vancouver, Empire Stadium
August 23	Los Angeles, Hollywood Bowl
August 24–25	Rest Days
August 26	Denver, Red Rock Stadium
August 27	Cincinnati, The Gardens
August 28	New York, Forest Hills Stadium
August 30	Atlantic City, Convention Hall
August 31–September 1	Rest Days
September 2	Philadelphia, Convention Hall
September 3	Indianapolis, State Fair Coliseum
September 4	Milwaukee, Auditorium
September 5	Chicago, International Amphitheater
September 6	Detroit, Olympic Stadium
September 7	Toronto, Maple Leaf Gardens
September 8	Montreal, Forum
September 9–10	Rest Days
September 11	Jacksonville, Gator Bowl
September 12	Boston, Boston Gardens
September 13	Baltimore, Civic Center

September 14	Pittsburgh, Civic Arena
September 15	Cleveland, Public Auditorium
September 16	New Orleans, City Park Stadium
September 17	Rest Day
September 18	Dallas, Memorial Coliseum
September 20	New York City, charity performance

1964

BRITISH TOUR with MARY WELLS, TOMMY QUICKLY, REMO FOUR,
MICHAEL HASLAM, THE RUSTICKS, BOB BAIN

October 9	Bradford, Gaumont
October 10	Leicester
October 11	Birmingham
October 13	Wigan
October 14	Ardwick
October 15	Stockton
October 16	Hull
October 19	Edinburgh
October 20	Dundee
October 21	Glasgow
October 22	Leeds
October 23	Kilburn, London
October 24	Walthamstow
October 25	Brighton
October 28	Exeter
October 29	Plymouth
October 30	Bournemouth
October 31	Ipswich
November 1	Finsbury Park
November 2	Belfast
November 4	Luton
November 5	Nottingham
November 6	Southampton
November 7	Cardiff
November 8	Liverpool
November 9	Sheffield
November 10	Bristol

1964–1965
*BEATLES CHRISTMAS SHOW December 24–January 18 Hammersmith Odeon
with FREDDIE AND THE DREAMERS, THE YARDBIRDS, ELKIE BROOKS,
JIMMY SAVILE, MIKE HASLAM AND THE MIKE COTTON SOUND*

1965 European Tour

June 20	Paris, Palais des Sports
June 22	Lyons, Palais d'Hiver
June 24	Milan, Velodromo Vigonelli
June 26	Genoa, Palais des Sports
June 27	Rome, Adriana Hotel
June 30	Nice, Palais des Fêtes
July 1	Jerez, Spain
July 2	Madrid, Monumental Bullring
July 3	Barcelona, Barcelona Bullring

1965 American Tour

August 14	New York; taped *The Ed Sullivan Show* with Cilla Black
August 15	New York, Shea Stadium
August 16	New York, Shea Stadium
August 17	Toronto, Maple Leaf Stadium
August 18	Atlanta, Atlanta Stadium
August 19	Houston, Sam Houston Coliseum
August 20	Chicago, Comiskey Park
August 21	Minneapolis, Metropolitan Stadium
August 22	Portland, Portland Coliseum
August 23	Los Angeles
August 28	San Diego
August 29	Los Angeles, Hollywood Bowl
August 31	San Francisco, Cow Palace

1965 British Tour

December 3	Glasgow, Odeon
December 4	Newcastle, City Hall

December 5	Liverpool, Empire
December 6	Rest Day
December 7	Manchester, Ardwick, Apollo
December 8	Sheffield, City Hall
December 9	Birmingham, Odeon
December 10	London, Hammersmith Odeon
December 11	London, Finsbury Park Astoria
December 12	Cardiff, Capitol

1966 Summer Tour of Germany and Japan

June 24	Munich, Circus Krone
June 25	Essen, Grugahalle
June 26	Hamburg, Ernst Merck Halle
June 27	Journey to Tokyo
June 30	Tokyo, Budo Kan Hall
July 1	Tokyo, Budo Kan Hall
July 2	Tokyo, Budo Kan Hall
July 3	Journey to Manila
July 4	Manila, Araneta Coliseum
July 5	Depart for London

1966 American Tour

August 12	Chicago, International Amphitheater
August 13	Detroit, Olympic Stadium
August 14	Cleveland, Municipal Stadium
August 15	Washington, D.C., Washington Stadium
August 16	Philadelphia, Philadelphia Stadium
August 17	Toronto, Maple Leaf Gardens
August 18	Boston, Suffolk Downs Racetrack
August 19	Memphis, Memphis Coliseum
August 20	Cincinnati, Crosley Field
August 21	St. Louis, Busch Stadium
August 23	New York, Shea Stadium
August 24	New York, Shea Stadium
August 25	Seattle, Seattle Coliseum
August 28	Los Angeles, Dodger Stadium

| August 29 | San Francisco, Candlestick Park |
| August 30 | Depart for London |

The preceding hagiography, encapsulated history and tour information was compiled and edited by Mavis Smith, Carol Paddon and Richard DiLello.

APPENDIX III
A BEATLE DISCOGRAPHY

BEATLES SINGLES AS RELEASED IN THE UNITED KINGDOM

Love Me Do . . . . October 5, 1962
Please, Please Me . . . . January 12, 1963
From Me to You . . . . April 11, 1963
She Loves You . . . . August 23, 1963
I Want to Hold Your Hand . . . . November 29, 1963
Can't Buy Me Love . . . . March 20, 1964
A Hard Day's Night . . . . July 10, 1964
I Feel Fine . . . . November 27, 1964
Ticket to Ride . . . . April 9, 1965
Help! . . . . July 23, 1965
Day Tripper/We Can Work It Out . . . . December 3, 1965
Paperback Writer/Rain . . . . June 10, 1966
Eleanor Rigby/Yellow Submarine . . . . August 8, 1966
Penny Lane/Strawberry Fields . . . . February 17, 1967
All You Need Is Love/Baby You're a Rich Man . . . . July 7, 1967
Hello, Goodbye/I Am the Walrus . . . . November 24, 1967
Lady Madonna/The Inner Light . . . . March 15, 1968
Hey Jude/Revolution . . . . August 30, 1968
Get Back . . . . April 15, 1969
The Ballad of John and Yoko . . . . May 30, 1969
Something/Come Together . . . . October 31, 1969
Let It Be/You Know My Name . . . . February, 1970

BEATLES SINGLES AS RELEASED IN THE UNITED STATES

(As Compiled by the Official Beatles Fan Club)

Capitol/Apple Records

#	Title	Lead singer(s)	Released
5112	I Want to Hold Your Hand/I Saw Her Standing There	Paul & John/Paul	January 13, 1964
5150	Can't Buy Me Love/You Can't Do That	Paul/John	March 30, 1964
EAP-2121	Roll Over Beethoven/All My Loving/This Boy/Please Mr. Postman	George/Paul/John & Paul/John	May 11, 1964
5222	A Hard Day's Night/I Should Have Known Better	Paul & John/John	July 13, 1964
5234	I'll Cry Instead/I'm Happy Just to Dance with You	John/George	July 20, 1964
5235	And I Love Her/If I Fell	Paul/Paul & John	July 20, 1964
5255	Slow Down/Matchbox	John/Ringo	August 24, 1964
5327	I Feel Fine/She's a Woman	John/Paul	November 23, 1964
5365	Honey Don't/I'm a Loser/Mr. Moonlight/Everybody's Trying to Be My Baby	Ringo/John/John/George	February 1, 1965
5371	Eight Days a Week/I Don't Want to Spoil the Party	John/John	February 15, 1965
5407	Ticket to Ride/Yes It is	John/John	April 19, 1965
5476	Help/I'm Down	John/Paul	July 19, 1965
5498	Act Naturally/Yesterday	Ringo/Paul	September 13, 1965
5555	We Can Work It Out/Day Tripper	Paul/Paul & John	December 6, 1965
5587	Nowhere Man/What Goes On	John/Ringo	February 7, 1966
5651	Paperback Writer/Rain	Paul/John	May 23, 1966
5715	Yellow Submarine/Eleanor Rigby	Ringo/Paul	August 8, 1966
5810	Strawberry Fields Forever/Penny Lane	John/Paul	February 13, 1967
5964	Baby You're a Rich Man/All You Need Is Love	John & Paul/John	July 24, 1967

#	Title	Lead singer(s)	Released
2056	Hello Goodbye/I Am the Walrus	Paul/John	November 27, 1967
2138	Lady Madonna/The Inner Light	Paul/George	March 18, 1968
2276	Hey Jude/Revolution (*THE FIRST SINGLE ON THE APPLE LABEL*)	Paul/John	August 26, 1968
2490	Get Back/Don't Let Me Down	Paul/John	May 5, 1969
2531	The Ballad of John & Yoko/Old Brown Shoe	John/George	June 16, 1969
2654	Something/Come Together	George/John	October 1969
2764	Let It Be/You Know My Name	Paul/John & Company	March 2, 1970
2832	The Long & Winding Road/For You Blue	Paul/George	May 7, 1970

EPS, BY THE BEATLES AS RELEASED IN THE UNITED KINGDOM

The Beatles' Hits. . . . . September, 1963
Twist and Shout. . . . . June 26, 1963
Beatles Number 1. . . . . November 1, 1963
All My Loving. . . . . February 7, 1963
Long Tall Sally . . . . June 19, 1964
A Hard Day's Night . . . . November 4, 1964
A Hard Day's Night (No. 2). . . . . November 6, 1964
Beatles for Sale . . . . April 6, 1965
Beatles for Sale (No. 2). . . . . June 4, 1965
Beatles Million Sellers . . . . December 5, 1965
Yesterday. . . . . March 4, 1966
Nowhere Man . . . . July 8, 1966
Magical Mystery Tour (Double EP). . . . . December 1967

SINGLES BY INDIVIDUAL BEATLES AS RELEASED IN THE UNITED STATES

(As Compiled by the Official Beatles Fan Club)

Capitol/Apple Records

#	Title	Lead singer(s)	Released
1809	Give Peace a Chance/ Remember Love	Plastic Ono Band	July 1969
1813	Cold Turkey/Don't Worry Kyoko	Plastic Ono Band	October 1969

#	Title	Lead singer(s)	Released
1818	Instant Karma/Who Has Seen the Wind	Plastic Ono Band	February 1970
2969	Beaucoups of Blues/Coochy-Coo	Ringo Starr	September 1970
2995	My Sweet Lord/Isn't It a Pity	George Harrison	November 1970
1827	Mother/Why	Plastic Ono Band	December 1970

BEATLES ALBUMS AS RELEASED IN THE UNITED KINGDOM

Please, Please Me .... April 1963
(*Please, Please Me* remained No. 1 in the LP charts for 6 months.)
With The Beatles............................. November 22, 1963
A Hard Day's Night.................................... July 1964
Beatles for Sale................................. November 1964
Help! .... August 1965
Rubber Soul .... December 1965
Revolver .... August 5, 1966
Sgt. Pepper's Lonely Hearts Club Band................... June 1, 1967
Magical Mystery Tour .... December 1, 1967
The Beatles.................................. November 21, 1968
Yellow Submarine............................... December 1968
Abbey Road .... September 26, 1969
Let It Be .... May 8, 1970

BEATLES ALBUMS AS RELEASED IN THE UNITED STATES

(As Complied by the Official Beatles Fan Club)

Capitol/Apple Records

#	Title	Lead singer(s)	Released
ST 2047	*MEET THE BEATLES*		January 20, 1964
	I want to Hold Your Hand	John & Paul	
	I Saw Her Standing There	Paul	
	This Boy	John & Paul	
	It Wont' Be Long	John	
	All I've Got to Do	John	
	All My Loving	Paul	
	Don't Bother Me	George	
	Little Child	John	
	Till There Was You	Paul	
	Hold Me Tight	Paul	
	I Wanna Be Your Man	Ringo	
	Not a Second Time	John	
St 2080	*THE BEATLES SECOND ALBUM*		April 10, 1964
	Roll Over Beethoven	George	
	Thank You Girl	John & Paul	
	You Really Got a Hold On Me	John	
	Devil in Her Heart	George	
	Money	John	
	You Can't Do That	John	
	Long Tall Sally	Paul	
	I Call Your Name	John	
	Please Mister Postman	John	
	I'll Get You	John & Paul	
	She Loves You	Paul & John	
UAS 3366A	*A HARD DAY'S NIGHT*	(UNITED ARTISTS)	June 26, 1964
	A Hard Day's Night	Paul & John	
	Tell Me Why	John	
	I Cry Instead	John	

#	Title	Lead singer(s)	Released
	I Should Have Known Better	Instrumental	
	I'm Happy Just to Dance with You	George	
	And I Love Her	Instrumental	
	I Should Have Known Better	John	
	If I Fell	John & Paul	
	And I Love Her	Paul	
	Ringo's Theme – This Boy	Instrumental	
	Can't Buy Me Love	Paul	
	A Hard Day's Night	Instrumental	
ST 2108	*SOMETHING NEW*		July 20, 1964
	I'll Cry Instead	John	
	Things We Said Today	Paul	
	Any Time at All	John	
	When I Get Home	John	
	Slow Down	John	
	Matchbox	Ringo	
	Tell Me Why	John	
	And I Love Her	Paul	
	I'm Happy Just to Dance with You	George	
	If I Fell	Paul & John	
	Komm, Gib Mir Deine Hand (I Want to Hold Your Hand)	Paul	
STBO 2222	*THE BEATLES' STORY* (Double Album)		November 23, 1964
	On Stage with the Beatles		
	How Beatlemania Began		
	Beatlemania In Action		
	Man Behind the Beatles— Brian Epstein		
	John Lennon		
	Who's a Millionaire?		

#	Title	Lead singer(s)	Released
	Beatles Will Be Beatles		
	Man Behind the Music—		
	George Martin		
	George Harrison		
	A Hard Day's Night—		
	Their First Movie		
	Paul McCartney		
	Sneaky Haircuts and More		
	About Paul		
	The Beatles Look at Life		
	"Victims" of Beatlemania		
	Beatle Medley		
	Ringo Starr		
	Liverpool and All the		
	World!		
ST 2228	*BEATLES '65*		December 15, 1964
	No Reply	John	
	I'm a Loser	John	
	Baby's in Black	Paul & John	
	Rock and Roll Music	John	
	I'll Follow the Sun	Paul	
	Mr. Moonlight	John	
	Honey Don't	Ringo	
	I'll Be Back	Paul & John	
	She's a Woman	Paul	
	I Feel Fine	John & Paul	
	Everybody's Trying to Be		
	My Baby	George	
ST 2309	*THE EARLY BEATLES*		March 22, 1965
	Love Me Do	Paul	
	Twist and Shout	John	
	Anna	John	
	Chains	George	

#	Title	Lead singer(s)	Released
	Boys	Ringo	
	Ask Me Why	John	
	Please, Please Me	John	
	P.S. I Love You	Paul	
	Baby It's You	John	
	A Taste of Honey	Paul	
	Do You Want to Know a Secret?	George	
ST 2358	*BEATLES VI*		June 14, 1965
	Kansas City	Paul	
	Eight Days a Week	John	
	You Like Me Too Much	George	
	Bad Boy	John	
	I Don't Want to Spoil the Party	John	
	Words of Love	Paul, John & George	
	What You're Doing	Paul	
	Yes It Is	John	
	Dizzy Miss Lizzie	John	
	Tell Me What You See	Paul & John	
	Every Little Thing	John	
SMAS 2386	*HELP!*		August 13, 1965
	Help!	John	
	The Night Before	Paul	
	From Me to You Fantasy	Instrumental	
	You've Got to Hide Your Love Away	John	
	I Need You	George	
	In the Tyrol	Instrumental	
	Another Girl	Paul	
	Another Hard Day's Night	Instrumental	
	Ticket to Ride	John	
	The Bitter End/You Can't Do That	Instrumental	

#	Title	Lead singer(s)	Released
	You're Going to Lose That Girl	John	
	The Chase	Instrumental	
ST 2442	*RUBBER SOUL*		December 6, 1965
	I've Just Seen a Face	Paul	
	Norwegian Wood	John	
	You Won't See Me	Paul	
	Think for Yourself	George	
	The Word	John, Paul & George	
	Michelle	Paul	
	It's Only Love	John	
	Girl	John	
	I'm Looking Through You	Paul	
	In My Life	John	
	Wait	Paul & John	
	Run for Your Life	John	
ST 2553	*YESTERDAY . . . AND TODAY*	June 15, 1966	
	Drive My Car	Paul & John	
	I'm Only Sleeping	John	
	Nowhere Man	John	
	Dr. Robert	John	
	Yesterday	Paul	
	Act Naturally	Ringo	
	And Your Bird Can Sing	John	
	If I Needed Someone	George	
	We Can Work It Out	Paul	
	What Goes On	Ringo	
	Day Tripper	Paul & John	
ST 2576	*REVOLVER*	August 8, 1966	
	Taxman	George	
	Eleanor Rigby	Paul	
	Love You To	George	

#	Title	Lead singer(s)	Released
	Here, There and Everywhere	Paul	
	Yellow Submarine	Ringo	
	She Said, She Said	John	
	Good Day Sunshine	Paul	
	For No One	Paul	
	I Want to Tell You	George	
	Got to Get You into My Life	Paul	
	Tomorrow Never Knows	John	
SMAS 2653	*SGT. PEPPER'S LONELY HEARTS CLUB BAND*	June 2, 1967	
	Sgt. Pepper's Lonely Hearts Club Band	Paul	
	A Little Help from My Friends	Ringo	
	Lucy in the Sky with Diamonds	John	
	Getting Better	Paul	
	Fixing a Hole	Paul	
	Sgt. Pepper's Lonely Hearts Club Band – Reprise	Paul, John & George	
	She's Leaving Home	Paul	
	Being for the Benefit of Mr. Kite	John	
	Within You, Without You	George	
	When I'm Sixty-Four	Paul	
	Lovely Rita	Paul	
	Good Morning, Morning	Good John	
	A Day in the Life	John/Paul of Bridge	
SMAL 2835	*MAGICAL MYSTERY TOUR*	November 27, 1967	
	Magical Mystery Tour	Paul & John	
	The Fool on the Hill	Paul	
	Flying	Instrumental	

#	Title	Lead singer(s)	Released
	Blue Jay Way	George	
	Your Mother Should Know	Paul	
	I Am the Walrus	John	
	Hello Goodbye	Paul	
	Strawberry Fields Forever	John	
	Penny Lane	Paul	
	Baby You're a Rich Man	John & Paul	
	All You Need is Love	John	
SWBO 101	*THE BEATLES* (Double Album)		
	(THE FIRST ALBUM ON THE APPLE LABEL)		November 25, 1968
	Back in the USSR	Paul	
	Dear Prudence	John	
	Glass Onion	John	
	Ob-La-Di, Ob-La-Da	Paul	
	Wild Honey Pie	Paul	
	The Continuing Story of Bungalow Bill	John	
	While My Guitar Gently Weeps	George	
	Happiness Is a Warm Gun	John	
	Martha My Dear	Paul	
	I's So Tired	John	
	Blackbird	Paul	
	Piggies	George	
	Rocky Raccoon	Paul	
	Don't Pass Me By	Ringo	
	Why Don't We Do It in the Road	Paul	
	I Will	Paul	
	Julia	John	
	Birthday	Paul	
	Yer Blues	John	
	Mother Nature's Son	Paul	

#	Title	Lead singer(s)	Released
	Everybody's Got Something to Hide Except Me and My Monkey	John	
	Sexy Sadie	John	
	Helter Skelter	Paul	
	Long, Long, Long	George	
	Revolution #1	John	
	Honey Pie	Paul	
	Savoy Truffle	George	
	Cry Baby Cry	John	
	Revolution #9	Beatles & Company	
	Good Night	Ringo	
SW 153	*YELLOW SUBMARINE*	January 13, 1968	
	Yellow Submarine	Ringo	
	Only a Northern Song	George	
	All Together Now	Paul	
	Hey Bulldog	John	
	It's All Too Much	George	
	All You Need Is Love	John	
	Pepperland	Instrumental	
	Sea of Time/Sea Of Holes	Instrumental	
	Sea of Monsters	Instrumental	
	March of the Meanies	Instrumental	
	Pepperland Laid Waste	Instrumental	
	Yellow Submarine in Pepperland	Instrumental	
SO 383	*ABBEY ROAD*		November 1, 1969
	Come Together	John	
	Something	George	
	Maxwell's Silver Hammer	Paul	
	Oh! Darling	Paul	
	Octopus's Garden	Ringo	
	I Want You/She's So Heavy	John	

#	Title	Lead singer(s)	Released
	Here Comes the Sun	George	
	Because	Paul, John & George	
	You Never Give Me Your Money	Paul	
	Sun King	John, Paul & George	
	Mean Mr. Mustard	John	
	Polythene Pam	John	
	She Came in Through the Bathroom Window	Paul	
	Golden Slumbers	Paul	
	Carry That Weight	Paul – Ringo, John & George	
	The End	Paul	
	Her Majesty	Paul	
SW 385	*HEY JUDE*		February 26, 1970
	Can't Buy Me Love	Paul	
	I Should Have Known Better	John	
	Paperback Writer	Paul	
	Rain	John	
	Lady Madonna	Paul	
	Revolution	John	
	Hey Jude	Paul	
	Old Brown Shoe	George	
	Don't Let Me Down	John	
	Ballad of John & Yoko	John	
ARS 34001	*LET IT BE*		May 15, 1970
	Two of Us	Paul & John	
	Dig a Pony	John	
	Across the Universe	John	
	I Me Mine	George	
	Dig It	John	
	Let It Be	Paul	
	Maggie Mae	John	

#	Title	Lead singer(s)	Released
	I've Got a Feeling	Paul	
	One After 909	John & Paul	
	The Long and Winding Road	Paul	
	For You Blue	George	
	Get Back	Paul	

APPLE RECORDS: NON-BEATLE SINGLES AS RELEASED IN THE UNITED STATES

(Compiled by the Official Beatles Fan Club)

#	Title	Lead singer(s)	Released
1800	Thingumybob/Yellow Submarine	Black Dyke Mills Band	August 26, 1968
1801	Those Were the Days/Turn, Turn, Turn	Mary Hopkin	August 26, 1968
1802	Sour Milk Sea/The Eagle Laughs at You	Jackie Lomax	August 26, 1968
1803	Maybe Tomorrow/And Her Daddy's a Millionaire	The Iveys	January 27, 1969
1804	Road to Nowhere/Illusions	Trash	March 3, 1969
1805	Carolina in My Mind/Taking It In	James Taylor	March 17, 1969
1806	Goodbye/Sparrow	Mary Hopkin	April 7, 1969
1807	New Day/Thumbin' a Ride	Jackie Lomax	June 2, 1969
1808	That's the Way God Planned It/What About You	Billy Preston	July 7, 1969
1810	Hare Krishna Mantra/Prayer to the Spiritual Masters	Radha Krishna Temple	August 21, 1969
1811	Golden Slumbers – Carry That Weight/Trash Can	Trash	October 15, 1969
1812	Give Peace a Chance/Living Without Tomorrow	The Hot Chocolate Band	October 17, 1969
1814	Everything's All Right/I Want to Thank You	Billy Preston	October 24, 1969
1815	Come and Get It/Rock of All Ages	Badfinger	January 12, 1970
1816	Temma Harbour/Lontano Dagli Occhi	Mary Hopkin	January 29, 1970

#	Title	Lead singer(s)	Released
1817	All That I've Got (I'm Gonna) Give It to You)/As I Get Older	Billy Preston	February 16, 1970
1819	How the Web Was Woven/I Fall Inside Your Eyes	Jackie Lomax	March 9, 1970
1820	Ain't That Cute/Vaya Con Dios	Doris Troy	March 16, 1970
1821	Govinda/Govinda Jai Jai	Radha Krishna Temple	March 24, 1970
1822	No Matter What/Carry on Till Tomorrow	Badfinger	October 1970
1823	Que Sera, Sera/Fields of St. Etienne	Mary Hopkin	June 15, 1970
1824	Jacob's Ladder/Get Back	Doris Troy	September 21, 1970
1825	Think About Your Children/ Heritage	Mary Hopkin	October 12, 1970
1826	My Sweet Lord/Little Girl	Billy Preston	December 3, 1970

APPLE RECORDS: NON-BEATLE ALBUMS AS RELEASED IN THE UNITED STATES

(Complied by the Official Beatles Fan Club)

#	Title	Lead singer(s)	Released
ST 3351	*Postcard*	Mary Hopkin	March 3, 1969
ST 3352	*James Taylor*	James Taylor	February 17, 1969
ST 3353	*Under the Jasmine Tree*	Modern Jazz Quartet	February 17, 1969
ST 3354	*Is This What You Want*	Jackie Lomax	May 19, 1969
ST 3359	*That's the Way God Planned It*	Billy Preston	September 10, 1969
STA03360	*Space*	Modern Jazz Quartet	November 10, 1969
ST 3364	*Magic Christian Music*	Badfinger	February 16, 1970
ST 3367	*No Dice*	Badfinger	October 15, 1970
SMAS3369	*The Whale*	John Tavener	October 15, 1970
ST 3370	*Encouraging Words*	Billy Preston	October 15, 1970
ST 3371	*Ain't That Cute*	Doris Troy	October 1970
SW 3373	*Yoko Ono/Plastic Ono Band*	Yoko Ono/Plastic Ono Band	December 11, 1970

APPLE RECORDS: ALBUMS BY INDIVIDUAL BEATLES AS RELEASED IN THE UNITED STATES

(Compiled by the Official Beatles Fan Club)

#	Title and content – artist		Released
T 5001	*TWO VIRGINS* (TETRAGRAMMATION)— JOHN & YOKO		November 1968
ST 3350	*WONDERWALL MUSIC* – GEORGE HARRISON		December 2, 1968
	Microbes	Party Seacombe	
	Red Lady Too	Love Scene	
	Tabla & Pakavay	Crying	
	In the Park	Cowboy Museum	
	Drilling a Home	Fantasy Sequence	
	Guru Vandana	Glass Box	
	Greasy Legs	On the Bed	
	Sking	Wonderwall to Be Here	
	Gat Kirwani	Singing On	
	Dream Scene		
ST 3357	*UNFINISHED MUSIC NO. 2: LIFE WITH THE* *LIONS* – JOHN & YOKO		May 26, 1969
		No Bed for Beatle John	
	Cambridge 1969	Baby's Heartbeat	
		Two-Minutes Silence	
		Radio Play	
ST 3358	*ELECTRONIC SOUND* – GEORGE HARRISON		May 1969
	Under the Mersey Wall	No Time or Space	
SMAX 3361	*WEDDING ALBUM* – JOHN & YOKO		October 20, 1969
	John & Yoko	Amsterdam	
SW 3362	*THE PLASTIC ONO BAND LIVE PEACE IN* *TORONTO* – PLASTIC ONO BAND		December 12, 1969
	Blue Suede Shoes	Don't Worry Kyoko	
	Money	John, John	
	Dizzy Miss Lizzie		

#	Title and content – artist	Released

Yer Blues
Cold Turkey
Give Peace a Chance

STAO 3363 *McCARTNEY* – PAUL McCARTNEY   April 20, 1970

The Lovely linda   Oo-You
That Would Be Someting   Momma Miss America
                Teddy Boy
Valentine Day   Signalong Junk
Every Day   Maybe I'm Amazed
Hot as Sun   Kreen-Akrore
Glasses
Junk
Man We Was Lonely

SW 3365 *SENTIMENTAL JOURNEY* – RINGO STAR   April 23, 1970

Sentimental Journey   Blue, Turining Grey
Night and Day   Over You
Whispering Grass (Don't   Love is a Many Splendored
Tell the Trees)   Thing
Bye Bye Blackbird   Dream
I'm a Fool to Care   You Always Hurt the
Stardust   One You Love
             Have I Told You Lately
             That I Love You
             Let the Rest of the
             World Go By

SMAS 3368 *BEAUCOUPS OF BLUES* – RINGO STARR   September 21, 1970

Beaucoups of Blues $15 Draw
Love Don't Last Long   Wine, Women and
Fastest Growing Heartache Loud Happy Songs
in the West   I Wouldn't Have You
Without Her   Any Other Way
Woman of the Night   Loser's Lounge
I'd Be Talking All the   Waiting
Time   Silent Homecoming

361

#	Title and content – artist			Released
STCH 639	*ALL THINGS MUST PASS* – GEORGE HARRISON			November 27, 1970

I'd Have You Anytime	Beware of Darkness	(Sides 5 & 6 Apple Jams)
My Sweet Lord	Apple Scruffs	Out of the
Wah-Wah	Ballad of Sir	Blue
Isn't It a Pity	Frankie Crisp	It's Johnny's
	Awaiting on	Birthday
What is Life	You	Plug Me In
If Not for You	All Things Must	
Behind That	Pass	I Remember
Locked Door		Jeep
Let It Down	1 Dig Love	Thanks for
Run of the Mill	Art of Dying	the Pepperoni
	Isn't It a Pity	
	(version two)	
	Hear Me Lord	

#	Title and content – artist		Released
SW 3372	*JOHN LENNON/PLASTIC ONO BAND* – JOHN LENNON/PLASTIC ONO BAND		December 11, 1970

Mother	Remember
Hold On	Love
I Found Out	Well Well Well
Working-Class Hero	Look at Me
Isolation	God
	My Mummy's Dead

362

APPENDIX IV
HAPPY BIRTHDAYS

John Ono Lennon was born on October 9, 1940, in Oxford Street Maternity Hospital, Liverpool.

James Paul McCartney was born on June 18, 1942, at Walton Hospital, Liverpool.

George Harrison was born on February 25, 1943, at 12 Arnold Grove, Wavetree, Liverpool.

Ringo Starr was born on July 7, 1940, at 9 Madryn Street, Dingle, Liverpool.

Great to have you with us
George Harrison
Paul McCartney
John Lennon

About the Author

As of the year 2000 Richard DiLello is alive and well. He lives in Los Angeles, California with his wife and daughter. Some days he writes, some days he tries to write, some days he does not. He is currently taking guitar lessons. Progress is slow.